Habermas and Theology

Other titles in the Philosophy and Theology series include:

Habermas and Theology

Maureen Junker-Kenny

t &t clark

Published by T&T Clark International
A Continuum Imprint
The Tower Building, 11 York Road, London SE1 7NX
80 Maiden Lane, Suite 704, New York, NY 10038

www.continuumbooks.com

British Library Cataloguing-in-Publication Data
A catalogue record for this book is available from the British Library

ISBN 13: 978-0-567-03322-2 (Hardback)
          978-0-567-03323-9 (Paperback)

Typeset by Newgen Imaging Systems Pvt Ltd, Chennai, India
Printed and bound in Great Britain

For Aedan O'Beirne,
1915–2010
Godfather and oldest friend
in gratitude for his presence and wisdom

Contents

Contents

Part 2   Habermas's Theory of Communicative Reason in Philosophical Debate

Contents

Contents

Introduction

The launch of a new series on 'Philosophy for Theologians' indicates that English-speaking academic publishing has discovered a need; it is addressing it with dedicated monographs on selected modern and postmodern authors and themes treated in contemporary theology. From Adorno to Zizek via Kierkegaard and Heidegger, human rights and Nietzsche, the choice reveals the range and diversity of concerns which engage theology at present. Resources are sought and found in different and opposite approaches. It would be anachronistic to conclude that theology has rediscovered its link to the *lumen naturale* with which God endowed the human creature and is taking up again the task of *fides quaerens intellectum* by developing philosophically mediated proposals for understanding and justifying God's self-revelation. While theology continues to take part in contemporary intellectual dialogue, the light of reason has dissected into many different rays, and faith seeking understanding has no singular defined counterpart to connect with. While previously, its dialogue partners were relatively homogeneous in that all related to 'reason', now a plurality of starting points and radically different interpretations of the project of philosophy exist.

The work of the German social philosopher Jürgen Habermas has been written in dialogue with and critical contestation of several of the authors covered in the series. How he relates to such seminal predecessors and their responses to the great movements of Western thought will appear at different stages in the context of the questions pursued in this book. His career in post-war philosophy, in the new democratic structures of the Federal Republic of Germany emerging from the ruins into which Hitler's European-wide reign of terror had collapsed, began in 1953 with a critical review in the *Frankfurter Allgemeine Zeitung* of Martin Heidegger's publication of his lectures of 1935.[1] After Max Horkheimer and Theodor W. Adorno's, two of the surviving Jewish founders of the Frankfurt School of critical social theory, had returned from their exile in California to Germany, Habermas became Adorno's first *Assistent* at the Institute for Social Research at the University of Frankfurt in 1956. Returning to Frankfurt as a professor in 1964, he took up the interdisciplinary programme of enquiry; a programme previously begun by the Institute for Social Research in 1934 but ultimately abandoned. Under the conditions of emigration and of powerless reception of the news from Europe of the horrors of the Holocaust, the second phase of critical theory was expressed in the *Dialectics of Enlightenment* (1941) in which Horkheimer and Adorno tried to identify the deep currents that led to civilization 'sinking into a new kind of barbarism'.[2] Reconnecting with the initial vision of critical theory, Habermas shaped its third phase by continuing to create and inspire its interdisciplinary research directions from 1971 to 1982 at the Max Planck Institute in Starnberg for the Study of the Conditions of Life in the Scientific-Technical World. He completed his teaching as professor in Frankfurt in 1994, 40 years after completing his doctorate on the German idealist philosopher Friedrich Wilhelm Joseph Schelling.

The core of his academic and public enterprise, communicative action, can be read as a sustained attempt supported by interdisciplinary efforts to elaborate the human orientation towards cooperation against Friedrich Nietzsche's vitalistic reduction of agency to the will to power. Interactive agency built on presuppositions of equality and the capacity for mutual role-taking, directed at finding universally justified norms and shaping democratic life, is a counter-proposal to Nietzsche's division of humanity into a noble, healthy and vigorous elite, and those deemed inferior, and to his justification of the power of the stronger. The relevance of Søren Kierkegaard's analyses of the self appears in the controversies about the permissibility of future genetic interventions. Against the philosopher Peter Sloterdijk's affirmation that the possible feasibility of 'elective breeding' was making Plato's and Nietzsche's dreams come true,[3] Habermas restates the principle of human dignity as the basis for human rights, especially in the asymmetric relationship of parents given the power to enhance their children's genes. His interpretation of Kierkegaard in *The Future of Human Nature* admits that the postmetaphysical mode of philosophy which Habermas subscribes to does not have to mean postreligious. His constructive use of the theological concept of creation is a case in point for the unspent 'semantic potential' he credits religious intuitions with. His work engages with and has inspired new research initiatives in philosophy, sociology and law, political and social sciences, cultural studies, theories of democracy and modernity, as well as theology.

The development of his thinking has been the theme of several recent overviews.[4] Rather than repeat or compare their analyses, my aim is not to make them unnecessary to consult by offering an even more complete overall account, but to deepen them by highlighting important theory decisions together with their philosophical critiques. They form the intellectual background from which the theological engagement with his work originates. With a commitment to cultural dialogue typical both for Protestant and Catholic Continental theology, the interest in his work has been strong throughout its different phases, including the first where the sacred is supposed to be transformed into communicative rationality. In his treatment of religion, three phases can be distinguished: its supersession by communicative reason, an abstemious co-existence, and genuine cooperation in the task of sustaining the normative project of a universalist modernity in the face of its pathologies. Changes in the relationship to religion are thus indicative for a reassessment of the power and internal variety of reason. The repositioning has diagnostic value.

Part 1 will treat the reception and critique of the first two phases of his work by theology. Before following the major turns he proposes and their reception in German-speaking philosophy in Part 2, the attraction of his work for theology and its different disciplines will be explained. Part 3 will be devoted to the most recent phase of his thinking on religion, marked by cooperation and 'translation'. This decade of a new engagement with religion seen as a resource for the public sphere begins in 2000 with lectures which were published in *The Future of Human Nature* in 2001, and with his speech *On Faith and Knowledge* on receiving the Peace Prize of the German Book Trade in 2001. *Between Naturalism and Religion*, first published in 2005, lays out the task of finding a way of not succumbing either to naturalism or to religious fundamentalism by debating Kant's philosophy of religion and moral philosophy, the demands of John Rawls's concept of public reason for religions, the prepolitical foundations of the state, in dialogue with Cardinal Joseph Ratzinger, as well as the issue of freedom and determinism. A panel discussion in 2007, published in 2008 entitled *An Awareness of What is Missing,* concludes the series of texts which are outspoken on the need to take religion seriously. The resonance which these new impulses and argumentations have had is manifested in articles and books, as well as in symposia to which he has responded. Especially 2009, the year of his eightieth birthday, has been an occasion for assessing the achievements of his philosophical work over more than five decades in which he has given more than two generations of philosophers and theologians the chance to form their thinking on modernity and religion.

Part 1

The Theological Reception and Critique of Habermas's Work in the First Two Phases of Its View of Religion

Throughout its different stages, theologians have engaged in intensive dialogue with Habermas's work. Their ongoing interest in his project throws a light on the way in which the self-understanding of theology developed in response to cultural changes surfacing in the late 1960s, among them the students' revolts of 1968. Factors in the reception of his theory of communicative action in the disciplines of theology were manifold: support for its interdisciplinary reconstruction of modernity and for the universalist scope of his discourse ethics with core categories such as 'repression-free communication'; its innovative methodology of combining a theory of action with an analysis of the democratic public sphere, the potential of his research methods for analyzing and redirecting the forces at work in a technological and scientific culture, and the reorientation of philosophy towards the individual sciences with an interest in participation and emancipation; political sympathy for his support of the critique and renewal that emerging social movements were bringing to the political system; and the rediscovery of roots shared with critical theory in the heritage of Jewish religious questioning. Thus, even at the stage where the unifying function of religion was handed over to communicative rationality, theologians were in dialogue with his enterprise. The questions they raised were reflected in his move away from an account of reason fulfilled in secularization, to a second phase of separate continued existences of both reason and religion.

Chapter 1

Attraction and Critique of Habermas's Theory of Communicative Action in the Disciplines of Theology

While text-oriented disciplines in biblical and theological studies had sharpened their hermeneutical consciousness in dialogue with philosophers like Hans-Georg Gadamer and Paul Ricoeur, the rediscovery of the understanding of theology as a whole as *scientia practica* explains the topicality of Habermas's theory of communicative action.[1] I shall trace the influence of his diagnoses of the contemporary age, the analytic purchase of his distinctions and their critiques in four different disciplines: in a systematic theology that reconceptualized itself as a practical fundamental theology (1), in practical theology with its different subdisciplines (2), in the theory of religious education (3) and in theological ethics (4).

1. Systematic Theology Oriented Towards Christian Praxis

For theologians dissatisfied with the role of their churches as service providers in the social and educational system and as representatives of Gospel values in an unquestioned bourgeois setting, the reconceptualization of the relationship between theory and praxis was highly significant. They welcomed the reversal of the previous order of praxis following theory as theologically overdue since it realized the priority of a practical faith in God's self-communication, as testified to in Scripture, to its subsequent

doctrinal reflection. In close connection with the rise of liberation and feminist theologies against the oppression by military
dictatorships in Latin America, against structural poverty and
patriarchy, political theology was founded as a movement in which
orthopraxis became the new criterion to balance and test ortho-
doxy.[2] Marked by their biographical experiences at the end of the
Second World War,[3] for Jürgen Moltmann, Johann Baptist Metz
and Helmut Peukert, the insight of critical theory into the need
to enquire into the context of origin and the context of use of
all theory production was irrefutable.[4] Theology had to conduct
its reflection in critical distance to political powers, and it had
to examine the basic conditions of agency to find out whether
there could be any capability for transformative, innovative action.
While the second phase of critical theory had diagnosed a
'universal context of delusion',[5] Habermas's design of a new
interdisciplinary programme of research into human agency was
promising important points of shared interest with theology.

At the same time, they were arguing from a different understanding of truth, not one that could be established by consensus[6]
but that depended on God's prior action towards humanity. It is
significant that already in 1972, political theology, with its high
profile in social movements for emancipation and justice, pointed
out the dilemma between 'relevance' and 'identity', 'emancipation'
and 'redemption'. With *The Crucified God* following his engagement with the work of the Marxist philosopher Ernst Bloch
in *Theology of Hope*, Moltmann set out the problem of theology
as either becoming sterile by just repeating doctrine in order to
safeguard its identity, or of losing the distinctive ground of its
hope by completely aligning itself with current movements of
liberation. The solution he proposed to this dilemma was to find
the identity of the Christian faith in the cross of Christ whose
solidarity with victims went as far as accepting death.[7] Dorothee
Sölle's book *Die Hinreise* turned to the resources of meditation to
replenish and redirect the political struggle against war, oppression,
hunger and the repression of memories.[8] In 1972, Johann Baptist
Metz surprised his colleagues at a conference of the German-
speaking dogmatic and fundamental theologians with a complete
rejection of 'emancipation' as the 'epoch-constituting catchword
for our contemporary experience of the world'. As a 'universal,

quasi-historico–philosophical category in the history of freedom' it is a 'programmatic . . . total and uncompromising' term of 'self-liberation', which rules out redemption which Marxism sees 'as an illusion distracting men from winning real freedom for themselves'. Metz's critique did not stop with the Marxist origins of the modern use, but included the Frankfurt School: 'These dialectics, far from minimizing the aspirations towards totality and inexorability in the notion of emancipation, actually make it more unassailable, less tractable and immunize it against external criticism'. He saw the 'attempt to reassimilate' the contradictions also at work in Habermas's analysis: 'The distinctions developed in the dialectics of emancipation between work and interaction, between technique and praxis, between empirical fact and anti-cipation . . . are conceptual tools for a dialectical analysis of social contradictions in the interest of total emancipation'. For him, there was no space left in this project for any questions that humans could not tackle themselves. He concluded: 'There is no theological foothold in the crevices of these dialectics of the history of emancipation'![9]

While the attraction of the new phase of critical theory lay in its starting point, the capacity of language to reach a consensus in discourse on norms, the critical reservations of its theological dialogue partners were voiced at an early stage. I shall present their distinct objections in conversations with Habermas which have been sustained over the decades, beginning with two Catholic fundamental theologians whose counterargument to his developing theory can be summarized in the term 'anamnestic reason'. While Johann Baptist Metz's position is built on a sharp contrast between 'Israel' and 'Athens' and on subordinating 'argumentative' to 'narrative' theology in which the memory of suffering and of liberation is prior to the systematizing role of theology, Helmut Peukert encounters the third phase of critical theory from the unanswered religious questions of the first and second phases, put forth by Walter Benjamin, Max Horkheimer and Theodor W. Adorno. From his work of tracing the sequence of problems in theory of science, existential, analytic and language philosophy, he supports Habermas's attempt to develop a renewed understanding of reason as communicative rationality and of modernity as an unfinished project. While Metz's critique concerns the constitution of agency, Peukert's also exposes its limits, especially when action is taken to aim beyond reciprocity and to be sustainable also in asymmetrical conditions through its advocatory, creative and transformative potential.

a. Practical Reason as Constituted by the Memory of Liberation

Metz's counterproposal to Habermas is located at the level of the context of origin which critical theory sought to uncover with an ideology-critical intention. Questioning Habermas's naturalizing link of language to the history of evolution, he traces practical reason back instead to the history reflected on in biblical monotheism.[10] Emancipative reason is based on memory, it is anamnestic. Memory has a foundational role; it is not an object but an 'inner aspect of all critical consciousness' which owes its origin to specific experiences of liberation from which the 'interest in freedom' arose. Thus, there is a 'cognitive primacy of narrated memory'. It functions as a

> precondition of a critical reconstruction of history by
> argumentative reason: Those traditions in which the
> interest in freedom originated . . . are in their basic
> narrative features, i.e. as a narrated history of freedom,
> not the object but the presupposition of any critical
> reconstruction of history by argumentative reason, the
> inner enabling moment of any critical consciousness.[11]

Metz credits Habermas with recognizing the role of memory by referring to historical struggles: 'The experience of reflection . . . recalls the thresholds of emancipation in the generic history of man'.[12] Yet, his account 'in fact conceals the connection that is revealed in memory between communicative action and historical frames of reference . . . the interests of knowledge (emancipation and coming of age) are naturalized . . . as linguistic structures that are remote from history'. His evolutionary account is rejected and contrasted with a task for hermeneutics: The 'critical treatment of memory has therefore clearly run into some of the unsolved problems of hermeneutics'.[13] By leaving it to hermeneutics to explore the relationship between communicative action and historical frames of reference, Metz avoids the objection that he is collapsing a human capacity, namely memory, into specific contents coming from history.

Metz's alternative genealogy is that the interest in freedom arose because the content of this memory is one of suffering: the 'memory of freedom is primarily a *memoria passionis*'.[14] The 'memory of suffering . . . becomes an orientation for action towards freedom . . . history – as the remembered history of suffering – has the form of a dangerous tradition'.[15] It is here that the 'dangerous memory of Jesus Christ's life, passion and resurrection', which witnesses to God's greater possibilities, is inscribed into the history of freedom as a starting point.

What is remarkable in this rediscovery of the category of memory is that its classification as a phenomenon of life, spirit, mind or perception by the different philosophical approaches surveyed is left behind by making it part of the 'problem of constitution of practical reason'. The 'process of remembering' is defined precisely as the 'medium of reason becoming practical as freedom'.[16] Under the category of freedom, agency can be thematized as imputability and singularity, subject to asymmetry, vulnerability and suffering. He grounds the universalist and 'polycentric' character of this orientation in the tradition of an 'empathic monotheism':

> For this monotheism, God is either a theme for all
> humanity or it is not a theme at all. This God cannot
> be 'my' God if God cannot also at the same time be
> 'your' God. God cannot be 'ours' if God cannot also
> be the God of others, indeed, of all the others. Thus
> we Christians would turn out, in a certain sense, to
> be the last universalists in the era of the postmodern
> fragmentations.[17]

In his response to Metz's article on memory and to his subsequent contribution to his *Festschrift*,[18] Habermas recognizes that there is a 'political as a well as a mystical' dimension to the 'biblical vision of salvation' which 'also implies collective liberation from situations of misery and oppression'. The 'eschatological drive to save those who suffer unjustly connects up with those impulses towards freedom which have characterized modern European history'.[19] The contribution of religion to struggles for liberation is now recognized; the political dimension which Metz had emphasized against the privatization of faith, which was implicit in Habermas's previous account of processes of emancipation, is no longer a point of disagreement. What Habermas contests, however, is the way in which reason is linked to memory. He discusses Metz's diagnosis of the need to retrieve biblical memory over against a monoculturally European conception of church in the context of the hellenisation debate: 'a Hellenised Christianity has cut itself off from the sources of anamnestic reason . . . Metz insists on the rational content of the tradition of Israel; he regards the force of historical remembrance as an element of reason'.[20] Yet Habermas disagrees with his polarization of Israel against Athens, for philosophical reasons: it 'is not just the grounding role of anamnestic reason which appears contestable. The picture of the philosophical tradition is flattened out, too. For this tradition cannot be subsumed under the category of Platonism'.[21] What follows is an intriguing account of the history of European thinking as marked by 'protests' against 'ontological thought and its epistemological and linguistic transformations', counterproposals which bring to bear the 'practical intuitions' of hope in salvation. The list of counter-movements to the ontological thought identified with 'metaphysics' contains 'nominalism and empiricism, . . . individualism and existentialism, . . . negativism or historical materialism. They can be understood as so many attempts to bring the semantic potential of the notion of a history of salvation back into the universe of grounding speech'.[22]

Habermas's assessment of the movements of European thinking as profoundly marked by biblical monotheism will be significant in the discussions of subsequent chapters; among them Chapter 3, in which Dieter Henrich's questioning of the opposition between metaphysics and modernity will be one of the philosophical critiques treated, and Chapters 7 and 8 on Habermas's proposal of cooperative translations between believers and non-religious fellow citizens and the theological responses to it.

b. The Paradox of Anamnestic Solidarity

While Metz tried to retrace the origins of critical consciousness to the 'dangerous memory' of God's saving interaction with humans in history, Helmut Peukert takes the long road of working through the stages and aporias of twentieth-century theory of science which arrives at ordinary language as the basis of its theoretical enquiries. Scientific rationality finds its foundation in a theory of communicative interaction. Focusing on the moral universalist core of Habermas's theory of society based on the orientation of language towards consensus, he points out the aporia at the heart of the norm of unconditional recognition when it is not limited to the present and the future but includes what can no longer be changed: history and its victims are the ultimate scope of a critical theory of universal solidarity. From this limit reflection at the abyss of practical reason, he develops fundamental theology as a theory of communicative action which is enabled through the proclamation, ministry and destiny of Jesus to face up to the questions posed by Kant, Benjamin and Horkheimer, problems that no normative account of praxis can escape: the antinomy of practical reason in the face of the gulf between our best intentions and our finite possibilities, and the concrete experience of history not as linear progress, but as the devastating sight of a mountain of ruins to flee from.[23] The conditions of intersubjectivity on which each person's identity are built become paradoxical once the irretrievability of the victims whose similar hopes were betrayed is considered.[24]

Peukert's main theological work, published in 1976, offers an immanent critique to Habermas's theory at an early stage of its development. It reads his core concepts on the background of the two previous stages of critical theory and brings their unanswered questions back on the agenda. It takes the universalist scope of his theory design seriously and understands recognition in the unconditional moral sense. Its key terms are deepened and extended to include the transformative quality of action and its unconditional character which does not wait for symmetrical responses but risks one-sided initiatives. Having moved from theology in Münster to a chair in theory of education at the University of Hamburg, he defines 'intersubjective creativity' as the task of a programme of education. Agency is understood as the fundamental human capacity to design and transform the identity of the self and 'to jointly create reality and re-invent a culture'.[25] The discipline of pedagogics combines analytic and normative levels of enquiry into the genesis of the capability to act. Dependent on mutual recognition but obligated to respect the other also when no response is forthcoming, the quest to become a self is precarious. Under the current conditions of spiralling systems of power accumulation the question of the resources for a self-understanding in solidarity is crucial.

Peukert's work in theology and theory of action radicalizes the project Habermas set out to investigate by including an unresolved history and a future shaped by forces which outpace the available level of institutions of reasoned agency.[26] On the backdrop of a history marked by the break of civilization and culture through the Shoah, and in the face of financial and technological globalization, capabilities are needed that sustain a cosmopolitan ethics and jointly create a world of shared meaning and perspectives. In this search for resources, Peukert turns to the anticipatory character of the proclamation and praxis of Jesus. In the Beatitudes, Jesus calls the 'poor and the hungry beatific and thus already anticipates and practically claims for them the unconditional, immediate attention of God'.[27] A theory of action must encompass the capability for conversion and reconciliation, and even the readiness to love one's enemy. He shows the possibility of such action in the way in which Jesus links apocalypse with genesis: basing the apocalyptic hope in God as 'the saving power whose range of action does not end at the threshold of death', who can 'call even the dead to life and make up for past injustice', on the goodness of creation which God is in the midst of restoring. His eschatological intervention is happening at present, 'the evil nexus has already been broken. ("I watched Satan fall from the sky like lightning", Luke 10.18). God has begun to reign in unconditioned goodness and to restore creation'. From this proclamation of the reign of God as already present, transformative action becomes a possibility. One 'should realize this prevenient goodness of God practically: in the unconditional affirmation of the other, even the one who may be an enemy. For this person, too, has been affirmed unconditionally'.[28]

In Peukert's reconception of the contours and depth dimensions of agency several issues are named where communicative ethics encounters theology. In the final part of his keynote lecture at the conference held at the University of Chicago in 1988 with Jürgen Habermas on the theme of 'Critical Theory: Its Promise and Limitations for a Theology of the Public Realm', he indicates future research directions. The 'task of reconstructing theology from a theory of intersubjectivity' points to outstanding issues for a theology that wants to do justice 'both to the claims of its tradition and to its own historical situation', as issues that can only be solved collaboratively. The first conclusion drawn from the ongoing need for theology to work with 'the formal sciences, the natural sciences, with the human sciences in their genetic-reconstructive method and with philosophy' is that they point to the question of the 'foundations of ethics'. In contrast to the starting point of Karl-Otto Apel's and Jürgen Habermas's theories of communication, the 'already fully developed autonomous subject', he sees the need to 'establish the ground of ethics on a deeper level', which does not presuppose but 'aims at the genesis of subjects; . . . in situations of inequality and oppression, but also in therapeutic and pedagogical action . . . the possibility to agree . . . or contradict me in freedom . . . must first be created'.[29] The intended outcome, the hoped-for consensus, also should be conceived of as an open and unpredictable interaction of 'provoking freedom through freedom': as the process of '*finding* a possible consensus which is not unequivocally preformed by conventions, but which preserves its character of being an innovative process for all participants'.

The second point that is overlooked in an 'ethics that proceeds from the implications of the conversations about validity claims' is the 'danger of losing sight of the temporality of human activity'. Interpreting 'recognition' as not just relating to the other as a partner in argumentation, but as an individual whose possibilities are being discovered, he first spells out this temporal character as the commitment of the interaction to the future of the other: this 'recognition affirms in an unconditioned way a developing, yet still presumed integrity of the other which does not lie within the power of the one initiating the communication'. It 'trusts in more than what it could achieve by itself'. The temporality of human action already points to intentions which finite humans can extend, but cannot guarantee to each other.

The third concern relates to the 'tragical and antinomical character of ethical activity' when it renounces to 'strategic-manipulative action' and becomes 'vulnerable the more she or he is oriented to the freedom of the other' whose recognition 'is not at its own disposal. Innovative freedom thus exposes itself to the danger of being futile, indeed, of being extinguished.'[30] He confronts the theory of communicative action with the antinomy of practical reason which for Kant raises questions about the very foundation of morality and its possible absurdity unless there is hope that the postulate of the existence of God is not illusory.[31]

From this philosophical enquiry about the foundations of ethics the fourth inescapable question for a theory of action is posed, relating to actual history: the 'Holocaust, *the* experience of annihilation in our century' needs a response that goes beyond

> the moral demand that this must never be repeated. For communicative action, which in the face of the annihilated victims still anticipates the communicative realization of possible freedom in a practical way ... the question of the salvation of the annihilated victims arises: the quest for an absolute freedom, saving even in death.[32]

If this question is not to be left open, the only answer to it is theological. In his final three points Peukert clarifies that the idea of 'an absolutely liberating and saving love' is not, as the critiques of religion concluded, 'illusionary' and evasive. It 'does not lead us outside of our situation, but, rather, more radically into it'.[33] He insists on the difference of such a limit reflection which can only show the relevance of faith in God, not God's reality, from 'an objectifying metaphysics'. The last point shows that his reflection has been about the preconditions for an agency that has already been reinterpreted as the outreach of free and vulnerable selves. Aware of the unresolved legacy of histories of violence and the unanswered cry of victims, the task of ethics is daunting. The capability for agency has to be restored first. It is here that the biblical witness to the resurrection of Jesus becomes hermeneutically accessible as 'an event which first makes possible an existence in unconditional and unlimited solidarity'.[34]

Referred to as a 'classic',[35] *Science, Action and Fundamental Theology. Toward a Theology of Communicative Action* has been included into the *Lexikon der theologischen Werke* and described as 'one of the most important works in fundamental theology in the past century', treating the 'foundational questions of theology on the background of existing theological approaches (Bultmann, Rahner, Metz)'. Concluding his review, the systematic theologian Magnus Striet states: 'It has inspired especially Catholic theology to submit its foundation to a sharpened reflection from theory of science'.[36]

The starting point of Peukert's engagement has remained the question of the dimensions in which a theory of action has to be developed. With its basis in the human sciences and philosophy, it has made his dialogue with Habermas the bridge for many of the authors in the praxis-oriented disciplines in theology to be discussed in the following sections. The two volumes of *Theory of Communicative Action* do not bear any trace of the exchange with these theological critics. It marks religion unambiguously as a stage to be superseded by communicative reason.[37] Articles written by Habermas in the same period engaged with the religious elements of critical theorists like Horkheimer or of Jewish religious thinkers with whom they were in contact like Gershom Sholem;[38] yet, as the Christian ethicist Duncan Forrester shows in his treatment of the crucial passages of the debate between Benjamin and Horkheimer and the latter's subsequent recognition that 'it is vain to strive for unconditional meaning without God', Habermas's answer in the first phase of redesigning critical theory as communicative reason remains reserved. As philosophy, it cannot answer these questions but still insists on 'the moral point of view'.[39]

Whether Habermas's position has changed on this point will be investigated in Part 3 in his response to the reception and critique by systematic theology, as well as by philosophers on the interpretation of Kant. It will show which insights he has accepted from these exchanges and where he continues to disagree.

2. Practical Theology and Its Subdisciplines

The reception of Habermas's work in practical theology also predates his turn towards accepting that communicative reason is not able to replace religion. Theologians were interested in his theory formation also before it recognized the ongoing significance of religion, first because it endorsed the principles of a modernity which they saw as part of Christianity's history of reception. Secondly, his work argued against positions which many in theology found incompatible with the views of the human person, community and history implied in a Christian concept of God: positivism, scientism, a Nietzschean analysis of reality in terms of power, systems theory, integralist critiques of the neutrality of the state and a rejection of human rights. Thirdly, a specific reason for practical theology's interest lay in its conceptual debates on its distinctiveness as a practical discipline. It found itself between two dependencies: on the one hand, an inherited dependency on systematic theology and church law, on the other, a one-sided relationship with the new sciences its subdisciplines were using such as psychology in pastoral care, pedagogics in religious education, sociology and action research in pastoral planning. It seemed to be the applied part both of dogmatics and of empirical sciences, in danger of disintegrating into an aggregate, with no unifying perspective for its different fields, methods and subdisciplines. Thus, a theory which emphasized the dignity of praxis was a welcome candidate to be examined on whether it could be a fruitful social philosophical dialogue partner.[40] Rather than function merely as an appendix to dogmatics and as the transmission belt of doctrinal truths or empirical research results, it was searching for a self-understanding that would do justice to the contemporary experience of that faith in different fields of practice in church and society. Apart from the insight into the circle between theory and praxis, several elements of Habermas's research enterprise were promising: a critical theory of society and of modernity – the period in which the discipline and the first chair of practical theology were established; his intention to renew an encompassing and multidimensional concept of reason; the capacity of his work to unite research approaches from the human sciences with the incisiveness of philosophical questioning into a theory of communicative action; his theory of the public sphere, of the changing role of the media, and his analysis of society through the distinction between 'system' and 'lifeworld' which was of relevance for all the fields of practical theology from pastoral care, to community building, and to religious education. I shall discuss the relevance of his work for two practical themes, pastoral care (a) and church as local congregation (b), before turning to proposals for the self-understanding of practical theology as a discipline (c) which utilize some of his core categories whilst sharing Peukert's critique of the deficits and restrictions at work in their explication.

a. Theory of Pastoral Care

In its work of accompanying ministry by analysing the parameters and forms of interaction, by comparing praxis proposals and offering an integrated vision of the different tasks of church in its specific contexts, practical theology saw the need for a renewed theory of pastoral care as arising from two weaknesses: by focusing too much on the role of the minister, and on professionalized perspectives such as that of psychological counselling, relations were conceived in an asymmetrical way in which the believers' own contributions to a shared interpretation of faith hardly appeared. Secondly, by attending above all to the individual or family in need in times of personal crisis, the theory of pastoral care neglected the societal background of emergencies or ingrained pathologies, which remained unchanged.

Relating his analysis of conceptions of pastoral care to the concept of the 'lifeworld' with its philosophical origins and its social scientific career, Thomas Henke sets out to develop an 'action theory of pastoral care', defining it as communicative action. At the same time, he draws attention to the limits of the categories used in his approach: the proposition that 'Christian faith is crucially marked by a communicative structure of action . . . is not to be understood as reducing the praxis of faith to communicative actions, or faith to a formal concept of morality for which religion is a content that can be replaced'.[41] Instead of succumbing to 'apparent plausibilities' and expecting functions it cannot deliver, the term has to be enriched with 'new dimensions' and its theological use specified. 'Thus, a theological reflection of the term communicative action . . . does not take over the task of founding theology but serves to make sure the theological relevance and the theological dimensions of this concept'.[42] For him, this dimension is brought out by grounding the human dignity to which unconditional recognition is due in the creation of the human being by God.[43] Henke concludes by relating the foundational philosophical (*erstphilosophisch*) approach of Hansjürgen Verweyen to Helmut Peukert's position:

> Thus, in theological perspective, communicative action
> is understood as an anticipatory outreach (*Vorgriff*) to the
> God who saves and as an act of bringing history to
> fulfillment . . . it is dependent on faith in the sense of
> a relation to the absolute ground of making possible,
> realizing and giving meaning to (*Ermöglichungs-,*
> *Verwirklichungs- und Sinngrund*) communication between
> humans (and between them and God).[44]

Henke provides a differentiated account of the concept of the lifeworld, relating philosophical, sociological and social scientific reflections to each other; it exemplifies the gain in analytical and normative reflection which the move from pastoral to practical theology achieved. The 'clerical paradigm' which had reigned until these new debates on the distinctiveness of the practical disciplines in theology commenced, is left behind in a new awareness of the shared dignity of all the faithful who constitute the people of God. Thus, a new sense of religious empowerment is making itself felt which takes the believers' own faith reflection, as well as their contemporary background culture, seriously. The subject of practical theology is no longer circumscribed by the professional knowledge needed by church officials to carry out the transmission of the word of God and the celebration of the sacraments with believers seen mainly as recipients, but by the task of first exploring their contribution to the life of the congregation. The rediscovery of the local congregation as the site and agent of the Christian tradition coming alive in the challenges of the contemporary world has made Habermas's core concepts interesting also for the second field of practical theology to be treated as a test case, the community-building context of the parish.

b. The Local Congregation at the Intersection of Lifeworld and System

The distinction set forth in *Theory of Communicative Action,* 'lifeworld' and 'system', had an immediate plausibility as well in the analysis of the structural setting of the congregation.[45] A new emphasis on the ecclesial grassroots was complemented by the sociological insight into the crucial position of the local congregation at the intersection of system and lifeworld, which gave it the opportunity of being a bridgehead to society. Rather than isolated individuals, it was communities which could detect deficiencies, create alternatives and give voice to concerns which would otherwise remain silent. In Ulrich Kuhnke's practical theological analysis, such processes of identity formation 'in critical remembrance of its tradition . . . have "subpolitical character" in that they hardly increase effective participation in political decisions but change the normative framework of political decisions'.[46] Thus, discourses in which self-understandings are formed, here from the biblical, theological and ecclesial traditions, are not just an internal matter for church members but enlarge the available framework of reference for all citizens.

Writing his doctoral thesis at a time when the first phase of Habermas's initial dissolution of religion into communicative reason was giving way to the second phase of co-existence, Ulrich Kuhnke interprets the four basic theological functions of church community in such a way that *koinonia,* living together, becomes foundational and integrates *martyria, diakonia* and *leiturgia.* While this fourfold division indicates irreducible features of the identity of Christian community, it is his reconceptualization of the three latter functions as corresponding to the basic types of linguistically mediated interaction distinguished in *Theory of Communicative Action* that is striking. The witnessing of *martyria* is linked to 'propositional truth', *diakonia* to the dimension of 'practical norms', and *leiturgia* to the 'subjective, aesthetic-expressive' orientation. It is an alignment which in my view surrenders the critical position Kuhnke has taken by supporting Peukert's objections to a thoroughly different framework.[47] Already in philosophical perspective, the act of giving witness or testimony belongs to a different register than the objectivity-related function of uttering propositions of truth. The subjective investment true to witnessing has since been explored philosophically in the concept of 'conviction' and theologically in the acts of 'testifying' and 'confessing'.[48] Although Kuhnke's reception of Habermas through the critique of Peukert and his structural positioning of the local congregation leads to fruitful practical theological insights, by relating *martyria* to the objective truth function of epistemic reason he ignores Peukert's explicit rejection of any objectifying metaphysics. The character of *martyria* as testimony with its personal involvement is misrepresented as an epistemological truth claim. It could even lead to the misunderstanding that it was the intention of faith to prove God empirically. Instead, the local community's *martyria* could have been developed productively as an insight into the irreplaceable role of the believers' response to God's call. It could have challenged a theory focusing mainly on the validity of claims in their different spheres. The interplay between the 'ethical' and the 'moral', and between reflected personal evidences including religious ones and universal claims is left untapped. The way in which views of the 'good' relate to and invigorate the normative level of agreement on what is 'right' by interpreting and disclosing reality will be one major theme in the response of theological ethics to Habermas's developing theory.

c. Practical Theology Reconceptualized as a Theological Theory of Action

In the debates on the self-understanding of the discipline, practical theology has emerged as involving 'the highly philosophical turns of fundamental theology and the hermeneutical turns of systematic theology . . . It explores the theoretical interpretation of contemporary praxis in social theory with a method of mutually critical correlation'.[49] This correlational approach establishes a relationship of specifically determined, rather than external, critiques to an enterprise which links a theory of action conceived in an interdisciplinary framework with a theory of democratic participation within the conditions of a complex technological society.

One approach that demonstrates both the openness and the necessary redirection and deepening of the concepts involved is Norbert Mette's foundation of practical theology as a theological theory of action.[50] The mutually critical correlation is enacted by acknowledging the distinction between role and personal identity which Habermas suspects religions of ignoring; at the same time, the need is shown to reconnect social scientific theories of identity formation to a philosophical investigation of the self which uncovers its contingency and its openness to being anchored in God. Habermas's critique of the philosophy of subjectivity as a monological analysis of consciousness is left behind as unconvincing by drawing on the analysis of freedom undertaken in Kierkegaard's exploration of the self. Twenty-five years later, in the context of the question of genetic enhancement, the precedent of Kierkegaard's concept of self will acquire new significance for Habermas. At this stage, his interest is in guiding empirical research by generative ideas from philosophy.

One of the key distinctions in aiming for an identity that is up to the demands of reason is that between role and self-identity; Mette summarizes the manner in which religion is seen in this respect and presents an alternative understanding of religion's contribution to the self. An

identity constituted on the basis of religion can serve as a prime example of mere role identity. This is paramount to saying that an identity formation adequate for the structure of contemporary society cannot be reached on its basis. For religion – at least in its inherited and previously wide-spread form – hardly allows for reflexive identity formation. It obliges the individual to hold binding propositions of faith and norms, leading not to autonomy, but to heteronomy . . . In addition, religious institutions such as the churches with their hierarchical structure which relies on authority are anything but the repression-free space that forms the presupposition to reflexive identity formation . . . In short: religion cannot even come near doing justice to the central features of self-identity – which are intersubjectivity, reciprocal reflexivity, universalist orientation, transparency and revisability of contents.[51]

In this perspective, religion stands for instructions and behavioural patterns which have to be taken over passively and thus inhibit reflexivity and autonomy in the sense of independent judgement. Mette agrees to the criteria of autonomy-oriented self-identity and is ready to submit, and when necessary, correct the goals of religious socialization in light of them. Yet he also refocuses the problem of identity from a simplified alternative between autonomy and heteronomy to the deeper level of the anxiety of the self when it is faced with the realization of its facticity. In the light of God's unconditional affirmation, the self is enabled to form an identity that is freed from the opposite choices of self-assertion and self-denial, from the alternative of either 'desperately wanting to be a self' or 'desperately not wanting to be a self'.[52] The religious experience of the 'gratuity'[53] of God's love is the starting point for creating an identity as a unique and related self and maintaining it also through situations of crisis. The contribution which a theological theory of communicative action can make is to link agency and self and to pursue the question posed by religion of 'how subjects in a specific societal situation can find identity in interaction – speaking with Kierkegaard: the possibility of their being a self'.[54]

Mette puts this approach to the test in concrete fields of action such as the churches' social work, the religious socialization of children and youth initiatives. At the same time, he does not want to confine the theological theory of action to the institutional limits of the churches. Rather, it has questions to put to the secular disciplines with which it works. Their presuppositions, too, can be discussed fruitfully, and practical theology has to resist subordinating itself to them. Accepting their results

> as valid without questioning and applying them to its subject area, . . . would mean that it submits itself to their action-theoretical approaches and recognizes them almost as 'metatheories'. It would then have no alternative to limiting itself to those fields of action which are allocated

by other sciences to theology as the praxis it has to be responsible for.[55]

The mutually critical correlation between theology, philosophy and the human sciences as contributing to a shared project from starting points that differ but can be justified is thus kept going.

3. Theory of Religious Education

When criteria of reasonable identity were being sought, the suspicion emerged that religion survives by indoctrination. This concern becomes more acute when the subjects in question are not peers, but children. How can religious education of pupils as a mandatory school subject be defended and designed in a way that can counter the charge of teaching authority-derived contents which hinder emancipation? What positive contribution does the continued teaching of specific religious traditions have in primary and secondary education? The challenge to justify the teaching of this subject in view of such questions has helped to articulate arguments which might have been left implicit if it had been enough to point to the status of religion as a school subject until age fourteen in the German Constitution.

Two assumptions have made it difficult for religions to argue for their cultural standing as forms of humanism. First, that Habermas's theory identifies universalism with a 'postconventional' stage of morality, understanding this as the necessity to leave background traditions behind.[56] Secondly, with the goals of education set as emancipation, reflexivity or the ability to cope with ambiguity, a hermeneutical and comparative perspective has been missing; that self-identity can include a mutual understanding of the cultural and religious components of each other's identities was not yet on the horizon. The semantic and motivational potential of religion for solidarity was also still undiagnosed. At this stage of the 'linguistification of the sacred'[57], only the role of religion to console in times of loss made it, for the time being, irreplaceable.

A problem for any theory of education was the focus of discourse ethics on symmetric communication. For the purposes of spelling out the presuppositions already at work when entering into the praxis of giving reasons, and thus of recognizing each person's equality, this was appropriate. Yet, its effect was to actually restrict reflection to discursive interaction between fully-fledged subjects. Against this, Helmut Peukert had already reoriented the theory towards the *genesis* of subjects through the anticipatory, advocatory and creative structure of communicative action. Re-dimensioned in these terms, it became accessible for theories that dealt with asymmetric relationships. The challenge internal to pedagogics had already been formulated memorably by Theodor W. Adorno: 'Whoever wants to educate towards autonomy, has to presuppose it'.

The theorist of education Hermann Nohl called this structure of having to presuppose what is still to be jointly created, 'the pedagogical paradox'.[58] Unlike the paradox of anamnestic solidarity however, it does not confront one with the limits of human ability since it is not dealing with a past that cannot be changed, that is, with a history in which others to whom one is indebted, have suffered and perished. The pedagogical paradox is oriented towards the future and can be resolved by an adequate structuring of the interaction which respects the emerging identity of the younger dialogue partner. The anticipatory constitution of the pedagogical relationship can draw on something that is not irretrievably lost but already there: the capability already of children to co-construct a world. From this perspective, the possible contribution of religion to identity formation appears in a different light. As long as religious or other contents are not imposed, they present an opportunity for creating a world with a more encompassing framework.[59] The case can be made that 'also a society that is no longer predominantly religious needs the encounter with religious concepts of interpreting the world'[60]. To give children access to this heritage, is not limiting, but opens up another world of reference in which they can explore their self-understanding. All this, however, only holds if it is eventually up to them to validate this offer. Everything depends on the scope given to critically and selectively appropriate a tradition, or to reject it on reflection. Thus, the position which characterized the first phase of Habermas's view of religion, a dogmatically consti-tuted content not open to critical reflection, turns into a question which religion has to put to itself. It becomes its own problem, not one posed by outside critics. As the theorist of religious education, Markus Tomberg, has put it with reference to Mette, there is a 'conflict immanent in the theory of religious education: It intends to mediate *normative contents as liberating orientation*'.[61] Norbert Mette shows that the conflict is radicalized within a theological theory of religious education: the contents to be taught can only be freely appropriated. It thus needs a type of teaching that aims at more than the 'cognitive level', namely at a 'process of transformation' by reviewing current and prior stages of the self.[62] The benchmark of its teaching is that it allows the space for engagement which can end with the decision to leave a faith community. Here, Habermas's principled insistence that processes of education have to able to be reviewed and rejected by the person herself is a helpful support for a faith that has turned from the objectivist position of 'error has no right' to the truth of the person.[63]

Habermas reiterates the need for input to be revisable a quarter of a century later, in the context of a different controversy, that of parents choosing the genetic specificity of their offspring. To be able to distance oneself from the choices of one's parents is critical for self-identity. Here, a crucial difference emerges between genetic and 'environmental', choices enacted on a child, including choices involving education. Previously, it was religious education that had to make it clear that shaping a child's intellectual and social orientation by traditions endorsed by parents and schools was not an authoritarian imposition. What if such prior choices are incarnated into the genetic make-up no longer inherited from, but selected by parents? If the requirement is paramount that the child, who is at the receiving end, has to be able to eventually consent or distance himself, the only permissible choices exercised on his behalf, without consulting him, are ones that can be revised. Habermas's rejection of enhancement as undermining the intended symmetry between parents and children and his defence of the right of the child to his or her own unmanipulated self will be returned to in Chapter 7.

By this stage, at the turn to the twenty-first century, the discussion has shifted. It has taken on board, as we shall see in the next section, the importance of the 'ethical' dimension and has examined the 'genealogy' of the modern foundation of morality on mutual recognition in the heritage of the encounter of biblical monothe-ism with antique thought. But for all these background traditions, the point remains the same: individuals must actively take a stance towards them. Habermas correctly insists that the only way in which world views can survive in modern pluralistic societies is by convincing their young members of their capability to deal with the problems of their world. The vitality of the different subcultures cannot be guaranteed from the outside (although it could be added that the conditions for education and participation provided in the life of civil society will make a difference). The strength of a world view is based on its potential to engage a per-son's self-understanding and to be validated by their reflection.

> A tradition must be able to develop its cognitive potential in such a way that the addressees are convinced that this tradition is really worth pursuing ... A culture can be conceived as an ensemble of enabling conditions for problem-solving activities. It furnishes those who grow up in it not only with elementary linguistic, practical and cognitive capacities, but also with grammatically prestruc-tured world views and semantically accumulated stores of knowledge. However, a culture cannot be maintained through conditioning or crass indoctrination; neither can it be maintained solely through the implicit habituation of the young to corresponding language games and practices. Rather, traditions preserve their vitality by insinuating themselves into the ramified and interlinked channels of individual life histories and, in the process, passing the critical threshold of the autonomous endorsement of every single potential participant. The intrinsic value of a tradition can manifest itself during adolescence at the earliest. Young people must be convinced that they can lead a worthwhile and meaningful life within the horizon of an assimilated tradition. The test of the viability of a cultural tradition ultimately lies in the fact that challenges can be transformed into solvable problems for those who grow up within the tradition.
> ... In pluralistic societies, cultural groups can pass on their heritage from one generation to the next only via the

hermeneutic filter of the affirmations of individual members who are in a position to say 'no' to a range of genuine alternatives. For this empirical reason, collective rights can strengthen the cultural self-assertion of a group only if they also accord the individual members the latitude to use them realistically in deciding on reflection between critical appropriation, revision or rejection. The guarantee of the internal latitude necessary to assimilate a tradition under conditions of dissent is decisive for the survival of cultural groups. A dogmatically protected culture will not be able to reproduce itself, especially not in an environment replete with alternatives.[64]

Thus, religious education has the task of introducing a faith tradition in a way that appeals to the child's response. Its reception cannot be taken for granted; the process of a free commitment to a tradition, in the face of the possibility to opt against it, cannot be substituted for and includes its transformation and renewal. The task of religious education then is not to transmit a tradition as a *depositum fidei* in the sense of an objectified body of knowledge but to disclose its resources - from the different genres of the Bible to depictions in art, from theological reflection to its symbols and celebrations - as a framework for an individual's and a community's self-understanding in their global situation. It 'has to strive in its content and method to make itself understandable to the child as ... affirming his or her freedom ... In this way Christian education has to correspond to its contents, the Gospel'.[65]

4. Theological Ethics

The systematic theological engagement with the theory of communicative action has shown that the ground of a universalist ethics has to be laid at a deeper level than a reciprocal recognition built into the structures of interaction can provide. This insight has been affirmed in theological ethics, as the first author I shall discuss, Andreas Lob-Hüdepohl, shows. My second author, the theological ethicist Hille Haker, examines the theory as it had developed by 1996 for the significance it gives to the personal quest for a flourishing life and to cultural traditions of formation in relation to moral identity.

a. Beyond Reciprocal Requirements: The Risk of Advance Unilateral Action

The procedural and intersubjective turn which Kant's testing of maxims for action has been given in discourse ethics has been accepted insofar as it operationalized the principle of universalization over against self-interest. It does not, however, pretend that an agreement reached even under idealizing conditions constitutes the ultimate decision on what is right. Thus, especially the distinction of an 'actual' from a 'true' consensus has found resonance in theology since it keeps the outcomes revisable and open to further, arguably more universal insights. The Kantian core of recognizing each individual's dignity can be accepted as a philosophical reformulation of the universal equality and singularity implied in the theological designation of being made in the image of God. Yet, the procedure of discourse ethics has only gone as far as reconstructing conditions for deciding on what was right in practical argumentations. Its shortcoming has been that these conditions do not capture the readiness to offer opportunities to others when they might not be reciprocated. Lob-Hüdepohl points to the everyday relevance of such generosity which at the same time has to remain an initiative that is free and not owed, as an

> agency that opens up new perspectives for action,
> widens narrow systematizations and thus adds in concrete
> situations to the improvement of real relationships of
> interaction. This, however, is something to which agents
> precisely *cannot oblige each other*; at best, they *can hope* for it
> from the respective other.[66]

He illustrates this attitude that cannot be institutionalized as a precondition of argumentation with the following examples:

> the victim's act of forgiveness . . ., reconciliatory
> action which overcomes separations and disruptions of

cooperation prior to the atonement for possible guilt; . . . the act of trust which in spite of all disappointment or in spite of extended mistrust unilaterally offers trust in advance; . . . the act of renouncing to one's own interests . . . although they would be of equal standing and justifiable. To these and other forms of innovative action no legal titles can ever be extended, and yet there are manifold situations in which it is likely that only through them a new beginning can be made by which joint action can first recommence . . . However, the failure of innovative action is especially fatal for the subject of such action since it has divested itself far more of its protective spaces and exposed itself to the strategic games and the self-interest of the others involved.[67]

The risk of these actions points to the relevance of faith in a God who rescues those who are betrayed, threatened and terrorized, and 'opens up the space for a praxis of solidarity'.[68] Yet it raises doubts about the parameters in which the theory of communicative action is spelt out. Its reconstruction of morality is incomplete if it is kept at the level of specifying conditions for the solution of practical conflicts through argumentation. If these normative demands are reclaimed for morality, then a similar question arises as the one put to religious traditions in the previous section. How can such normative demands be appropriated by children, adolescents and adults? Habermas's response to the different aspects of this problem remains the same: the depth dimensions which go beyond reciprocity are classified as 'supererogatory', that is, morally heroic actions, and left to an existential realm which cannot be theorized; they are beyond the scope of competence of philosophy. A similar answer is given in relation to the issue of motivation, as lying before philosophy appears on the scene to reconstruct what is operative in communication:

It is true that a philosophy that thinks postmetaphysically cannot answer the question . . . : why be moral at all? At the same time, however, this philosophy can show why this question does not arise meaningfully for communicatively socialized individuals. We acquire our moral intuitions in our parents' home, not in school.[69]

It is in relation to this problem, moral identity, that the Christian social ethicist Hille Haker compares the answers of different philosophical approaches: those of Jürgen Habermas, Axel Honneth, Charles Taylor, Hans Krämer, and Paul Ricoeur.

b. Personal *or* Universalizable? The Disjunction between the Ethics of the Good Life and Normative Morality

Haker's enquiry is based on the premise that the constitution of personal identity is significant for morality. She first distinguishes normative from descriptive accounts of identity and observes that 'a functionally oriented sociology is skeptical against construing a prior moral target for the concept of identity because it tries to make do without a normative concept of social action'. She adds that the 'priority and totality claim of the description itself then become normative'.[70] In distinction to descriptive social studies, a normative approach sees as the 'target of identity formation the autonomous subject, a person capable of moral responsibility, . . . or groups who are able to justify their interactions morally and to engage in actions which are morally desirable'.[71] This is the perspective taken, among others, by Habermas, which she endorses but wants to link with the modern interest in individuals as the 'subjects of life stories'.[72] Apart from the aesthetic sense of literary fiction, there are two major senses to this term: the history of a person's life marked by 'temporality and irreversibility', and its biographical narration marked by changing perspectives and oriented towards 'reversibility and the ability to correct evaluations'.[73]

On the one hand, the change in retrospective evaluations from new thresholds can be seen as an expression of what was described before in the context of the theory of religious education, as the need to reorganize at each new stage one's complete self-understanding. On the other hand, a total disconnection to prior stages of the self is problematic. Haker points out the danger posed by the

> discontinuity of evaluation, at first only in relation to one's own life history. It radically endangers the formation or

maintenance also of moral evaluative attitudes, so
that *nolens volens* ethics has to pay attention to these
developments.[74]

Anyone interested in people's practical orientation has to pay heed
to their subjective evaluations and to philosophical approaches to
them. The question of identity arises first at the level of 'ethical'
evaluation of what one considers 'good' before these judgements
become the matter of justification by the standard of universalizability. Her main objection to Habermas's theory is that it leaves
the good and the right separate and bereft of a transition that
could be reflected on rationally. One model of mediation is offered
by the communitarian philosopher Charles Taylor who overcomes
the separation by having 'strong evaluations' perform this link.
They 'cannot be grasped independently from a person's identity',
who articulates in them her guiding ideals, making it possible to
'discuss more concretely'[75] what is at work in the move from
personal evidence to justifiability. For Taylor, this is the place
where 'strong evaluations', in their quality of being second-order
reflections on spontaneous preferences (called 'weak evaluations')
allow us to establish a prioritized order of goods. What could be
a juncture, however, remains a place of philosophical silence for
Habermas, who merely distinguishes the three different uses of
practical reason and considers the hermeneutical clarification of
biographical turns as related to an 'authenticity' which cannot be
further elucidated. As a consequence of this reticence, discourse
ethics has a problem both with the transition from 'good' to 'right',
and from 'justification' to 'application'.[76] In each case, Habermas
first separates the two sides rigorously:

> Moral practical discourses . . . require a break with all of
> the unquestioned truths of an established, concrete ethical
> life, in addition to distancing oneself from the contexts of
> life with which one's identity is inextricably interwoven.[77]

He subsequently has to 're-integrate' in a second move what has
been disconnected before. This is due, in Haker's analysis, to a
specific understanding of universalization which is not shared by
Kant. The requirement to distance oneself from the perspective of

one's background tradition asks for more than Kant did in his more demanding foundation of moral obligation.

> The Kantian principle of universalization does not presuppose this; it only demands to transcend in a fictive way the perspective of self-interest and of being bound to a specific situation of action, in order to clarify one's motives ... Since (in Habermas's conception) ... moral theory is to escape from the grips (*Fängen*) of a normative tradition, individual life histories, respectively life forms, are easily reduced to the aspect of hypothetical obligations and declared morally irrelevant. In a second step, however, they again have to be re-integrated since the moral perspective remains dependent on the 'support' (*Entgegenkommen*) of life forms, and since without the perspective from a life history the problem of motivation appears unsolvable.[78]

c. At the Intersection of the Good and the Right: Churches as Communities of Interpretation

Such exchanges on the starting point of ethics have relevance for disciplines beyond theological ethics. They clarify anthropological presuppositions regarding capabilities for ethical and moral reflection, as well as the role of traditions in the formation of identity and indirectly of morality. Theory decisions made here are significant for the connection with the theological interpretation of humanity and history in terms of creation and redemption, nature, sin and grace, as well as for the understanding of churches as ethical communities and as formative traditions. The question of their vitality was posed when discussing religious education. It is in relation to the apparent need to choose between modernity and tradition that Johann Baptist Metz addresses a series of questions to discourse ethics and its theory of democratic consensus which he sees as being in need of revitalization through religious memory:

> Is a society in which the project of modernity has been ... achieved necessarily and irreversibly a post-traditional society, as it is being suggested by the current Frankfurt School? ... Are there no discourse-guiding traditions anymore which

can protect these discourses from their own formalisms and from the desiccation of their contents (*inhaltliche Verödung*)? ... Are there any institutions left on the soil of modernity which understand themselves as accumulated memories, which keep a reservoir of memory accessible that is able to structure diffuse, communicatively untameable lifeworlds? Religious institutions which harbour a core that can rescue freedom exactly by presenting the *memoria passionis* represented by them as memory of alien suffering? ... Does the capability for democracy and pluralism not in the end depend on the presupposition of a 'remembering' which overcomes the self-referentiality of individuals through respect of the suffering of others and thus becomes ... a cultural resource (*Reserve*) of liberal democracy?[79]

Not all of Metz's dichotomies have to be accepted in order to endorse the thrust of his objections. Hille Haker has shown that other philosophical approaches find it possible to attribute greater internal rationality to life forms. For Charles Taylor, while they are not completely transparent, they are at least in part rationally analyzable with orders and priorities of goods which are accessible and can be interpreted. They have a mediating, formative function for morality. For Paul Ricoeur, the programmatic understanding of modernity as an alternative to tradition put forward by Habermas undervalues the historical status also of the Enlightenment from which he argues.[80] This opposition has only recently given way to a dialectical understanding.[81] The gulf declared between modernity and tradition, the interpretation of the priority of the 'right' as a 'postconventional' stage beyond particular historical formations and biographical evaluations of the 'good', leaves important elements of individual and political life without reflection; among them are the narrative generation of continuity in the identity of individuals and communities, including the relationship between memory and forgetting.

Perhaps resulting from his move in 2000 to embed the universalistic level of practical discourse in a 'species ethics', Habermas has recently spoken of the value of religious 'communities of interpretation'. The proposal put forward by Francis Schüssler Fiorenza at the 1988 conference in Chicago now appears relevant:

that churches could provide an institutional basis for publicly discussing questions in which normativity and self-understanding, the right and the good intersect.[82] The idea of a discourse community of the churches that Fiorenza suggested with reference to Seyla Benhabib's point that conceptions of striving for a flourishing life could at least be articulated, has finally been taken up by Habermas. Under conditions he now interprets as 'postsecular', the 'growth in the significance of religion in national publics' goes beyond their 'effective self-presentation in the media'; it is owed to the fact that 'religious communities increasingly take over the role of communities of interpretation'. They contribute to public opinion and will formation on 'conflicts of values' in pluralist societies where the state of argumentation does not fall into neat camps. Habermas observes that controversies no longer follow the usual divisions in politics as the scene has become more complex with argumentations from different value intuitions. If it is the case that 'it is by no means a priori settled which party can call in the right moral intuitions',[83] the role for religious communities which Fiorenza proposed in 1988, of providing space for such debates, is a crucial form of their ministry within contemporary culture and politics. It opens up the prospect of religions contributing to the public sphere as a laboratory in which future self-understandings are worked out.

Theology's reception of Habermas's theory of communicative action well before he began to appreciate religion as a critical resource was motivated by several features: its conception of agency as mediated by language, its universal moral scope, its integration of the social and human sciences, as well as its insistence on the crucial role of the lifeworld and of the self-understandings of citizens and communities for the processes of democracy.[84] On closer examination, however, it became clear that even as a theory of action it had deficiencies. It ignored the type of innovative action which theology takes as central for enabling relationships of mutuality and for renewing worn foundations of intersubjectivity – forgiveness, perseverance after disappointment, generosity in renouncing to an equal share and outreach towards the enemy. It banishes such action to the personal sphere, keeping what really are questions to the foundations of ethics at arm's length by classifying them as 'existential'. At the same time, it did not account for the individual motivation and interest arising from a person's striving for a self that would fulfill her ideals. So, while it figured unchallenged as *the* theory of action approach, it lacked the very drive that it could only have found by taking its foundation not in language as such but in human good will, striving for a flourishing life or autonomy oriented towards authenticity. Yet, Habermas's project of renewing critical theory has made it possible for new and far-reaching theory connections to be worked out, such as the decisions treated in the next chapters. In response to criticism, it has carried out major self-corrections. With so many pieces and junctures of his work already alluded to through the theological reception to it, it is now time to reconstruct its major moves together with the philosophical critiques to which it reacted. After investigating his project on its own terms and following its reception on the grounds of its own discipline in Part 2, it will be possible to examine the revised view of religion and its assessment in philosophically mediated theological critiques in Part 3.

Part 2

Habermas's Theory of Communicative Reason in Philosophical Debate

The core insight with which Habermas challenges the theories of Karl Marx, Max Weber and the *Dialectic of Enlightenment* phase of critical theory is that work, purposive and instrumental reason only capture one side of the capacity of humans to engage with the challenges of their natural constitution. The other equally original capacity that still has to be unfolded is communicative reason, based on the natural, specifically human capacity for language. The duality of work and interaction as two different types of agency which cannot be reduced to each other gives rise to the technical rationality of the subject–object relation, and to a rationality able to create cooperation based on the understanding of shared meanings. This relationship of subjects to each other is taken as the critical standard to judge the structures and practices that have been created historically. A critical theory of society is implicit in taking the capacity for intersubjective agreement as the normative starting point. Habermas combines theories from different origins in his new enterprise that seeks to reconstruct the realms and direction of societal organization with an inbuilt normative benchmark, and to test them through empirical research: (1) an anthropology focused on the practical competencies developed to cope with the task arising from human needs to be met by a society surviving over time through its structures of reproduction; (2) a standard of critique for the structures and modes of exchange created in responding to this task; here, the idea of taking one's measure from an analysis of human existence as proposed by Heidegger meets Marx's critical analysis of being dominated by the interest-driven logic of economics[1]; (3) the hermeneutical and the linguistic turns which recognise the embeddedness in language that already forges mutual under-standing but which, as Habermas insists in his debate with Hans-Georg Gadamer, also enables critical self-reflection.[2] This is a step beyond Gadamer's concept of the classic as a tradition enveloping the individuals more than they can ever elucidate. Habermas takes the prior linguistic mediatedness of all subjects – which makes philosophical analyses of consciousness appear to him as solipsist ventures – not in the sense of binding traditions but as implying validity claims which people direct towards and accept from each other. (4) The reconstructive character of this multidisciplinary theory design is evident in the integration of empirical social sciences, which, for example, investigate condi-tions and processes necessary for successful identity formation. Here, recognition of the other can be shown empirically as the constitutive presupposition of autonomous agency.

The guiding assumptions on which this framework is built already leave some alternatives behind: for instance, Hobbes' analysis of society as a means to ensure survival against one's violent neighbour, based on the vitalist assumption that the all-encompassing need is that of defending one's life. Equally put to one side are positions that begin with isolated individuals, rather than understand them as linguistically socialized fellow-humans which already share meanings in their intersubjectively constituted life worlds.

With its definitive new departures, Habermas's approach has to justify the connections and ruptures it chooses to make: the move to tie reflexivity to language, to conceive of philosophy as a partner in a joint interdisciplinary venture, the break of modernity with metaphysics, and the translation of morality into presuppositions of discourse. They have been received contro-versially by different philosophical perspectives, for example, postmodern, feminist, systems theoretical and Neo-Aristotelian. I have chosen authors whose critiques are concerned with normative concepts of agency, self and other, and with an under-standing of philosophy which can deliver on these themes. These core concepts are necessary implications of the Christian testimony to God's self-revelation in Jesus Christ. The theological requirement to their conception in philosophy is that they are suitable to be further determined by a faith perspective, while the requirement for the Christian faith is to make its option understandable to a general consciousness of truth.

I begin my review of the resonance and the critiques which Habermas received for the moves he proposed with the paradigm change from the philosophy of consciousness to language theory (Chapter 2). It is followed by the debates on the exclusion of metaphysics from a modern philosophical framework (Chapter 3) and on philosophy's new role as 'placeholder' and 'interpreter' (Chapter 4). The steps of the foundation of discourse ethics and its understanding of recognition will be treated subsequently (Chapter 5). Probing into the motivation for moral agency, especially in view of its aporias, Chapter 6 will complete Part 2.

Chapter 2

The Paradigm Change from the Philosophy of Consciousness to Language Theory

What reasons have led Habermas to the position that nothing less than a paradigm change is needed (1), and how have representatives of the philosophy of subjectivity, which language theory is to replace, responded to them and to the new presuppositions which he introduces instead (2)?

1. Language as an Alternative to the Dualisms of the Philosophy of Consciousness

For Habermas, the principal deficit of the philosophy of consciousness lies in its failure to give an adequate place to the role of language. He formulates his critique in view of the ending of the first phase of critical theory in the 'blackest book' of its second phase, the Dialectic of Enlightenment.[3] Its diagnosis of the inescapable structures of domination is not only due to its historical context, which makes it understandable that the authors lost their hope in the enlightening power of reason. It is also caused by the constraints of their philosophical approach with its dualist categories of subject and object, reason and nature. It is this opposition which leads to reason being conceptualized as pure domination. The possibility to revise this singularly instrumental understanding of reason stems from another human capacity that has to be brought into play, 'anchored as deeply in the history of the human species', namely, language:

> The human interest in autonomy and responsibility
> (*Mündigkeit*) is not mere fancy, for it can be apprehended a
> priori. What raises us out of nature is the only thing whose
> nature we can know: *language*. Through its structures,
> autonomy and responsibility are posited for us. With
> the first sentence the intention of a universal and
> unconstrained consensus is unmistakeably expressed.[4]

The normative idea of communicative rationality arises from an emphatic counter-stance to domination based on understanding language as being oriented towards intersubjective exchange and agreement. It is devised to overcome two major deficits which Habermas identifies in the paradigm to be surpassed.

(a)   Philosophy of consciousness takes as its starting point the solitary subject who relates to the *world* through the operation of *knowing*, setting up a subject-object dichotomy between consciousness and everything outside it, world and fellow-humans. Typical dualisms, such as essence-appearance, *res cogitans – res extensa* are the consequence of this schematization. This subject-object dichotomy also reappears in its self-reflection. It finds itself as the *object* of this reflective turn, although it intended to grasp the spontaneity of its reflective capacity.[5] It remains in a dual position of subject *over against* the world and as object *in* the world.

(b)   It isolates consciousness from the prior conditions that make it possible: embodiment, intersubjective constitution, situatedness, and stylizes it as giving independent access to the world: it 'disengaged the entirely dependent moment of self-consciousness from the network of linguistic interactions. Self-consciousness was inflated into an autonomous, solitary point of reference'.[6] In contrast, philosophy of language embeds consciousness in an already functioning world of shared references and repositions the previously monological subject as emerging from an intersubjectively constituted world.[7] The decisive insight is reached by linking speech act theory with the symbolic interactionism of

George Herbert Mead. The self is constituted in the performance of the roles of speaker and listener by taking over the perspective of the other with the help of the grammatical pronouns 'I' and 'you'. The methodological advantage of a pragmatic theory of language is its 'reconstructive analysis of publicly accessible grammatical facts' over against the 'introspective analysis of facts of consciousness'.[8] What it attributed to the subject's a priori faculties of synthesis, has to be relocated to the resources of the lifeworld which already provides shared meanings and common traditions.

Thus, the visible, public features of grammar make it possible to move beyond the 'introspection' of the subject, and the stores of cultural self-understandings assembled in the lifeworld allow the theory to let go of the need to assume a transcendental ego. The first correction is owed to philosophy of language, the second to hermeneutics.[9] As a result, subjects are seen as interacting and enriching a lifeworld to which they owe their intersubjective constitution. 'A circular process comes into play between the life-world as the resource from which communicative action draws, and the lifeworld as the product of this action; in this process, no gap is left by the disappearance of the transcendental subject'.[10]

Philosophy of consciousness is superseded by combining two partly alternative approaches in such a way that their problematic points are cancelled out. Against a purely immanent analysis of language, the historical constitution of linguistically mediated life forms is emphasized; against the danger of the hermeneutical attention to different traditions to succumb to a relativizing perspectivism, the necessity of critical evaluation is maintained.[11] The place of tradition is taken by the possibility of linguistic interaction to rationalize the lifeworld. Rationality consists not in consenting to culturally given contexts, but in taking a Yes or No stance.[12] This capacity for self-reflection is given an institutional location: the social sciences. What philosophy strove to do on its own, appealing to the human capacity for critique and enlightenment, is now allocated to the differentiated enquiries of individual sciences, such as sociology, psychology and language theory.

The insights from the philosophical approaches Habermas puts to use, such as the embodiment of reason in structures of language and its situatedness in a shared culture, do not have to be contested. But is a paradigm change necessary to do justice to them? And can his counter-proposal offer more satisfying solutions for the problems which could at least be formulated at the level of reflection reached by the philosophy of consciousness, or does it in turn reduce problems and restrict questions? Which premises and unresolved issues have his philosophical colleagues detected in his proposal of a new framework for modern theory?

2. Objections from Philosophers of Subjectivity

The first critique, whether the resources of the philosophy of consciousness have not been underestimated in declaring its failure, focuses on two points: its alleged solipsist or monological nature in relation to specific authors, and the way in which Habermas subordinates subjectivity to intersubjectivity (a). The second question about the explicit and the tacit premises of the new approach is discussed under the heading of 'naturalism' (b). The exchanges portrayed are important for understanding the reservations against his reinterpretation of Kant's moral philosophy in his discourse ethics which will be treated in Chapter 5, and for his later return to Kierkegaard in response to developments in genetic technologies, discussed in Chapter 7. Both enquiries concern assumptions and conclusions that affect the scope of practical reason which has been at the core of Helmut Peukert's theological critique, and are relevant for the openness of the theory for theological interpretations of human life and agency.

a. Intersubjectivity against Solipsism?

What is at stake in the corrections by colleagues who share with Habermas the commitment to modernity is how self and other, freedom and nature, moral responsibility and history, are to be understood. The first port of call to test his far-reaching thesis that a paradigm change is needed is current reconstruction of the historical positions of Kant and Johann Gottlieb Fichte. Whether

Habermas's judgment of their analyses of the subject as solipsist is adequate, is not only a question of historical justice, but also instructive for understanding his approach and his use of core concepts, such as recognition, with less emphasis on its normative content. The critique accompanying the interpretation and integration of his theory of communicative action by theologians into their theories of communicating the gospel may then emerge as reinstating the fuller meaning put forward by the philosophy of subjectivity with which he wants to part.

With regard to Kant, one has to distinguish between the different functions of the focus on the individual subject of reflection in the *Critique of Pure Reason* and the *Critique of Practical Reason*. In the first Critique, Kant's method of going back from 'visible' intellectual performances to the 'invisible' conditions of their possibility in the subject can be called 'introspective'; but since it aims at elucidating general presuppositions which are true for any act of knowing, it is not merely 'subjective'. The act of testing maxims for their universalizability in the *Critique of Practical Reason* appears monological to Habermas, who transfers this examination to the discourse between actual conversation partners. Here, the philosopher Reiner Wimmer makes the point that Kant's underestimation of the need to 'think together', which earns his procedure the label 'monological', may be connected to his famous formula that Enlightenment means to be able to use one's own independent understanding and insight, over against 'a thinking that remains bound by authority and tradition'.[13] Thus, the lack of regard for a joint and plural process of deliberation is due to his intention to distinguish from given and shared assumptions the capability of each individual's reason to examine, judge and validate them herself.

Also for Paul Ricoeur, Kant's method in practical reasoning cannot be captured as an interior monologue. In the view of

> the Habermasians, the principle of universalizability
> is ... applied in an immediately dialogical situation,
> whereas for Kant it remains confined to an inner
> monologue (something, let me note in passing, that is
> highly contestable and certainly wrong with respect
> to the Kantian philosophy of right).[14]

If Kant as a prime representative of the philosophy of consciousness develops a theory of ethics with reference to plurality, and if
his transcendental method does not exclude the prior linguistic
mediatedness of concrete subjects, then some of the apparent
alternatives can be resolved as matters pertaining to different levels
of analysis. The point that remains controversial then is whether
individual consciousness, or conscience, is the authority which
justifies validity, or whether it arises from the empirical process of
examination by concrete historical subjects. Karl-Otto Apel and
Habermas opt for the second; Henrich and, as far as moral conscience is concerned, Ricoeur opt for the first possibility.

Regarding Fichte, the well-known dilemma of self-reflection
quoted by Habermas in his exchange with Henrich was put
forward by this classical thinker of consciousness himself, who
subsequently proposed as a different method of foundation, the
constitution of the I from the recognition of the other. Habermas
does not mention his analyses of the mutual recognition of
freedoms.[15] So if the relation between self and other in the
philosophy of subjectivity is more complex than Habermas's
labelling as 'monological' admits, then the transcendental method
of enquiring into the condition of the possibility of linguistic
and social acts should not be written off before further interpretative effort has gone into it. The internal possibility in the
subject of the achievements attributed to language should no
longer be left unexplored.

Equally, the question, posed neither by Habermas nor by
George Herbert Mead, of what is implied and what makes it
possible to take the perspective of the other needs to be reconsid-
ered. Here the relationship between individuality and sociability,
self-reflection and intersubjectivity has to be investigated. For
Henrich, the thesis on which Habermas has 'made his whole work
dependent . . . , the primacy of the community of interaction'[16] is
radically one-sided by attributing the constitution of the self
completely to one of two distinctive factors. Instead of giving
'primacy' to one of them, Henrich suggests 'equal primordiality'
between linguistic interaction and reflexivity. This is to restore the
balance which Habermas has tipped to one side by stating that
'original self-consciousness is not a phenomenon inherent in the
subject but one that is communicatively generated'.[17] Henrich

wants to show that communication is unthinkable without self-relation. The

> functioning of linguistic communication presupposes a
> self-relation on the part of the 'speaker' – as one of its
> constitutive pre-conditions, one which is no less
> fundamental than the subject–predicate form of the
> proposition . . . Habermas finds . . . that the linguistically
> organized lifeworld, which for its part is self-sufficient,
> can generate self-relations – and hence the identity of
> speakers – out of itself . . . Such a view . . . would be
> incapable of describing or understanding language and
> communication . . . rather, . . . the capacity of language can
> only develop *along (in einem) with* the spontaneous
> emergence of a self-relation. This emergence in turn
> requires explanation. And this would require us to speak of
> an implicit self-relation, which already appears or functions
> at the most elementary level of language acquisition.[18]

The simultaneity of imitation and spontaneity is characteristic already for children's first acquisition of language. Their learning of their mother tongue would be misunderstood as rote learning and accumulation of meanings. Here, Henrich's analysis is close to Friedrich Schleiermacher's reflections in his hermeneutics on the complementary elements of 'divinizing' (guessing), and comparing, in the effort to discover the meaning of a word. Children in their second year have to guess two things at once and make an inventory leap between the general unity of meaning of a word (*Einheit der Bedeutung*), and its local determination by the context (*Localwerth*). Their amazing performance can only be understood if their 'learning' is grasped as this spontaneous double reconstruction.[19] Henrich describes it in similar terms as 'spontaneous attempts . . . oriented towards an example' in which 'eventually understanding along with the capability (to speak the language) emerge spontaneously'.[20] Although the use of the personal pronoun 'I' is learnt at a later stage – a year later than the first words – there are other elements that show the implicit self-relation at work: 'the mastery of demonstratives, the correct use of one's own name, the developed use of negation, and thus one of the elementary conditions for the understanding of truth'.[21] Henrich is making the point that imitation and repetition of words only represent one part of children's language acquisition; the other part is invisible but nonetheless effective, namely the capability to relate them to themselves even before they are able to say 'I'. The same is true for the ability to change perspectives in the mutual role-taking which Habermas assumes from Mead. How can it be internalized without confusing self and other? It has to presuppose as the internal condition of its possibility a prior familiarity with oneself which is at the basis of reflexivity.

The 1985–1987 dispute, conducted in articles and in Habermas's contribution to the *Festschrift* for Henrich, and preceded by Henrich's *Laudatio* for Habermas in 1974, spells out an abiding disagreement on how to understand what is implied in conscious life, and whether its reconstruction needs a transcendental or a reconstructive method allied to empirical investigations. The question of the transformation of categories from the philosophy of consciousness into ones of a theory of communication concerns the most decisive juncture of any theory, the selection of its guiding paradigm. Henrich's emphasis on the significance of the choices involved is apposite: they relate to 'the question of whether Habermas relies on adequate or inadequate assumptions regarding a life which has to be led in the light of reason. Anyone who has a relation to his work of some kind must try to get clear about this issue'.[22]

b. Descending into Naturalism?

The objection that specific theory decisions give the enterprise naturalist underpinnings relates to two different periods of Habermas's work: to its nascent stage represented by *Knowledge and Human Interests* (1968), with the 1969 commentary of another interlocutor throughout the phases of his work, Michael Theunissen, and to its 1981 elaboration in *Theory of Communicative Action*, scrutinized by Henrich in the 1980s. It is a discussion important for being able to trace the background to and assess the position Habermas takes in *Between Naturalism and Religion* in 2005, but also more generally about the status of his theory in its combination of disciplines with different methods.

What is at stake in Theunissen's debate of his early work is where the measure of the critique of current social structures, and the move for change, come from. The problem for Henrich is the alliance with language theory which promotes a descent into naturalism by decoding achievements due to consciousness, as activities of language. Tasks to be carried out by reason are assumed to have been completed by the 'lifeworld' taken as an immediate, conflict-free zone. I shall portray each of their argumentations separately and then examine what points they share.

Theunissen's perceptive analysis of an enterprise, the 'underlying intentions' of which he 'endorses', concludes with the judgment that despite his counter-measures, Habermas ends up with abso-lutizing 'both subjective nature and nature in itself'.[23] On the one hand, his critique of the *Dialectic of Enlightenment* was that it 'entails that nature has a selfhood independent of subjectivity' in its 'objectivistic ontology'[24] which he saw as arising from the subject-object-split of the philosophy of consciousness. Habermas's rejection is at first borne out by two theory decisions which provide protection against hypostasizing nature as an objectivized power which grounds subjectivity. The first is the distinction, against Marx, between labour and interaction, which differentiates societal praxis into instrumental and communicative action. Here, he 'breaks the monopoly of labour by renewing Aristotle's distinction between *poiesis*, or *techne*, and *praxis*'.[25] The second is the interpretation of the 'dimension of interests in which labour and interaction are located in Kantian terms, as an "achievement (*Leistungen*) of the transcendental subject"'.[26] Another Kantian formulation is chosen when Habermas presents 'knowledge-guiding interests' as furnishing 'the conditions of possible objectivity', in distinction from 'particular interests';[27] they are taken by Theunissen as pointing to the wish to steer clear of any natural objectivism: there 'can be no place for an objectivistic ontology of nature in a picture which portrays the being of every entity as constituted by a transcendental subject'.[28] How is it possible then, that he falls prey to the temptation of naturalism after all?

Here, Theunissen assembles the evidence for his diagnosis that Habermas ultimately interprets both objective and subjective nature in a way in which nature wins out over history. The decisive move is that Habermas anchors precisely the transcendental achievements of the subject once again in *objective* nature, as in this crucial quote: '"The achievements of the transcendental subject have their basis in the natural history of the human species" (TWI, 161)'. For Theunissen, this 'solidifies nature . . . into the being that grounds the subject' and concedes to it a preponderance which pushes history aside. The argument which Habermas marshals as a defence against a 'naturalistic misunderstanding of this thesis', that 'labour and interaction go beyond the natural principle of self-preservation in which they are grounded' is so weak that what could be more than nature remains unclear.[29]

The same tendency reappears in Habermas's interpretation of *subjective* nature. In a subtle way, it is again nature that trumps history by relating back to its natural basis what should count as human historical achievements. What Theunissen wants to see expressed in categories of free agency as the mover in historical struggles, is objectified into 'invariant frameworks' (*Bezugsrahmen*) for labour and interaction. Thus,

> nature creeps upwards into the subject from its base,
> eventually objectifying it from the inside . . . Nature
> penetrates the very activities of consciousness, and petrifies
> the transcendental horizon of world constitution into
> what Habermas so often refers to as a 'frame of reference',
> which is inherently something static . . . which man carries
> around with him, like a snail its shell.[30]

Another proof of this reduction of options open to freedom to the naturally given basis of such 'frameworks' is Habermas's response to Herbert Marcuse's critique of current uses of science. Marcuse stresses the ability to choose between historical alternatives, and to move from a science which exploits nature to one that cares for nature; Habermas refers to 'anthropologically fixed structures', which do not allow for such conscious counter-options: 'There can be no question of a historicity that is at work in the cultural determination of human beings' (*Geschichtlichkeit, die in die kulturellen Bedingungen des Menschseins eingriffe*). For Theunissen, Arnold Gehlen's emphasis on institutions as the anthropological counterpart to animal instinct wins out over the critical theory of Herbert Marcuse: it is 'no accident that Habermas invokes Gehlen against Marcuse'.[31]

Apart from these responses which regularly come down on the side of natural givenness, the other great give-away for Theunissen that Habermas makes standards of self-reflection dependent on natural structures is the much-quoted passage from his inaugural lecture in Frankfurt 1965, on the structure of language and its implications. The Kantian concepts used seem to distance it completely from any suspicion of naturalization. Yet, although the standards of evaluation are described as 'theoretically certain' and as 'a priori intelligible', it is exactly their being claimed as a priori, and not historical, that marks the transition into naturalizing thinking: it 'cannot be seen as anything other than a manoeuvre that tries to cover over the historicality of these standards'.[32] The problem is that they are not recognized as stemming from processes of self-reflection in historically changing self-understandings, but that they are attributed to the gradual unfolding of natural presuppositions of the species.

Theunissen's uncovering of the naturalism at work in the 1960s relaunch of the research programme of the first phase of critical theory can be summarized as follows: despite all his criticism of the subject-object dualism and of the concept of nature in the *Dialectics of Enlightenment,* Habermas, following Marx, allocates to *objective nature,* the position of being the independent ground of the history of humanity. Regarding *subjective nature*, the achievements of consciousness, attitudes to and projections of the world are taken as the anthropological heritage of the natural history of the species in the shape of invariant frameworks. They are thus deprived of their origin in human self-understandings and of the dynamics of conscious historical transformation. Habermas's reference to language and agreement between humans is perceived as forming part of the tendency towards naturalization of phenomena which can only be interpreted adequately in categories of freedom and history.

If Theunissen's interest is ultimately practical, resisting a naturalization that results in 'a limiting of the possibilities of real historical transformation',[33] Henrich's critique of the stage of work reached by 1981 is that the commitment to modernity which they share needs a different approach that does not abandon previously achieved differentiations. The real danger for continuing the project of modernity does not lie in metaphysics, but in opening up the road towards naturalism by taking over uncritically the conceptual framework of language theory. It veils conflicts which before, in a more dialectically aware analysis, were able to be expressed. Symptomatic in Habermas's programmatic combination of theories is his unproblematic use of the term 'life-world'. For Henrich, it 'is a term which has this avoidance written into its profile. For it declares the essential point of departure for all speech acts to be a totality which is in principle harmonious' with 'resources' that are 'ultimately reliable and valid'.[34] It thus unifies alternative positions which should be argued out.

For Henrich, 'conscious life' defies such assumptions of 'immediacy' and reliability. The 'problem . . . it represents for itself' is 'finding a stable description of itself',[35] since it is marked by conflicts between different self-descriptions and concepts of world that cannot all be true, but have to be resolved with reasons at a level beyond the primary contradictions: 'Whoever reflects has already understood that he is at home not only in one world, and that he cannot merge seamlessly with the world'.[36] Henrich's objection to Habermas is not that he expressly promotes naturalism, but that he avoids these conflicts and the pressure of the problem of naturalism by treating concepts with a history of diverse interpretation as if they were unequivocal. Henrich's criterion is which tradition of thinking is better able to do justice to the spontaneity and irreducible primordiality of conscious life in the unavoidable transformation of primary descriptions into disputes at the level of philosophical reflection.

For ethics and theology, two of his insights are especially relevant: first, the tension between different orientations of action and self – examples given are, 'taking as criteria for our actions, norms which cannot be derived from the interest in survival', or 'revealing ourselves in a relation of trust' which is more than 'honestly communicating', viewing a relationship not just 'from the standpoint of strictly universal norms'; secondly, the misleading attribution of 'totality' to the lifeworld.

The first query derives from the everyday experience that 'the self-understanding of human beings leads to conflicts between equally convincing self-descriptions' which 'force us to seek some more comprehensive dimension in which these conflicts could finally be resolved, one which would make possible a self-description which reconciled the primary self-descriptions'.[37] Henrich illustrates the depth of these enquiries by pointing to Kant's question, 'What is man' (*Was ist der Mensch?*), which can only be put radically enough as the question of a precarious synthesis: what can we know, what ought we do, and what can we hope for? Henrich shows that individual answers to each of these questions 'at the first level, in relation to only one layer of self-description' miss the point. The 'explosive force of the question arises from the fact that it aims at a synthesis'.[38]

In comparison to the task which the philosophy of subjectivity poses to itself, reconciling such divergences, the clarifications achieved by analyses of different speech acts, examined one by one for their validity claims, remain at a different level. Yet if they are taken to exhaust the remit of philosophical reflection, the conflicts arising when, e.g., 'normative' and 'expressive claims' intersect or clash, will be ignored. Henrich uncovers these claims to be linked to 'self-descriptions'. His quest for resolution or integration at a higher level only makes sense if the conflict posed by simultaneous claims and options of agency is admitted. And does the alternative option become clear in Habermas's analysis between a life led by self-interest and one led by the moral respect for oneself and others which needs hope to be sustained? In Chapter 5, the answers which his discourse ethics give to the different aspects of these questions will be examined. In his response to theologians, however, mentioned in Chapter 1, a dividing line was drawn between philosophical and 'existential' questions which Henrich's approach does not seem to support.

The second point, Henrich's perception of the role of the lifeworld, is of importance to theology in its task to spell out the biblical witness that God's salvation of humanity has already begun and continues to the end of time. If the lifeworld, in which all matters have already found some kind of answer, constitutes the ultimate horizon and takes the place of the responsibility for the 'totality' of the history of humanity, then the scope of reason suffers an immense reduction. In contrast to Kant who understood reason as the faculty of principles including the open and unanswered questions this leads to, this move would cut off all questions, strivings and hopes beyond the contemporary lifeworld, and abolish the platform shared by philosophy and theology in grappling with the conflicts and contradictions of human life and history. It is a problem I shall return to in the discussion of philosophy's role as interpreter of the lifeworld in Chapter 4.

The parallels between Theunissen's and Henrich's critique lie in their diagnosis of the naturalization of subjective nature. Although the authors with whom Habermas dialogues change, the tendency remains the same: the achievements of subjectivity in creating knowledge, orientation and norms, are traced back to a different ground than consciousness, be it anthropologically given frameworks, or the resources of the lifeworld. The urgency of Henrich's concern with theory decisions which abandon the project of modernity to its naturalist opponents can be explained by his awareness that there is no safety net to stop its fall, nor any other platform from which it could rebound. If philosophy fails in its role of illuminating everyday experiences of conscious life, there is no other level which could recoup these self-understandings. The precariousness of the project of modernity is also reflected in Theunissen's diagnosis that critical theory, enlarging subjectivity into the human species and 'overburdening' it with the role, taken over from God, as subject of world history, 'collapses back' into an 'apotheosis of nature'.[39] Thus, the heritage of modernity which is owed to some degree to monotheism, as Habermas admits in the passages quoted in Chapter 1 on the continuing impulses of 'Israel' on 'Athens', can also be lost again. If the foundations of the life-world turn out to be less secure than at first assumed, the defence of modernity and its achievements, especially its morality of mutual recognition, will need other resources. Therefore, as the second round of questions put to Habermas, the relationship of metaphysics to modernity will be explored.

Chapter 3

The Relationship of
Metaphysics to Modernity

Which understanding of metaphysical thinking leads Habermas to reject it (1), and how are his reasons to be judged (2)? How do philosophers who do not agree to relinquishing metaphysics in modernity define it instead (3)? And how do its respective interpretations affect theology's situation of dialogue (4)?

1. Habermas's Concept of Metaphysics

Three features mark the metaphysical mode of thinking in Habermas's analysis: it is defined by 'identity thinking', that is, identifying being and thinking; it puts forward a doctrine of ideas; and it has a 'strong concept of theory'; this third element is traced as continuous from Plato via Descartes to Kant and Hegel.[1] The first feature, 'identity thinking', in which 'the one is both axiom and essential ground, principle and origin', can take different conceptual shapes: that of a 'a world-transcendent creator-god', of 'the essential ground of nature, or, lastly and most abstractly', of 'being' from which 'things and events . . . in their diversity' appear as 'ordered multiplicity'. The typical tension of idealism is between 'two forms of knowledge', such as 'idea and appearance, form and matter'. Its new foundation in modernity, after the 'shift in paradigms from ontology to mentalism', is 'subjectivity'. The 'precedence of identity over difference and that of ideas over matter' is retained. In the philosophy of consciousness, identity thinking and doctrine of ideas undergo a transformation that ends with reason becoming absolute:

> In the contempt for materialism and pragmatism there
> survives something of the absolutistic understanding of

theory, which is . . . elevated above experience and the specialized scientific disciplines . . . Therein is completed the circuit of an identity thinking that self-referentially incorporates itself within the totality it grasps, and that wants in this way to satisfy the demand for justifying all premises from within itself. The modern philosophy of consciousness sublimates the independence of the theoretical mode of life into a theory that is absolute and self-justifying.[2]

It comes as no surprise that a metaphysics which insists on such exaggerated claims cannot be reconciled with modernity. Accordingly, this tradition was put into question only 'from outside', through developments in society in which the 'procedural rationality' of the natural sciences, the 'formalism' of moral and legal theory and the 'historical-hermeneutical sciences' became effective.[3] This controversy between current philosophical approaches in which Habermas profiles the need for his postmetaphysical venture, acquires a political edge when the return to metaphysical thinking is interpreted as a fruit of the 'neo-conservative *Zeitgeist*'.[4]

2. Questions Regarding Its Adequacy

How are the concept and the transformations of this tradition, sketched from a specific understanding of modernity, to be evaluated? It speaks for the discourse ethicist's differentiated perception that he does not simply identify metaphysics and the philosophy of subjectivity:

Metaphysics had emerged as the science of the universal, immutable, and necessary; the only equivalent left for this later on was a theory of consciousness that states the necessary subjective conditions for the objectivity of universal synthetic judgements a priori. If we stick with this way of using these words, then under modern conditions of the philosophy of reflection there can be no metaphysical thinking in the strict sense, but at most the reworking of the metaphysical problems that have been transformed by the philosophy of consciousness.[5]

He also acknowledges the components of modern self-understanding which can be attributed to metaphysics in the larger sense; it is significant, however, that he emphasizes the element of self-determination but not of the mutual recognition of subjects: 'Under the headings of self-consciousness, self-determination, and self-realization, a normative content of modernity has developed that must not be identified with the blind subjectivity of self-preservation or the disposition over oneself'.[6]

On the other hand, the precision of his presentation can be questioned on three decisive points:

(a)   Acutely different, even oppositional theories are summarized under the title 'metaphysics' as an apparently unified position. Thus, Kant's critical idealism can be subsumed under 'identity thinking' and 'objective teleology'. The description given of 'idealism' might capture Berkeley's version, but not Kant's. Hegel and Kant are pictured as two variants of the same type of thinking instead of as alternative basic philosophical conceptions which are in competition until today. It is telling as well that faith in a 'world-transcendent creator-god' is aligned with Greek identity thinking, as if biblical monotheism had not challenged it profoundly. Chapter 7 will show how Habermas moves to a different appreciation of the relationships of freedom established by creation, over against Neo-Platonic emanation. The thesis that metaphysical thinking is superannuated can only be supported due to this broad-brush sketch which can be contested by scrutinizing the different historical positions more closely.

(b)   The generalizing presentation creates the impression that with an edifice of thought as monolithical as metaphysics the only possible attack is from the outside. A typical expression is used, insinuating an unexamined complex of tradition: 'The basic concepts of religion and metaphysics had relied upon a syndrome of validity that dissolved with the emergence of expert cultures in science, morality and law on the one hand, and with the autonomization of art on the other'.[7]

This description treats metaphysics as a unified block and ignores the succession of theory designs which constitutes its history in each era. Insofar as its positions followed each other in mutual criticism, the judgment has to be questioned that its absolute claim runs counter to the modern insight into the fallible and revisable nature of knowledge. It is true that challenges to metaphysical thinking arose in the context of developments within society, but they did by no means only arise from outside. As will be seen in the next subsection, also Herbert Schnädelbach, a critic of Neo-Aristotelianism and of religion, portrays the history of metaphysics as a history of its transformations.

(c)   Above all, characterizations such as 'totalizing and self-referential' theories raise major doubts as to whether they capture the self-understanding of classical positions like Kant's, Fichte's and Schelling's. Speaking of 'a subjectivity that makes possible the world as a whole'[8] overlooks the distinction between the world's given existence and ways of knowing it in Kant. Only the concepts of world and objectivity as such stem from subjectivity, but not that what is given to which they refer. Moreover, the radical insight into the facticity of reason itself shows Habermas's marking of this position as 'absolute and self-justifying' as false. For Habermas, it is only through the linguistic and the pragmatic turns that it becomes 'possible to attack a problem that cannot be solved using the basic concepts of metaphysics: the problem of individuality'.[9] Here, he shows with reference to Wilhelm v. Humboldt, how the pragmatic turn gives space to individuality by going beyond grammatical rules and leaving 'room for individual nuances and innovative unpredictability in the use of these expressions'. He sees a moral regard for the other embodied in the structures of language: 'The grammatical role of the personal pronouns forces the speaker and the hearer to adopt a performative attitude in which the one confronts the other as *alter ego*; only with a consciousness of their absolute difference and irreplaceability can the one recognize himself in the other'.[10]

The hope that the problem of mutual recognition can be solved by transforming it into the roles given by grammatical structures will be discussed in greater detail in Chapter 5 on discourse ethics.

Yet in the context of his debate of metaphysics, the contrast is striking between the incapability attested to it with regard to grasping individuality, on the one hand, and the appreciation of its significance for the emergence of core concepts of modern self-understanding, such as self-determination, on the other.

What Habermas projects as 'metaphysics', in order to reject it subsequently, is owed to a combination of individual concepts which can be found in specific authors, but which cannot be unified into one coherent position. The ironic suspicion voiced by Herbert Schnädelbach 'that one identifies what cannot be supported any longer with "metaphysics as such"' is quite apposite. 'The following strategy does not make sense: What one rejects philosophically gets called metaphysics, and the metaphysics on which one relies oneself, is not identified as such'.[11]

3. Modern Understandings of Metaphysics

Following Kant, for Theunissen and Henrich, and, as will be seen, for Schnädelbach, it is an essential trait of humans to question beyond what can be analyzed empirically. As we have seen, for Henrich the 'self-relation of conscious life' unavoidably implies metaphysical questions. The subject experiences the world and itself in multiple conflicting ways which it seeks to integrate. To show 'the internal lack of homogeneity in, and the conflict between, the primary world conceptions and self-descriptions . . . so that they can then be translated into synthesizing second-stage conceptions[12] are 'figures of thought' and tasks which 'Habermas is wrong to think that his own theoretical enterprise can do without'.[13] A metaphysics of 'resolving closure' (*Abschluss*) which at the same time renounces to the claims of 'absolute knowledge',[14] corresponds to a 'latent interest of every human being' since '(n)either reason, nor a life oriented towards reason . . . can simply remain in this state of incompletion and in such contradictions . . . It is a concern of reason, and as such a concern of humanity'.[15]

Also Schnädelbach highlights the difference to scientific knowledge. He defines metaphysics as 'the effort to reach a cognitive comprehensive orientation with interpretative means'.[16] 'Interpretive' signifies that what is at issue is not a knowledge claim regarding the world, as in the sciences, but a question of the 'meaning of it all' (*Sinn des Ganzen*).[17] He distinguishes between responses which meanwhile may have become dated, and abiding questions: 'I still regard metaphysical questions as irrefutable (*unabweisbar*) since they are "given to us by reason itself" (Kant); if certain types of answers are no longer acceptable, it cannot mean that these questions can no longer be asked'.[18] If – as in the case of the foundations of the lifeworld which cannot be researched any further – questions which transcend what can be answered in the framework of one specific approach are no longer admitted, Schnädelbach fears that the result of overcoming metaphysics is the opposite of the enlightenment its detractors hope for:

> Could it not be that a thinking that has purged itself from anything that reminds one of metaphysics no longer deserves the label 'thinking'? Does not the 'postmetaphysical age' only begin when we – flooded by media and other tranquilizers – simply stop asking certain questions?[19]

Since for both contemporary philosophers, thinking itself is oriented towards a metaphysical outreach, it cannot be overcome, but only transformed:

> For factual and historical reasons I advocate regarding the cause of metaphysics as a matter that cannot be closed in principle; the 'ending' of metaphysics should finally end . . . this farewell to the rhetorics of completion should then free the view towards the transformations into which the spectacular collapses of metaphysics flowed. We are learning today to see the history of metaphysics with increasing clarity as a history of the criticism of metaphysics . . . My thesis is: a critical deconstruction which really affects metaphysics in its core is only possible as its reconstruction.[20]

If one were to apply Schnädelbach's understanding of metaphysics as the 'effort to reach a cognitive comprehensive orientation from critical reason with a practical intent'[21] and as a sequence of mutually critical projects, to Habermas's theory of communicative rationality, it could count as metaphysics *par excellence*: its orientation towards enlightenment and autonomous responsibility, intersubjective recognition and undamaged individuality as much as its evolutionary underpinnings are features of a comprehensive orientation which one can also call metaphysics. Henrich's concern to reconnect the different segments and concepts of world to each other is replicated in the task which Habermas ascribes to philosophy, to mediate between the differentiated spheres of the objectified knowledge perspective of the sciences, and the hermeneutical, self-reflective, and normative insights of the Humanities. The 'interpretive' and 'place-holding' roles of philosophy to be investigated in the next chapter reformulate tasks which other contemporary thinkers call 'metaphysical'.[22] We shall see how Habermas holds on to a universal remit of reason but situates it in the lifeworld. For Schnädelbach, however, his procedure does not show any serious engagement with this heritage. In his analysis of different types of farewell from metaphysical thinking he classifies him together with Marx and Nietzsche under the 'ideology critical' type.

> The ideology critical attack on metaphysics is based on a containment strategy: the critic discontinues dialogue and regards it *en bloc* as a symptom that has to be treated and fought including its causes . . . We still find this today in the concern that a positive understanding of metaphysics amounts to a strengthening of neo-conservativism and to sabotaging the project of modernity.[23]

Habermas's principled rejection stands and falls with how the counterpart is portrayed. Schnädelbach's definition does not include the three contested elements: what Habermas 'considers as no longer sustainable in metaphysics – identity thinking, idealism and the claim of "strong", i.e., immediately action-guiding theory – is not, anyhow, linked to this concept'.[24]

Does it make any difference for theology if contemporary philosophers defend the abiding significance of some version of 'metaphysics' against Habermas's critique? I shall summarize the salient point of the disagreement, and conclude by comparing Schnädelbach's metaphysics-friendly but theology-critical approach with Habermas's ongoing 'postmetaphysical' but theology-friendly position.

4. (Post)metaphysical Thinking and Theology

The key point of the disagreement on whether metaphysics can, or cannot, be critically transformed, is what role is to be allocated to subjectivity. Both Schnädelbach and Henrich see this mode of thinking as arising from inescapable questions of the subject or of 'conscious life'. To abolish, supersede or circumvent it would level human self-perception and autonomous praxis; it would hand over victory to competing systems of world explanation, especially to naturalism, against which Henrich directs his approach, a non-absolutist 'metaphysics of completion', but also to tradition-centred alternatives.[25] In their view, the three elements identified in metaphysics have already undergone multiple transformations.

Habermas replaces the first, identity of being and thought, post-metaphysically by the different methods of enquiry of the natural sciences and the humanities; they are held together by the 'placeholding' and 'interpretive' functions of a philosophy that explicates a concept of rationality which is still universal but supported by the communicative structures of the lifeworld.[26] Thus, the new form of reason is situated, but still assumed to be normative and critical. The second element, idealism, is brought down from its Platonic disconnectedness, but also from Kant's (and Henrich's) transcendental enquiry to the content of validity claims which is shown to be context-transcendent. The replacement of the third aspect, the strong concept of theory, creates interesting openings for actual religions and theology. Once philosophy loses its extraordinary status and assumes its place in the lifeworld, it no longer presumes to be able to judge which life forms are preferable. Because of its fallibilistic self-understanding, it does not rule out religion as incompatible with modernity. At the same time, since it lacks the capacity of metaphysics to endow the world with meaning,[27] it needs the resources of religion as one formation in civil society to

> mobilize modern reason against the defeatism lurking
> within it. Postmetaphysical thinking cannot cope on its own
> with the defeatism concerning reason which we encounter
> today both in the postmodern radicalization of the 'dialectic

of the Enlightenment' and in the naturalism founded on a naive faith in science.[28]

What is positive for theology is Habermas's acknowledgement of the function which concrete historical traditions and communities of faith have in the symbolic and motivational household of a society. The expectations directed to them will be discussed in the subsequent chapters. Before the objections formulated by Henrich, Theunissen and Schnädelbach are followed up in the postmetaphysical reconceptualization of philosophy in the next chapter, one point should be made clear in conclusion: the differences between each of their positions towards religion show that there is no direct link between defending metaphysics and supporting religion. While both Theunissen and Henrich have remained dialogue partners for theology, Schnädelbach remains a 'pious', that is, not a 'militant . . . atheist'[29] for whom philosophy of religion can take over the function of theology. He ends his review of metaphysics and religion with the following 'provocation': theology is

> the reflexive form of religion. Religion is what one
> lives and thus believes and confesses; theology is the
> interpretation of what is lived, believed and confessed . . .
> In their interpretive character theology and metaphysics
> are comparable; both strive for a cognitive comprehensive
> orientation, although on different foundations. Whether
> the religious is a suitable basis for this has to be decided by
> the theologians. What I see as valid – and the provocation
> I want to conclude with – is: religion is what one has.
> Theology is what one thinks about it. Reflecting on what
> one has – or thinks one has – is philosophy. Thus principled
> systematic thinking about religion is philosophy of religion.
> If you ask me: there is no need for theology.[30]

Here, the relationship between theology and philosophy is seen as one of competition at the interpretive level. One background for discounting theology is his conclusion from human finitude that all responses have to be kept open. The 'cognitive comprehensive orientation' is only seen as possible in 'critical metaphysics' if it remains 'negative, . . . without a link to an "unconditional" meaning'.[31] Here, even his two philosophical colleagues would disagree. His refusal of an ongoing role for theology results from its link to a concrete historical religion – Christianity – which in his view has had overwhelmingly negative effects.

The counterpositions of Schnädelbach and Habermas are informative for theology in two respects: Habermas's acceptance of theology as an intellectual enterprise recognizes, on the one hand, that theology is more than reflection on religion as such, and that its link to a historically individuated tradition of believing in God cannot be substituted. Thus, the internal differentiation between dogmatic theology, fundamental theology and philosophy of religion is not put into question; the distinctive tasks of interpreting the identity of a faith tradition in its hermeneutical development, contemporary forms of the question of meaning, and philosophical approaches to the concept of God are not collapsed. The problem that Habermas's programme of superseding metaphysics poses for theology, on the other hand, is that it abolishes a shared level of reflection on the task arising from the tension between divergent 'self-descriptions' (Henrich) and world concepts. If their relevance is no longer accepted as a theme for philosophy, or relegated to an existential private sphere, theology loses the possibility to justify its position with reasons to the *lumen naturale*, the general human consciousness of truth. Theology could still articulate its convictions among other voices in pluralism; civil society and the neutral state may even appreciate it as a facilitator of discussions on moral and ethical self-understandings. But it has a truth claim about the reality and the nature of God which it needs to be able to legitimate to reason, not least in view of classical and current critiques of religion. If the level of reflection to which it could contribute has been abolished by the paradigm change from consciousness to language, it loses the condition of the possibility of reasoned explanation of the practical option to believe in God.[32]

Chapter 4

Postmetaphysical Philosophy as Stand-in and as Interpreter

Prior to elaborating the postmetaphysical self-understanding of his theory in his exchange with Henrich, Habermas had redesigned the role of philosophy. His contribution to the Hegel-Congress in Stuttgart in 1981 has been characterized as 'one, if not *the* key to his whole work'.[1] In keeping with the exigencies of modernity, philosophy is reconfigured from 'usher' (*Platzanweiser*) to 'stand-in' (*Platzhalter*) which brings its universalizing quest to bear within the individual sciences, and from 'judge' (*Richter*) to 'interpreter' between the lifeworld and the sciences. On the one hand, in comparison with its classical modern reconceptualization by Kant, this is a reduction. On the other hand, against postmodern and conventionalist positions, Habermas seeks to hold fast to the 'unity of reason' and to a 'moment of unconditionality'. I shall analyze the proposed new understanding of philosophy in its two functions in relation to the individual sciences (1) and to culture (2), and assess how the self-understanding of the third phase of critical theory and the basis of communication with theology are affected by it. As the debate on metaphysics has shown, restrictions on the type of problems philosophy can treat have a bearing on theology's theoretical and public status; its contribution to foundational questions of the self and its contingency, its relation to others and to agency in history are discredited when these questions are abandoned. Yet, if science as a decisive power within the contemporary world could be submitted to an analysis by the means of philosophy, a lot could be gained by reconnecting it to the other segments of a differentiated modernity, and ultimately to the needs, aspirations and democratic ownership of citizens. It could help establish a structured two-way dialogue between disciplines that investigate life as an object, and those that enquire into the origins of historically achieved normative self-understandings, [2] kept available by humanity's capability for religious and cultural memory.

1. The Role of Stand-in for Universalistic Questions in the Individual Sciences

The emergence in the nineteenth century of new methods of scientific research has changed the role of philosophy. It is no longer the single unitary representative of reason. Rationality has diversified into the distinct methods of individual disciplines of enquiry which no longer derive their foundation from the power of an encompassing reason. In *Theory of Communicative Action*, Habermas has already looked back on Kant's three critiques from the sociological perspective of Max Weber. In this programmatic address held in the same year in which its two volumes were published, he acknowledges on the one hand Kant's transformation of philosophy as a response to the scientific achievements of his day, especially the physics of Newton, but distances himself on the other hand from Kant's insistence on the independent role, subject area and method of philosophy. It is the critical delimitation of the sphere of knowledge to what understanding (*Verstand*) in combination with the senses can establish – in effect, the 'Copernican turn' – that earns Kant's proposal the designation of 'usher', who accompanies the sciences to their place. For Habermas, this demarcation from above of the sphere of the sciences is no longer possible, and the independent method of philosophy, transcendental as opposed to empirical enquiry, has to be given up together with the attitude of the 'master thinker'. At the same time, he does not want to follow Richard Rorty completely who, together with Willard Quine and Donald Davidson, made the Stuttgart panel into one great apology for Hegel, in Hauke Brunkhorst's analysis.[3] Despite Habermas's critique of the separation of philosophy from the sciences through Kant's 'foundationalist' method, he does not agree that 'it must also surrender the function of being the "guardian of rationality"' together with 'ideas like truth or the unconditional with their transcending power' which need to be retained as 'a necessary condition of humane forms of collective life'.[4]

Before comparing his conclusion that, as a consequence of the scientific turn, philosophy loses its own subject area and method, to those of other colleagues, such as Karl-Otto Apel and Walter Schulz, I shall review his argumentation for rejecting the remit of philosophy as it was critically reconceived by Kant. The first reason

> why the Kantian view of philosophy's vocation has a dubious ring today . . . has directly to do with the foundationalism of epistemology. In championing the idea of a cognition *before* cognition, Kantian philosophy sets up a domain between itself and the sciences, arrogating authority to itself. It wants to clarify the foundations of the sciences once and for all, defining the limits of what can and cannot be experienced. This is tantamount to showing the sciences their proper place. I think philosophy cannot and should not play the role of usher.[5]

However, it can still 'retain its claim to reason, provided it is content to play the more modest roles of stand-in (*Platzhalter*) and interpreter'[6] by assuming a reconstructive and assisting role, submitting itself to falsifiability, and replacing foundational concepts with 'third categories' such as action, embodiment, and lifeworld. This new form of philosophy that puts its 'strong universalistic claims' to work within the sciences is exemplified by 'fertile minds' such as

> Freud . . . Durkheim, Mead, Max Weber, Piaget and Chomsky. Each inserted a genuinely philosophical idea like a detonator into a particular context of research. Symptom formation through repression, the creation of solidarity through the sacred, the identity-forming function of role-taking, modernization as rationalization of society, decentration as an outgrowth of reflective abstraction from action, language acquisition as an activity of hypothesis testing – these key phrases stand for so many paradigms in which a philosophical idea is present in embryo

(*einen philosophisch zu entfaltenden Gedanken*) while at the same time empirical, yet universal, questions (*empirisch bearbeitbare, aber universalistische Fragestellung*) are being posed.[7]

In this new reconstructive role, 'transcendental and dialectical modes of justification' are not excluded, but only with the more modest (*ermäßigt*) remit of offering reconstructive hypotheses for empirically observable competences.[8] Among the examples of fruitful cooperation are the links 'between cognitivist ethics and a psychology of moral development, between philosophical theories of action and the ontogenetic study of action competences'.[9]

In this integrated work with science philosophers function 'as suppliers of ideas' (*Zuarbeit*) for the individual disciplines which start 'primarily from the intuitive knowledge of competent subjects – competent in terms of judgment, action and language – and secondarily from systematic knowledge handed down by culture (*überlieferte kulturelle Wissenssysteme*)', to 'explain the presumably universal bases of the rationality of experience and judgment, action and linguistic communication'.[10] In this assisting role, philosophy becomes subject to the same fallibility as the social, human and natural sciences: 'Fallibilistic in orientation', it rejects 'the dubious faith in philosophy's ability to do things single-handedly (*im Alleingang*), hoping instead that . . . success . . . might come from an auspicious matching of different theoretical fragments'.[11]

The final departure from the concept of self-reflection of the philosophy of consciousness is the renunciation to 'foundations' which are replaced with the

> web of everyday life and communication (*Nexus der Alltagspraxis und Alltagskommunikation*) . . . Purposive action and linguistic communication play a qualitatively different role from that of self-reflection in the philosophy of consciousness. They have no justificatory function any more save one: to expose the need for foundational knowledge as unjustified.[12]

A different conclusion from the success of *Wissenschaft,* the academic enquiries of the sciences and humanities, regarding the role of philosophy is drawn by Walter Schulz. Since their effectiveness results from pursuing isolated specified questions which are abstracted from everyday practices, they need to be both complemented and challenged by a mode of thinking that can diagnose and overcome the fragmentation resulting from their specialization. Philosophy no longer 'founds' or 'constructs them a priori',[13] but it identifies the different concepts of self and world used in the various disciplines and relates them to a 'practical-ethical' orientation; it also reintroduces the questions they no longer pose in their neglect of the 'mutual conditioning of self-relation and world relation',[14] such as the question of facticity.

It is especially on the points of giving up the transcendental method and accepting the possibility of empirical falsification where Karl-Otto Apel parts company with Habermas in his radical trimming of the prior self-understanding of philosophy. For Apel, its justificatory modes can only be retained if the distinction between transcendental and empirical methods is upheld. Here no 'falsification' is possible. I shall discuss Apel's objections in greater detail since they also relate to the justification of the principle of morality and thus throw a light on his critique of the parameters in which Habermas develops his version of their joint project of discourse ethics. Their shared conviction that the procedure of justification which remains monological in Kant has to be validated by concrete subjects will be treated in the next chapter. In an immanent critique of the theory decisions of his project partner he asks about the 'consistency' of a proposal the ambitions of which cannot be reached because the tools are not adequate.[15] If the shared goal is to continue developing a critical theory for the present conditions, then the standards of critique cannot be identical with the conventions of the lifeworld. On the one hand, Habermas distances himself from perspectives that give up on critique, such as Wittgenstein's 'therapeutic' approach and Rorty's which 'enjoys the benefits of all three types of farewell: therapeutic relief, heroic overcoming and hermeneutic reawakening':[16]

> The weakness of this particular farewell to philosophy is
> that it leaves the world as it is. For the standards by which
> philosophy is being criticized are taken straight from the

self-sufficient, routinized forms of life in which philosophy happens to survive for now.[17]

On the other hand, by leveling the distinction between two modes of enquiry, and between those presuppositions of communication that – as argumentation – are 'methodologically inescapable', and those that – as lifeworld – are 'practically inescapable' (*nichthintergehbar*),[18] he renders himself incapable of carrying out this assessment from a universalistic, rather than contextual, standard. He offers a mediating proposal which forces irreconcilable alternatives together: a rationality that is supposed to be both contextual *and* a critical standard. When philosophy's

> gaze is not fixated on the scientific system, when it reverses this perspective and looks back upon the thicket of the lifeworld . . . (i)t then discovers a reason that is already operating in everyday communicative practice. True, claims to propositional truth, normative rightness and subjective truthfulness intersect here with a concrete, linguistically disclosed world horizon; yet, as criticizable claims they also transcend the various contexts in which they are formulated and gain acceptance. In the validity spectrum of the everyday practice of reaching understanding, there comes to light a communicative rationality opening unto several dimensions; at the same time, this communicative rationality provides a standard for evaluating systematically distorted forms of communication and of life that result when the potential for reason that became available with the transition to modernity is selectively utilized.[19]

This attempt at solving the dilemma by postulating that the opposites coincide in the 'discovery' of a rationality that is both part of the thicket of the lifeworld and able to transcend it critically, is not convincing for Apel. As Henrich did before in the context of the naturalization dispute, he sees the need to make a decision between two positions that remain alternatives. The

> Habermasian strategy of avoiding a methodological distinction between philosophy and empirically testable reconstructive

science seems to me openly inconsistent: I suspect Habermas will have to make up his mind one day whether he wants to persist in the inconsistency or give back to philosophy its genuine *justificatory function*, together with its a priori universal and self-referential validity claims.[20]

The critical function which Habermas wants to defend against conventionalist approaches resides in the ability of agents to say yes or no to validity claims. This is where the moment of unconditionality is embodied:

> The validity claims that we raise in conversation – that is, when we say something with conviction – transcend this specific conversational context, pointing to something beyond the spatiotemporal ambit of the occasion. Every agreement . . . is based on (controvertible) grounds or reasons. Grounds have a special property: they force us into yes or no positions. Thus, built into the structure of action oriented towards reaching understanding is an element of unconditionality. And this is the unconditional element that makes the validity (*Gültigkeit*) that we claim for our views different from the mere de facto acceptance (*Geltung*) of habitual practices. From the perspective of first persons, what we consider justified is not a function of custom (*Lebensgewohnheiten*) but a question of justification or grounding (*Begründbarkeit*).[21]

The capacity to say yes or no would be worth investigating for what makes it possible. This does not happen, however, the reflective self-understanding behind the capability to take a stance to what one encounters is not elucidated. And even when the element of unconditionality is seen to take an embodied, public form, it seems impossible to test empirically whether it is present or absent in the positions taken by the discourse participants. This is also implied in Apel's critique. The idea of unconditionality is not accessible to procedures of empirical proof.

Especially because of its relevance for the principle of morality which Apel wants to distinguish from the justification of norms in concrete instances, he is scathing about submitting philosophy to the fallibility and falsification claims of empirical sciences. Habermas's readiness to accept the possibility of falsification misconstrues the relationship between the two 'autonomous, methodically different, and thus "complementary" procedures of justification'.[22] Since transcendental reflection relates to the pre-suppositions of empirical verification, it is logically prior. The condition of the possibility of falsification cannot be falsified itself: 'Naturally, it makes no sense at all to require empirical testing in the latter case'.[23] The types of justification required for the principle of morality and for 'concrete, situation-related norms' are at different levels. His objection to Habermas's strategy of argumentation is similar to Theunissen's twenty years earlier on the normative implications of language: first, two levels, one nature, the other normative agency in history, are distinguished, and then both are related back to the prior level of nature as their ultimate foundation. Here, the place of nature is taken by the lifeworld, or the existing ethos of linguistic exchange, and the place of historical achievements created by free action falls to the principle of morality that cannot be deduced from its context: Habermas

> likewise wants to distinguish between the standard of
> morality as it cuts into the ethical lifeworld and the latter's
> settled, concrete norms, which are more or less receptive to
> such morality. Now what sense can these distinctions
> possibly have if, in the final analysis, the formal principle of
> discourse morality is also supposed to stem from a histori-
> cally contingent presupposition of communicative action in
> the lifeworld – a presupposition that one must constantly
> check by submitting it to widespread empirical testing?[24]

In summary, the downgrading of the role of philosophy from 'usher' to 'stand-in' for universalistic questions in the individual sciences is in danger of unwillingly relinquishing the normative function of critical theory. Renouncing to a method of its own, and assimilating transcendental and empirical levels of investigation leads to the loss of a standard for legal orders, systems of value and belief, life forms, etc., that can be vindicated as independent and not only as contextually bound. The principle of morality which would have to be justified not empirically, but transcendentally, which could guide such a critique of existing structures seems to have been reduced to existing ethical life.

The question of the method and criteria of legitimating theoretical and practical truth claims receives an ambivalent answer.

In all three cases of limiting the claim of philosophy by denying it its own method, by submitting it to the postulate of falsification, and by replacing foundational categories deemed as 'dualistic' by 'third' ones, the emerging orientation is directed towards an ideal of knowledge that is at one's disposition. In the close alignment of philosophy with individual sciences, the origin and status of its standards of critique become questionable.

The drive towards empirically testable knowledge revealed in the stand-in function is even more consequential when the 'integrating' and 'enlightening role of philosophy . . . directed toward the whole of life practices'[25] is at stake. The questions of humanity which metaphysics put on the map are now on the agenda of its role as interpreter.

2. From Judge to Interpreter

The 'domain of its own' which philosophy inserted between itself and the sciences is not acceptable for Habermas; it indicates an attitude of 'domination' to him.[26] Since the transcendental method not only gives a new foundation to epistemology, but also provides a critique of knowledge, it attributes the role of a judge to philosophy. Habermas interprets the tripartite division of Kant's *Critiques* into the critique of pure reason, of practical reason and of judgment as replacing the 'substantial concept of reason found in traditional metaphysics with a concept of reason the moments of which have undergone differentiation to the point where their unity is merely formal'. As much as he welcomes the 'theory of modernity . . . (i)mplied by Kant's conception of formal, differentiated reason', so does he reject the extension enacted by the *Critique of Pure Reason* to 'the abuses of this cognitive faculty, which is limited to phenomena'[27] to culture as a whole. By taking over Max Weber's translation of the types of reason of the three Kantian critiques into 'cultural value spheres', he comes to the conclusion that Kant makes philosophy the highest judge not only of the sciences, but also of culture:

He sets up practical reason, judgment, and theoretical cognition in isolation from each other, giving each a foundation unto itself, with the result that philosophy is cast in the role of the highest arbiter for all matters, including culture as a whole. Kantian philosophy differentiates what Weber was to call the 'value spheres of culture' (science and technology, law and morality, art and art criticism), while at the same time legitimating them in their respective limits. Thus Kant's philosophy poses as the highest court of appeal vis-à-vis the sciences and culture as a whole.[28]

Whether this objection to sitting in judgment, for example, over art, captures Kant's intention, the content of his theory of art in the *Critique of Judgment*, or the internal connection between the three critiques, need not be discussed here, since Habermas does not dwell on them. But the alleged role of judge has to be replaced with a more modest one, that of interpreter. The integrating function of philosophy is applied to two tasks: the mediation of the expert cultures among each other, and with the commun-icative practices of the lifeworld. It is to 'help set in motion the interplay between the cognitive-instrumental, moral-practical, and aesthetic-expressive dimensions that has come to a standstill today like a tangled mobile', to 'overcome the isolation of science, morals, and art and their respective expert cultures', join them 'to the impoverished traditions of the lifeworld' and establish 'a new balance between the separated moments of reason . . . in communicative everyday life'.[29]

In this role of translator, however, philosophy is acting on foreign soil. The restricting statements here are that it 'has lost its autonomy in relation to the sciences, with which it must cooperate', that also as interpreter it 'no longer directs its own pieces', and that it has to 'operate under conditions of rationality that it has not chosen': 'Today, the illumination of common sense by philosophy can only be carried out according to criteria of validity that are no longer at the disposition of philosophy itself'.[30]

This is a serious diminution of philosophy's area of competence. It cannot be made up by the fact that Habermas also argues against 'the scientistic background assumption that the natural sciences . . . do in general furnish the model and the ultimate authority for all knowledge that is still acceptable'[31] and against 'the unenlightened scientistic motive of elevating empirical scientific thinking itself to the position of an absolute'.[32] The only statement that seems to give some measure of independence to philosophy is the image of the tangled mobile which it is trusted with being able to stir. If it still has the capacity of providing a gentle therapeutic initiative from the outside, then it seems to operate from a level of its own, despite its dependence on the criteria furnished by the expert cultures.

It appears that the only integrating function which philosophy is able to carry out is in relation to the lifeworld. Here, the possibility is admitted that it may be able to reunite the segments into which reason has split: 'Everyday life, however, is a more promising medium for regaining the lost unity of reason than are today's expert cultures or yesteryear's classical philosophy of reason'.[33] It seems positive that in view of the restrictions conceded before at least this function is still left to it. Yet by disconnecting it from the previous task of investigating the 'grounds and abysses of the classical philosophy of reason', an additional limitation has been proposed. Not being allowed to follow it into its abysses, questions are removed which for Kant and his more demanding followers in the twentieth century constituted unavoidable questions of humanity. In comparison with the questions of facticity and of the antinomies of reason, from the undecidable alternative between freedom and determinism to the problem of meaning when moral initiatives fail in a hostile world, the new role of philosophy seems modest indeed: it 'might do well to refurbish its link with the totality by taking on the role of interpreter on behalf of the lifeworld'.[34] The question about the totality of everything that can be experienced which its classically modern predecessor was able to pose, has been reduced to the totality of the lifeworld. It is worth looking at Habermas's characterizations of the form of enquiry he sees as superannuated by the 'new type of procedural rationality' in the natural sciences, law and morality which was ushered in by external historical developments. They produced shifts in world orientation: 'The intrusion of historical consciousness rendered the dimension of finiteness more convincing in comparison to an unsituated reason that had been idealistically apotheosized (*idealistisch verhimmelt*)'.[35]

This portrait might fit one of the classical positions, namely the very proposal his levelling of the transcendental method and his own reliance on the communications embedded in the lifeworld gives credence to, that is, Hegel. Yet, the problem of finitude was not first introduced by the historical–hermeneutical sciences, but was a central insight of the philosophy of subjectivity itself in its reflections on the dialectic between finitude and infinity in the double constitution of human freedom. Over against Habermas's description of reason, quoted already in the metaphysics debate, 'as a simultaneously totalizing and self-referential reflection',[36] the succession of different projections of reason testifies to the problematizing of each proposal and the character of a quest, rather than of an absolutizing apotheosis. His reference to 'a subjectivity that makes possible the world as a whole'[37] finds a counterposition in his insight that 'synthetic accomplishments are attributed to a subject that must be *given* its material, both in cognition and in action'.[38] In view of the insights into the facticity of reason and of existence as such by Kant, Fichte, Schelling, Schleiermacher and Kierkegaard, the question should really be whether the naive world consciousness which Habermas privileges with the lifeworld does not deserve the label of 'foundationalism' more than these efforts of questioning all that is given.

Thus, on the one hand, the critical subject's question about totality and the ground of its existence has become limited to the lifeworld in its 'unproblematized, nonobjectified and pretheoretical . . . totality'; philosophy, as opposed to 'common sense', submits it to 'the subversive power of reflection and of illuminating, critical and dissecting analysis' and thus fulfils its role 'on *this* side of the scientific system . . . of an interpreter mediating between the expert cultures of science, technology, law and morality . . . and everyday communicative practices'.[39] On the other hand, despite this competence of reflection, analysis and mediation between widely differing segments, self-reflective capacities are attributed not to the questioning subject herself, but to the lifeworld:

As matter-of-course and as something about which we must be reassured, this totality of the lifeworld is near and far at the same time; it is also something alien from which insistent questions emerge – for example, 'What is a human being?' Thus, the lifeworld is the almost nature-like wellspring for problematizations of this familiar background to the world as a whole; and it is from this source that basic philosophical questions draw the relation they have to the whole, their integrating and conclusive character.[40]

Even the unconditional moment predicated of freedom now belongs to contingent historical conditions: 'built into the conditions of action oriented toward reaching understanding is an element of unconditionality'.[41]

Habermas's preference for 'public' rather than 'introspective' pursuits here almost amounts to moving the lifeworld into the vacant position of the transcendental subject, having thoroughly 'detranscendentalized' reason into empirical conditions of the possibility of action. Apel and other allied thinkers do not follow him in this and see it as a dangerous hegelianizing move which robs him of a standpoint from which to critique Neo-Aristotelianism and neo-pragmatist common-sense approaches, such as Rorty's.[42] What should be stated in conclusion, however, is the major turn which this new position marks within Habermas's own course of thinking. In comparison with the absolute role given to ideology critique in *Knowledge and Human Interests*, this move to a hermeneutically reflected position is to be welcomed. Michael Theunissen and Paul Ricoeur have voiced their critiques of the prior stage of his thinking which was directed towards an ideal of complete self-enlightenment and transparency:

Habermas pursues reflection both as the preferred object and as the vehicle of his Critical Theory, 'up to the point at which the self-consciousness of the human species, having become critique has wholly freed itself from ideological distortion . . . Since it thereby reaches completion, self-consciousness is also absolute, since instead of being content with criticizing, it has turned into critique . . . Completed self-reflection lays claim to absoluteness, in so far as it insists on the complete transparency of its interests. By contrast, it seems sensible to me to hold open at least

the possibility of an unilluminated remainder of interests,
a remainder in which the effects of the ideologically
distorted norms of existing society find expression. Only
thus could the admission of historical relativity be given its
full due, and only thus could Habermas meet his own
demand that critique must always also be self-critique.[43]

While Theunissen notes the closeness of this stage of Habermas's
approach to Hegel's, Ricoeur argues for understanding the
Enlightenment itself as a tradition in which ideology critique is
a moment. I shall come back to his position which provides
space for the historical self-understandings that created the
Enlightenment, including monotheism, in Part 3. If

the critique of ideology can partially free itself from its
initial anchorage in pre-understanding, if it can thus
organize itself in knowledge and enter into . . . theory,
nevertheless, this knowledge cannot become total. It is
condemned to remain partial, fragmentary, insular
knowledge; its non-completeness is hermeneutically
founded in the original and unsurpassable condition which
makes distantiation itself a moment of belonging . . . the
critique of ideology, supported by a specific interest, never
breaks its links to the basis of belonging. To forget this
primordial tie is to enter into the illusion of a critical
theory elevated to the rank of absolute knowledge'.[44]

How this realization of the embeddedness of reason in communicative practices affects the foundations of morality will be
examined in the next chapter.

Chapter 5

The Foundation of the Discourse Theory of Morality

Now that the contours of the theory design have become clearer, the new approach to social ethics which has given his project its name, 'discourse ethics', can be examined. After outlining the core concepts and steps of Habermas's foundation of the discourse theory of morality (1), I shall treat the exchange with fellow-critical theorist Albrecht Wellmer on how 'recognition' is to be understood (2).

1. Core Concepts and Steps of Habermas's Argument

Starting out from the concept of 'discourse', shared by his and Apel's proposals, in its relation to and distinction from the life-world, I shall explain the cognitivist and universalistic type of moral theory it represents (a), and then investigate the steps by which the principle of morality is founded (b).

a. Discourse as a Reflexive Form of Communicative Action

In the preceding chapters the significance of intersubjective exchanges in the lifeworld, helping to create rational identities in complex societies, has become clear. They can rely on shared cultural understandings, conceptions of values and norms, which function as background resources where the good and the right are not distinguished until disagreements arise which have to be dealt with in order to enable renewed cooperation. The capacity to move from shared understandings to their problematization and reflection from a standpoint of distantiation is seen as residing in language. Thus, '(d)iscourses are the continuation of everyday communicative action with the means of argumentation'.[1] Once a new consensus has been reached, the movement comes full circle by returning to the accommodating (*entgegenkommende*) form of life it needs as a condition and informs as a result:

> For unless discourse ethics is undergirded by the thrust of motives and by socially accepted institutions, the moral insights it offers remain ineffective in practice ... any universalistic morality is dependent upon a form of life that meets it halfway. There has to be a modicum of congruence between morality and the practices of socialization and education ... In addition, there must be a modicum of fit between morality and socio-political institutions ... Morality thrives only in an environment in which postconventional ideas about law and morality have already been institutionalized to a certain extent.[2]

Discourse is a temporary suspension of practices in which processes of mutual learning become possible by adducing, exchanging and agreeing on reasons that can be justified as universalizable. At this level, it is a cognitive moral theory, in the sense that moral problems can be decided on the basis of reasons. It is universalistic in claim and procedure by appealing to the general level of human reason and obliging the participants to rise above their contexts, personal interests and culture-specific ethical codes, and to accept only those reasons that pass the test of being generalizable interests. It is deontological by making the resulting norms binding on individuals due to their being bearers of practical reason, apart from being persons with different strivings and histories. 'U', the principle of universalization, is the counterpart to Kant's Categorical Imperative, as an explicit, public and plural form of testing which maxims or norms can be justified.[3] At the same time, 'U' has an internal connection to everyday practices since it is linked to 'D', the 'discourse principle' derived from the rules that can be identified as presuppositions of discourse which are already operative in linguistic interaction.

What has to be demonstrated is the priority of communicative action oriented towards understanding over uncooperative, strategic action.

> I call interactions *communicative* when the participants coordinate their plans of action consensually, with the agreement reached at any point being evaluated in terms of the intersubjective recognition of validity claims . . . the actors make three different claims to validity in their speech acts as they come to an agreement with one another about something. Those claims are claims to truth, claims to rightness and claims to truthfulness . . . I distinguish between communicative and strategic action. Whereas in strategic action one actor tries to *influence* the behaviour of another by means of the threat of sanctions or the prospect of gratification in order to cause the interaction to continue as the first actor desires, in communicative action one actor seeks *rationally to motivate* another by relying on the illocutionary binding/ bonding effect (*Bindungseffekt*) of the offer contained in his speech act.[4]

This is the task that 'universal pragmatics' has been charged with, to identify and reconstruct universal conditions of possible agreement.[5] Both Apel and Habermas point to the 'performative self-contradiction' of the strategist, the skeptic or the moral relativist who need to presuppose what they evidently deny: the existence of rules of engagement in discourse which call to respect each possible participant as a person who deserves equal rights of contribution.

Thus, the specific task of discourse ethics is to clarify the formal structures of rational conflict resolution on norms.[6] The decision on material ethical problems does not belong to the remit of the philosophical ethicist, but to real discourses between concrete conversation partners with opposing views. Subsequent to justifying the 'moral point of view', and to establishing the formal procedure by which it is to be operationalized, philosophy leaves application discourses completely to the insights and learning processes of the participants who are directed to the analyses which the individual sciences can provide.

> Any ethics that is at once deontological, cognitivist, formalist and universalist ends up with a relatively narrow conception of morality that is uncompromisingly abstract . . . Since the concept of morality is limited, the self-perception of moral theory should be correspondingly modest. It is incumbent on moral theory to explain and ground the moral point of view. What moral *theory* can do and should be trusted to do is to clarify the universal core of our moral intuitions and thereby to refute value skepticism. What it cannot do is to make any substantive contribution. By singling out a procedure of decision making, it seeks to make room for those involved, who must then find answers on their own to the moral-practical issues that come at them, or are imposed upon them, with objective historical force. Moral philosophy does not have privileged access to particular moral truths . . . philosophy cannot absolve anyone of moral responsibility. And that includes philosophers, for like everyone else, they face moral-practical issues of great complexity, and the first thing they might profitably do is to get a clearer view of the situation they find themselves in. The historical and social sciences can be of greater help in this endeavour than philosophy.[7]

Also foundational norms are part of the contents that are delivered over to the outcome of real intersubjective processes of agreement. For Kant, this foundation was the formal principle of the Categorical Imperative: the character of each human being as an end in herself, as its humanistic formulation stipulates. In discourse ethics, the participants, and the dynamics of voicing, encountering and weighing up arguments, are entrusted with jointly establishing and safeguarding these foundations.

> All contents, no matter how fundamental the action norm involved may be, must be made to depend on real discourses (or advocatory discourses conducted as

substitutes for them). The moral theorist may take part in them as one of those concerned, perhaps even as an expert, but he cannot conduct such discourses by *himself alone* (*nicht in eigener Regie*).[8]

The question then is whether the foundation of the universalization principle succeeds, or whether abolishing the distinction between the empirical-pragmatic and the transcendental levels will affect this decisive juncture.

b. Justifying 'U', the Principle of Morality: Two Versions and Their Implications

The foundation of 'U' in 'Discourse Ethics – Notes on a Programme of Philosophical Justification' underwent a correction after the first edition that has far-reaching implications for the kind of recognition the principle aims at. I shall compare the steps of argumentation in the first and revised versions, and link their difference in the second section to Albrecht Wellmer's critique.

Together with the whole book, the article is dedicated to Karl-Otto Apel for his 60th birthday, thanking him for 'three decades of teaching' and identifying him as the thinker among contemporary philosophers who has had the greatest sustaining effect on the direction of his own thoughts.[9] In it, he seeks to 'elaborate the shared problematic that distinguishes cognitivist theories from noncognitivist approaches', such as Alasdair MacIntyre's. With other neo-Kantians he shares the 'intention of analyzing the conditions for making impartial judgments of practical questions, judgments based solely on reasons',[10] rather than, for example, traditions or consequences. The new foundation is to replace earlier ones – among them the attempt to which the early theological critiques responded – in which the presuppositions of argumentation were described as 'the defining characteristics of an ideal speech situation'.[11] The article tries to give an answer to 'the fundamental question of moral theory . . .: how can we justify the principle of universalization itself, which alone enables us to reach agreement through argumentation on practical questions'?[12] Thus, the aim is not to justify individual norms of action, but to show the justifiability of norms in general.

The first step of argumentation is a reminder of the rules of discourse, as described by Robert Alexy. They summarize the formal requirements of a communication in which any 'coercion other than the force of the better argument' is excluded, and which is committed to a 'cooperative search for truth':

(3.1) Every subject with the competence to speak and act is allowed to take part in a discourse.

(3.2) a. Everyone is allowed to question any assertion whatever.
        b. Everyone is allowed to introduce any assertion whatever into the discourse.
        c. Everyone is allowed to express his attitudes, desires and needs.

(3.3) No speaker may be prevented, by internal or external coercion, from exercising his rights as laid down in (3.1.) and (3.2).[13]

To show that these rules are 'inescapable presuppositions', rather than 'mere *conventions*', Habermas gives examples for the 'performative contradictions' which a person who contests them runs into, such as the 'semantic paradox' of the statement: 'Using lies, I finally convinced H that p'. [14]

The second step is to try to derive 'the universalization principle (U)' both from these rules, presupposed and accepted in every discourse, and from a 'weak idea of normative justification (i.e. one that does not preclude the matter).[15] It is here, with regard to the second premise, that the first version of the argument has encountered the objection of logical circularity, and has been altered subsequently. The specification is given a different direction. In the first formulation, the decisive sentence is as follows (*my emphasis*):

If every person entering a process of argumentation must, among other things, make presuppositions whose content can be expressed in rules (3.1) to (3.3) and if we **further understand justified norms in the sense that they regulate societal matters in the common interest of**

all who might be affected, then everyone who seriously tries to discursively redeem normative claims to validity intuitively accepts procedural conditions that amount to implicitly acknowledging (U) . . .[16]

In the corrected version of the derivation the second premise is changed to:

If every person entering a process of argumentation must, among other things, make presuppositions whose content can be expressed in rules (3.1) to (3.3) and if we understand **what it means to discuss hypothetically whether norms of action ought to be adopted**, then everyone who seriously tries to *discursively* redeem normative claims to validity intuitively accepts procedural conditions that amount to implicitly acknowledging (U). It follows from the aforementioned rules of discourse that a contested norm cannot meet with the consent of the participants in a practical discourse unless (U) holds, that is,

Unless all affected can *freely* accept the consequences and the side effects that the *general* observance of a controversial norm can be expected to have for the satisfaction of the interests of *each individual*.[17]

In the original proposition, the two premises from which the universalization principle is to be derived are (1) the discourse rules and (2) the condition of meaning that 'justified norms' are to solve controversial issues 'in the common interest of all who might be affected'. The problem of this second premise is that it already expresses what is to be derived from it, namely the universalization principle which is in need of justification. The second premise already guarantees that no particular interest is to decide the solution of practical conflicts, but only the universal interest of everyone affected. What was to be a formal premise for the derivation of the principle is in its content already the product of the derivation. In it, the universalization principle has already been fulfilled.

Subsequent editions replace the formulation which evidently already presupposes what still has to be justified by a different premise which expresses a far weaker claim. It now only refers to the shared self-understanding of the participants that they are engaging in a hypothetical discussion (*Erörterung*) on whether certain norms of action are, or are not, to be implemented.[18] Here, the generalization principle is not already introduced with the premises, but actually derived from them. But together with the logical correction, the claim of the argumentation has been reduced. While it remained undecided in the previous formulation, whether the symmetrical conditions of access meant the recognition of the discourse partners as persons or only as participants in argumentation, the new version seems to tip the balance towards hypothetical argumentations. The recognition as equals relates to the level of meeting for a practical discourse. The universalization principle derived in the logically correct steps is valid in the weak sense of the unlimited nature of discourse to which every bearer of reason has to be able to contribute in order to satisfy the criterion of an unrestricted quest for truth. What would have been thinkable, but is less likely now that the logical level of 'discussion' (*Erörterung*) has been emphasized, would have been a strong interpretation of the universalization principle in which the presupposition for the correctness of norms is the morally relevant recognition of every human being as a person who cannot be instrumentalized.

This observation is not an argument for returning to the first fraught method of justification, but for imagining what different type of correction the discovery of the *petitio principii* could have given rise to. It explains why recent accounts of his position, such as Rainer Forst's, diagnose a 'gap of justification (*Begründungslücke*)' between 'the "must" of a weak transcendental necessity', and the 'prescriptive "must" of a rule of action'.[19] Forst asks whether 'the foundation of a duty to discursive justification needs a stronger emphasis on discursive reason as *practical,* without striving for the "ultimate foundation" (*Letztbegründung*)'[20] that Apel proposes as the only sufficient method. It is clear that the route taken also in *Between Facts and Norms* has been to offer a reduced understanding of demands implied by morality:

> Unlike the classical form of practical reason, communicative
> reason is not an immediate source of prescriptions. It has as

normative content only insofar as the communicatively acting individuals must commit themselves to pragmatic presuppositions of a counterfactual sort. That is, they must undertake certain idealizations – for example, . . . assume that addressees are accountable, that is, autonomous and sincere both with themselves and others.[21]

These formulations are not emphatic ones of a morality that recognizes each other's dignity. The discussion – which is relevant for theology in that much of its reception and critique has been predicated on a more demanding understanding of mutual as well as anticipatory, unilateral recognition – is still ongoing. A perceptive early response will be outlined in the next section.

2. Recognition as What? Albrecht Wellmer's Critique

The 'gap' noticed by Forst was stated in an early comment by Albrecht Wellmer on a specific ambiguity in Habermas's justification of the principle of discourse ethics.[22] Does the insistence that every subject should be allowed to take part in discourse mean her recognition as a singular person? Are the 'pragmatic presuppositions' normative in this demanding sense? What does it mean that the presuppositions of argumentation are necessary and unescapable unless one commits a performative self-contradiction? Would it be a contradiction at the level of logics, or of morality? Which of these alternatives turns out to be true, makes a difference for how the claim and the scope of discourse ethics are to be evaluated.

Already in the first edition of his article, Habermas had clarified against Apel the difference between rules within discourse, and for actions in general.

It is by no means self-evident that rules that are unavoidable *within* discourses can also claim to be valid for regulating action *outside* of discourses. Even if participants in an argumentation are forced to make substantive normative presuppositions (e.g., to respect one another as competent

89

subjects, to treat one another as equal partners, to assume
one another's truthfulness, and to cooperate with one
another), they can still shake off this transcendental-
pragmatic compulsion when they leave the field of
argumentation. The necessity of making such presuppositions is not transferred directly from discourse to action.
In any case, a separate justification is required to explain
why the normative content discovered in the pragmatic
presuppositions of *argumentation* should have the power
to *regulate action*. One cannot demonstrate a transfer of
this kind as Apel and Peters try to do, namely by deriving
basic ethical norms *directly* from the presuppositions of
argumentation. [23]

Wellmer asks for clarification on the sense of 'obligation',
distinguishing between a 'rational' and a 'moral' intention.
He suspects that

the unavoidable presuppositions of argument do not
in themselves constitute *moral* obligations . . . What is
questionable, . . . is whether those norms of argument
which we cannot dispute without committing a
performative contradiction actually betoken obligations of
a moral nature. To put it another way, it is questionable
whether the 'must' entailed in the norms of argument can
be meaningfully understood as a *moral* 'must' . . . We seem
here to be dealing rather with a 'must' of the kind that is
associated with *constitutive rules*: I am unable to dispute this
'must' in my capacity as participant in an argument because
it is constitutive of the practice of arguing. Now norms of
argument are of course not rules of a game in which we
can participate or not participate as the mood takes us.
They are *inherently* connected with norms of rationality . . .
But precisely the fact that the inescapability of obligations
to rationality can be expressed through a 'principle of
avoiding performative contradictions' also shows that the
most general norms of rationality are not directly capable
of having a moral content. Obligations to rationality refer
to the acknowledgment (*Anerkennung*) of arguments, moral

obligations to the acknowledgment of persons. It is a requirement of rationality to acknowledge even the arguments of my enemy if they are good ones; it is a requirement of morality to permit even those people to speak who are not yet capable of arguing well. Overstating the point a little, we might say that obligations to rationality are concerned with arguments regardless of who voices them, whereas moral obligations are concerned with people regardless of their arguments (*Personen ohne Ansehen ihrer Argumente*).[24]

The misunderstanding of Wellmer's crucial distinction in Habermas's response is significant:

> The obligatory character of justified norms involves the notion that they regulate problems of communal life in the common interest and thus are 'equally good' for all affected. For this reason, moral obligations relate, on the one hand, to 'persons regardless of their arguments', if by this one understands 'without taking into account egocentric convictions that may be bound up with generally valid arguments from the perspective of individual persons'. On the other hand, the moral principle owes its rigorously universalistic character precisely to the assumption that arguments deserve equal consideration regardless of their origin and, hence, also 'regardless of who voices them'.[25]

This response does not engage at all with the question Wellmer has posed, whether in discourse ethics subjects count merely as purveyors of rational insights. Habermas misses the import of the phrase, people or persons 'regardless of their arguments', directed to the human dignity of the other person which is independent of the quality of their contributions to discussions. He even devalues it by interpreting it as taking seriously 'egocentric convictions'. The ultimate point of his foundation of ethics seems to be the insistence that in the situation of discourse, geared to finding universalizable norms for measures that affect all, everyone is equal. Even if this egalitarian pathos can be shared and its elaboration in a theory of the public processes of democratic opinion and will formation can be welcomed, the question remains what the content of such equality is. Is it the aim that in the interest of argumentation all aspects and perspectives can be expressed as far as possible, *or* that the recognition of human beings becomes practical in counting in their interests as equal?[26] For Kant, the 'universalistic content of the principle of morality' does not relate to argumentations but to humans respected as ends in themselves. Recognizing them as subjects would have the consequence that the principle of morality would have to make it obligatory to enter into argumentations in which the interests of all affected can be represented and argued out. Yet, in his effort to steer clear of Apel's insistence on the need for an ultimate justification, Habermas also weakens this requirement:

> No *direct* action-regulating force outside the context
> of argumentation may (or need) be ascribed to the
> 'normative' content of presuppositions of argumentation
> that cannot be denied without falling into a performative
> contradiction or to the moral principle based upon them.
> The moral principle performs the role of a rule of argu-
> mentation only for justifying moral judgments and as such
> can neither obligate one to engage in moral argumentation
> nor motivate one to act on moral insights.[27]

The altered form given to the derivation of the universalization principle in response to the critique of its logical circularity strengthened the impression that Habermas wants to restrict the mutual obligation of the interaction partners to recognize their accountability and sincerity to the situation of discourse, and to their roles as partners of argumentation. The misunderstanding of Wellmer's explicit contrast of two alternative readings of this principle now confirms this impression. At this stage of the development of his theory, the evident concern is to fend off morally more ambitious understandings of the obligations involved. The scope of the normative content of the presupposi-tions of argumentation remains circumscribed, as his debate with Apel has made explicit.

This reticence puts into question what in Apel's view is a sensible division of labour between universal pragmatics and transcendental pragmatics in the foundation of discourse ethics. Habermas's approach takes over the empirical-reconstructive part which draws on individual sciences to elucidate the constitution of the capacities, stages, and connecting systems of communication in their genesis and dependence in modern society; Apel's approach takes over the part of reflection on their validity or justification. This division of tasks, however, becomes a competition between two approaches once Habermas denies the need to extend reflection to the transcendental-pragmatic level of justification. In his analysis of the separate tasks to be carried out in the whole theory enterprise, Reiner Wimmer points to the consequence of Habermas's withdrawal from this division of roles: no longer affirming the need to reflect on the *validity* of the regulatory systems of competencies he has helped reconstruct as conditions of communicative action, he commits a 'naturalistic fallacy':

> At times, Habermas gives the impression that the problem of justification did not exist or became irrelevant once the question for the conditions of the possibility of discourses had been answered by way of a theoretical-hermeneutical reconstruction. Yet the mere reconstruction of 'basic norms of rational speech' which contents itself with the universalization principle as the 'ultimate (*allerletzten*) "fact of reason"' . . . incurs the suspicion of committing a naturalistic fallacy or of moving in a circle. What has to be added is the proof of the *normative* inescapability of the universalization principle.[28]

Thus, the objection of fellow-critical theorists is that he collapses the levels of the constitution and the justification of morality.[29] Loading the level of the factual with normative implications and identifying it with the level of the normative, is seen as committing the naturalistic fallacy of concluding from what is, to what ought to be. The relationship between empirical-reconstructive and transcendental methods becomes circular. This observation would explain why Apel's and other transcendental philosophers' efforts to argue for an ultimate justification seem superfluous to him. He sees normativity as given in the 'basic norms of rational speech' where they are always already operative as conditions of linguistic agreement; thus, the universalization principle is factually valid. Yet, the level of the modern justification of ethics established by Kant demands more, namely enquiring into its normative validity.

Habermas's proposal of founding discourse ethics can be summarized as follows: on the one hand, a social orientation is introduced with the premises of argumentation. In addition, the reliance of the principle of morality on 'accommodating forms of life' is expressly recognized. What appears here as the roots of morality in ethical life (*Sittlichkeit*), is spelt out in the standing which the lifeworld receives in his theory. On the other hand, Habermas remains reticent against determining the universalization principle that rules discourse at a properly normative level as a relationship of mutual recognition between human beings. This is why Ricoeur's characterization of his enterprise as 'ethics of argumentation' can be seen as the most apposite for its core content.[30]

Two questions have appeared at different stages that point beyond the framework in which Habermas addresses them: the issue of the source of motivation which is crucial for any theory of action, and becomes more pressing when faced with the problem of evil (1); the aporias of moral action that become especially acute when the scope of recognition is widened to include the past as well as the genesis of subjects. Habermas classifies them as 'existential', rather than as affecting moral reflection (2). Following Habermas's own classification of these questions, I shall treat them in a new chapter which will conclude the philosophical debate of Part 2.

Chapter 6

The Motivation for Agency and the Aporias of Morality

Discourse ethics have been dismissed on practical grounds as never-ending, decision-shy sequences of problematizing validity claims before the tribunal of communicative reason. However, in a memorable image that sinks this misconception of discourse,[1] Habermas locates the exercise of critique in a continuum of troubled agency:

> like all argumentation, practical discourses resemble islands threatened with inundation in a sea where the pattern of consensual conflict is by no means the dominant one. The means of reaching agreement are repeatedly thrust aside by the instruments of force.[2]

If discourses are just islands in an ocean of praxis marked by violent swells, these counter-experiences need to be thematized. Does philosophy have anything to say regarding the experience of the intention of morality failing? I shall follow the traces which lead Habermas back to the resources of the lifeworld and examine his theory of action in relation to the motivation to be moral (1). In my second enquiry, I shall analyze the answers Habermas gives to the question posed mainly by theologians, of the aporias of moral action which emerge once 'recognition' is understood as a relation offered by and to individuals in their capability and vulnerability (2).

1. Agency and Its Motivation

The symmetry of conditions of access to discourse has been so much at the centre that non-reciprocal constellations of action have hardly been mentioned. Yet when the expected reciprocity is not forthcoming, they are the ones that make the question of motivation acute. It was here that the need for 'innovative' action in situations of enmity, and for advocatory action had been suggested. The way in which the human experience of evil is treated will be discussed (a) before looking at how Habermas deals with the questions of why to be moral and whether expectations of anticipatory and unilateral action are justified (b).

a. Evil Will or Weak Will?

It belongs to the core intuitions of Habermas's renewal of critical theory that the cancellation of the project of interdisciplinary enquiry which the *Dialectic of Enlighenment's* had declared in the face of the experience of absolute evil could not be the final stance. Against this experience, and the dualistic categories of analysis inherent in the philosophy of consciousness, he has taken his starting point in the faculty of language to forge agreement and shown it to be more foundational than its strategic use. Against the resurgence of Nietzsche and analyses of human action solely in terms of power, he has elaborated the paradigm of recognition. Unlike John Rawls with his part neo-Kantian, part rational choice foundations of justice, there is no ambiguity in his discourse ethics between self-interest and orientation towards the other. His choice of a philosophical tradition that is oriented towards mutuality will not be questioned but endorsed. My scrutiny of his theory of action, first with regard to the experience of negativity, is directed at finding out how much an approach dedicated to reconstructing the genesis of competencies can deliver, and whether it needs to be complemented by a different avenue towards human agency.

In his political writings, inhuman conditions of action, violations of human rights as well as patterns of thought that promote enmity are identified. Yet in the context of discourse ethics, the main problem is not that of the evil will, but of the weak will:

> A valid moral judgment does indeed *signify* in addition an obligation to act accordingly, and to this extent every normative validity claim has rationally motivating force grounded in reasons ... But insight is compatible with weakness of will. Without the support of complementary processes of socialization and structures of identity, without a background of complementary institutions and normative contexts, a moral judgment that is accepted as valid can establish only one thing: that the insightful addressee then knows he has no good reason to act otherwise. The weak motivating force of moral insights is manifested empirically in the fact that someone who acts against his better judgment must not only face the moral rebukes of others but is also prey to self-criticism, and thus to 'bad conscience'.[3]

Every approach to ethics must face the question as to how the experience of evil is included into its framework. Certainly a proposal in the Kantian tradition cannot deny the problem posed to the foundation of ethics by negativity in the course of the world and the disappointment it causes to the legitimate expectation of happiness. For Kant, this antinomy of practical reason in which worthiness and actual happiness diverge threaten its foundation: '(N)o necessary connection, sufficient to the highest good, between happiness and virtue in the world can be expected from the most meticulous observance of the moral law'.[4] Habermas's answers to this question will be treated in section two. But what is also at stake is the origin of motivation. Can the 'rationally motivating force' invoked above be specified any further? Beyond pointing to 'bad conscience' as a result of the self-evaluation of the weakness of one's will, does he accept the question, 'Why be moral', and what is considered to be overtaxing?

b. Why be Moral, and to What Extent?

His answer to this question when posed to him by David Tracy at the Chicago conference in 1988 is indicative to the level at which he will respond also to the antinomy problem.[5] As indicated already in Chapter 1, he splits it into a part that has already found an answer, and one for which philosophy is not responsible for a different reason, in that it does not have the task of being a purveyor of meaning. Thus, it is classified as belonging to 'the question about the meaning of life' to enquire about

> a far-reaching engagement for the abolition of unjust structures and the promotion of forms of life that would not only make solidary action more likely, but first make it possible for this action to be reasonably expected. Who or what gives us the courage for such a total engagement that in situations of deprivation and degradation is already being expressed when the destitute and deprived summon the energy each morning to carry on anew? The question about the meaning of life is not meaningless.[6]

As far as the level of everyday morality is concerned however, it is not a meaningful point:

> it is true that a philosophy that thinks postmetaphysically cannot answer the question that Tracy also calls attention to: why be moral at all? At the same time, however, this philosophy can show why this question does not arise meaningfully for communicatively socialized individuals. We acquire our moral intuitions in our parents' home, not in school. And moral insights tell us that we do not have any good reasons for behaving otherwise: for this, no self-surpassing of morality is necessary.[7]

The question posed related to the unconditional character of morality; presumably, it could only be answered by the moral decision of human beings to radically respect their equally free counterparts. It now has been redirected into an enquiry about the conditions the lifeworld provides for socialization. Again we encounter the move, characteristic for Habermas, from the individual moral agent's will determination which could only be disclosed in a transcendental reflection, to empirically observable 'intersubjective' processes of socialization and democratic life forms. His fellow discourse ethicist Apel also criticizes this response as a return to the level of conventional ethical life which a person who asks this question has exactly left behind.[8] It demands an answer at a different level. The problem here is not that supportive forms of life are highlighted in their relevance for morality, but that this emphasis replaces grappling with those questions that present a test case for the depth and scope of an approach to ethics, those concerned with the extent of obligation under conditions of asymmetry or non-reciprocity. Again, a separation is drawn between what can be expected generally, and what is heroic or supererogatory, levelling the unconditional character of morality to the limits of reciprocal returns, and leaving any actions beyond this to stronger motivations, for example, religious ones:

> since [Friedrich] Schiller, the rigidity of the Kantian ethics of duty has been repeatedly and rightly criticized. But autonomy can be reasonably expected (*zumutbar*) only in social contexts that are already themselves rational in the sense that they ensure that action motivated by good reasons will not of necessity conflict with one's own interests. The validity of moral commands is subject to the condition that they are *universally* adhered to as the basis for a general practice. Only when this condition is satisfied do they express what all could will. Only then are moral commands in the common interest and – precisely because they are good for all – do not impose supererogatory demands. To this extent, rational morality puts its seal on the abolition of the victim. At the same time, someone who obeys the Christian commandment to love one's neighbour, for example, and makes sacrifices that could not reasonably be morally required of him, is deserving of our rational admiration. Supererogatory acts can be understood as attempts to counteract the effects of unjust suffering in cases of tragic complication or under barbarous living conditions that inspire our moral indignation.[9]

What makes this answer unsatisfactory is that he treats the unconditional nature of morality – a term he has defended on other occasions – as falling under the label of 'rigidity', a familiar objection to Kant's ethics; by identifying the two, Habermas is effectively denying the difference of morality to relations of calculable exchange. While some of Kant's moral judgements can rightly be critiqued for their rigorism and rigidity, what should be recognized is that he succeeded in distinguishing what is moral, from what serves one's self-interest. As the philosopher Herta Nagl-Docekal summarizes, unlike the

> principle of reciprocal benefit, the Categorical Imperative is not led by such symmetry. The point is to respect human dignity in the other and in myself (strict duty) and make the ends of the others my own as far as possible (wide duties), independently of the fact of whether others treat me in the same way. This is the point of the concept of moral autonomy, over against heteronomy.[10]

This difference is obscured in Habermas's reference to Kant's contemporary and poetic counterpart, the dramatist Friedrich Schiller who objected to Kant's negative view of 'inclinations'. Yet only if the demand of morality goes beyond self-interest, does the question of meaning show its edge. His answer to Apel's critique, however, makes it evident that he does not accept the problem of the meaning of morality as one that falls into the purview of philosophy. He dismisses as 'directives' what really are matters for philosophical-ethical reflections on nonreciprocal conditions of action. They would require an innovative agency with risks that can only be taken over freely. The fulfilment that it cannot guarantee itself, but has to anticipate, leads moral theory into the philosophy of religion, as theologians will remind him of against his restrictive answer to Apel:

> philosophy is overtaxed by what Apel terms 'the existential question concerning the meaning of being moral'. For moral despair demands an answer to the fundamental ethical question of the meaning of life as such, of personal or collective identity. But the ethical-existential process of reaching an individual self-understanding and ethical-political clarification of a collective self-understanding are the concern (*Zuständigkeit*) of those involved, not of philosophy. In view of the morally justified pluralism of

life projects and life-forms, philosophers can no longer
provide on their own account generally binding directives
concerning the meaning of life. In their capacity as
philosophers, their only resource is to reflective analysis of
the procedure through which ethical questions *in general*
(*überhaupt*) can be answered.[11]

These deflections of problems posed to him by fellow-Kantian
philosophers form a parallel to his answer to the theological
questions put to him by Helmut Peukert. Before analyzing this
debate, I shall draw a preliminary summary of his understanding
of the sources of agency.

To a certain extent, action is assumed to be motivated by
reasons, although the step from insight to realization is not taken
for granted. His emphasis can change with regard to what his
philosophical counterpart holds. Against Apel, he de-emphasizes
the moral nature of discourse; against political liberalism he insists
on a motivation that is willing to make sacrifices. His understanding
of public reason expects citizens 'as co-legislators to make active
use of their communication and participation rights, which means
using them not only in their enlightened self-interest but also
with a view to promoting the common good'. This implies
the 'willingness to take responsibility if need be for anonymous
fellow-citizens who remain strangers to us and to make sacrifices
in the common interest (*allgemeine Interessen*)'.[12]

On the one hand, the normative self-understandings and value
systems assembled in the lifeworld are expressly drawn on as a
resource, without, however, succumbing to specific current uses of
Hegel. Taking up 'Hegel's critique of Kantian morality', he wants
to 'provide a simple interpretation of the primacy of ethical life
(*Sittlichkeit*) over morality, an interpretation that is immune to
neo-Aristotelian and Neo-Hegelian attempts to ideologize it'.[13]
While the historical contribution of monotheism to modern ethical concepts is pointed out, and the different traditions that shape
the lifeworld are accepted as cultural resources, their difference
from the level of universalizable norms is emphasized:

> While cultural values may imply a claim to intersubjective
> acceptance (*Geltung*), they are so inextricably intertwined

with the totality of a particular form of life that they cannot be said to claim normative validity in the strict sense. By their very nature, cultural values are at best *candidates* for embodiment in norms that are designed to express a general interest.[14]

Thus, on the one hand, values and norms are allocated to different levels, but on the other, the possibility for values from particular life-forms to become generalizable norms is not excluded. Yet what remains unexplicated is the link at the individual level between self and agency, the striving, aspiration or drive that energizes action. An internal connection between ethical and moral self-understanding is not mentioned.[15] While before, the problem of meaning arising in the experience of failed moral intentions was taken seriously as referring to the existential level, the chance is missed to spell it out at the intersection of moral claim and ethical life project. Instead of developing an integrated philosophical account of agency from here, a stringent separation is made between the two at the level of theory:

> If we define practical issues as issues of the good life, which invariably deal with the totality of a particular form of life or the totality of an individual life story, then ethical formalism is incisive in the literal sense: the universalization principle acts like a knife that makes razor-sharp cuts (*einen Schnitt legt*) between evaluative statements and strictly normative ones, between the good and the just . . . a deontological ethics . . . deals not with value preferences but with the normative validity of norms of action.[16]

Here, no transition or reflective integration is envisaged which would allow for a more satisfactory understanding of the factors at play in creating motivation and moral selfhood, as proposed, for example, by Ricoeur in his structured combination of Aristotle's and Kant's approaches to ethics.[17]

2. The Scope of Recognition and the Aporetics of Moral Action

As we have seen in Habermas's exchanges with Wellmer and Apel, he intends to limit recognition to the duration of practical discourses on validity claims and to persons in their quality as participants. In contrast, the theological reception of his theory of action has seen recognition as extending to a universal dimension, including the unkept promises of the past, and as exploring the genesis of subjects whose autonomy still lies in the future. It has also insisted that these questions belong to philosophy's self-reflection on the limits of human reason and agency, as they were put on the agenda by Kant and by the first generation of critical theorists. By accepting these problems only as 'existential' ones, they are not being dismissed but moved to an area outside the reach of postmetaphysical thinking. Habermas's responses take account of the challenge which the victims of historical violence pose to one's moral existence but, disputedly, consider any hope for their sake that goes beyond human powers as the attempt to reinstitute a 'premodern certainty' or a 'confidence' (*Zuversicht*) that can no longer be kept open in contemporary philosophy.

As was shown in Chapter 1, Peukert redefines the task of a theory of action as pointing to an 'ethics of creatively finding – even inventing – an orientation for transformational praxis'.[18] Theory of education researches conditions and interactions that aim at the genesis of subjects. Their identity is challenged when they realize that the debt they owe to the past includes histories of prior subjects whose hopes remained unfulfilled and whose lives were cut short by violence. Regarding the problem posed once the dimension of temporality is included into the presuppositions of argumentation, Habermas spells out his view with reference to Helmut Peukert's book and Christian Lenhardt's article. He introduces it as one of the 'problems that flow from the self-limitation of every nonmetaphysical point of view':

> Discourse ethics does not see fit to resort to an objective teleology, least of all to a countervailing force that tries to negate dialectically the irreversible succession of historical

events – as was the case, for instance, with the redeeming
judgment of the Christian God on the last day. But how
can we live up to the principle of discourse ethics, which
postulates the consent of *all*, if we cannot make restitution
for the injustice and pain suffered by previous generations
or if we cannot at least promise an equivalent to the day of
judgment and its power of redemption? Is it not obscene
for present-day beneficiaries of past injustices to expect the
posthumous consent of slain and degraded victims to
norms that appear justified to us in light of our own
expectations of the future?[19]

Thus, the norm of including everyone into the process of reaching consensus can only be held for the present and the future, but
becomes 'obscene' when past suffering is taken into account, in
view of the irreversibility of history. A few years after the Naples
conference on 'Morality and Ethical Life' from which this text is
taken, at the conference held in 1988 at the Divinity School of
the University of Chicago, he gives an extended answer to his
theological critics. It states a point that will be repeated even in
2005 in his 'Reply to Objections, Reaction to Suggestions' to a
conference held with him in Vienna that will be further analyzed
in Part 3: 'One cannot draw a conclusion from the desirability of
such a power to its effective existence (*Wirksamkeit*)'.[20] It is worth
analyzing the text of 1989 not only because of its inclusion into
several collections of his articles, but also because it gives a good
indication of the stage of debate in the period of 'co-existence'
with religion recognized as a power that can console, and with
still unspent 'semantic potential'. His answer gives different
examples for a 'transcendence from within', and of its limit, and
is instructive in the range of interpretations it offers to the aporia
of human action in view of the victims of history and of the risk
of a recognition that remains unilateral:

I willingly repeat my position: 'As long as religious language
bears with itself inspiring, indeed, unrelinquishable
semantic contents which elude (for the moment?) the
expressive power of a philosophical language and still
await translation into a discourse that gives reasons for its

positions, philosophy, even in its postmetaphysical form, will neither be able to replace nor to repress religion.'

This does still not imply any agreement with Peukert's thesis that the discourse theory of morality gets so entangled in limit questions that it finds itself in need of a theological foundation. Of course, effective socializing or pedagogical praxis, which under the aegis of an anticipated autonomy (*Mündigkeit*) seeks to provoke freedom in the other, must take into account the appearance of circumstances and spontaneous forces that it cannot control. And, with an orientation toward unconditional moral expectations, the subject increases the degree of his or her vulnerability. Yet, the risk of failure, indeed of the annihilation of freedom precisely in the processes that should promote and realize freedom, only attests to the constitution of our finite existence. I refer to the necessity, which [Charles S.] Peirce emphasized again and again, of a self-relinquishing, transcending anticipation of an unlimited community of communication . . . The anamnestically constituted reason, which Metz and Peukert, rightly continually advocate in opposition to a Platonically reduced communicative reason that is insensitive to the temporal dimension, confronts us with the conscientious question about deliverance for the annihilated victims. In this way we become aware of the limits of that transcendence from within which is directed to this world. But this does not enable us to ascertain the *countermovement* of a compensating transcendence from beyond . . . It is, indeed, true, that whatever human beings succeed in doing they owe to those rare constellations in which their own powers are able to be joined with the favorableness of the historical moment. But the experience that we are dependent on this favorableness is still no licence for the assumption of a divine promise of salvation.[21]

Despite this range of interpretations and options, from 'spontaneous forces that it cannot control', to the 'constitution of our finite existence', from 'the favorableness of the historical moment' to the 'unlimited community of communication', the 'limits of that transcendence from within' are obvious. It becomes clear that they are not an adequate response to the question posed, 'about deliverance for the annihilated victims'. They indicate instead where action either transcends immanent conditions, or is supplemented by elements of serendipity. With regard to such instances of 'transcendence from within', however, the danger is that a secular interpretation of Peirce's 'unlimited community of communication' falls back into the problem of Feuerbach and Marx: the finitude of human existence cannot be compensated for by the 'infinity' of a species that is composed of such finite individuals.[22] 'Transcendence from within' should be more than the 'bad infinity' of adding up finite entities when the problem remains one of individual finitude.

A theology that emphasizes faith as a practical option of freedom will of course agree to the point that the step from the desirability of a redeeming power to asserting its existence can only be legitimated as an option of practical reason, not as a necessary theoretical presupposition. The intention of theological ethics or fundamental practical theology is not to give a moral proof of the existence of God, but to identify where the option of faith intersects with demands of reason: questions which may otherwise be abandoned since they cannot be fulfilled by human capacities. In ethics, this could mean the shrinking of the uncon-ditional demand of morality to a calculation of probable success. How many protests and social movements would have begun if the realm of the possible had been preshrunk in this way? Keeping questions open to which there is no human answer can be a service to political culture. It does not have to be read as theo-logical apologetics which uses human violence – despite the fact that some of it has religious origins – to make a case for God. Thus, there can be agreement on the point which Habermas has expressly stated subsequently, that religion is not a priori irrational, and that it keeps resources of meaning and critique alive. It is not necessary for grounding the obligation foundational for autonomous morality, but relevant for a realization in which the limits of human effort are not ultimately definitive.

What theologians will not accept is the interpretation of the practical option of faith as a return to 'premodern certainty' or an 'objective teleology'. It cannot be a regression to a premodern experience of self and world, if it presupposes the modern insight into the discrepancy between the finite chances of realization and the unconditional intentions of human freedom. Nor do 'certitude' or 'ascertaining' capture what remains a hope. There is a difference between the 'shape of a hoping question', as which Peukert puts it, and 'a hoping expectation', as Habermas reinterprets it in his reply of 1988. In conclusion, Habermas rejects what he sees as a theological attempt to move from the 'experience of a burning deficit' to the assumption of a saving God. Instead, he prefers that 'we give out utmost for the sake of the possible advances' which cannot give 'confidence for a praxis whose certainties have been taken away, yet can still leave it some hope'.[23]

For the purpose of this chapter's enquiry into the intersection between the ethical roots of agency and moral obligation, the conclusion from this response is: what was a question which theology saw as corresponding with Kant's understanding of morality as aiming for more than it could achieve by its own capabilities, is seen by Habermas as a matter of individual 'ethical' conviction. 'Confidence' (*Zuversicht*) in a God who saves belongs to the ethical level of world views. Regarding the future, the access of all to discourse oriented towards consensus is a moral question; regarding the past, which cannot be changed and to which individuals can only take a personal stance, mediated by their world views and value systems, it is an ethical question. On the one hand, Habermas's interpretation of hope in a saving God as 'ethical' can be seen as vindicating in different terms what I have referred to as the 'practical option' of faith. The element of a freely chosen individual commitment is paramount. The consequence for him, however, is, that 'no strong "moral" but only weak "ethical" validity claims'[24] are assigned to it. On the other hand, such 'ethical' claims are weak only as long as convictions are deemed secondary to a higher, normative level of consent. If 'conviction' were understood as already including the mediation of the normative level with biographical appropriations of particular traditions, then the 'ethical' would move from the weak claims of mere particularity to a more significant position. It would change the notion of discourse into aiming for a different type of normative consensus, into which subjects are invested as selves, not just as argumentation partners.

Part 3

The Current Phase: Cooperation and Translation in Theological Debate

The postmetaphysical mode which has been a signature of Habermas's thinking since the 1980s has shown its limitations by discontinuing philosophy's own treatment of questions of religion. Its willingness to learn is realized by dialogues as practical exchanges, rather than by questions internal to the philosophy of religion which is understood as belonging to a religion's apologetics:

> Certainly also philosophy of religion as the rational self-interpretation of a practiced faith with the means of philosophy is a worthy task (*verdienstvolles Geschäft*). But postmetaphysical thinking for which religious experience and the religious mode of faith maintain an opaque (*undurchsichtig*) kernel has to renounce to philosophy of religion. Nor does it try to *reduce* the rational content of religious traditions to what it can appropriate itself according to its own standards by translation into discursive speech.[1]

Philosophy has thus separated itself from a previously recognized domain; one that, in the disputed view of Herbert Schnädelbach, even made theology superfluous. However, the fallibility conceded by postmetaphysical reason has the advantage that religious worldviews cannot be ruled out a priori as unable to meet the demands of rationality. Once Habermas's cultural diagnosis has detected signs for tendencies that endanger the standards of enlightened, egalitarian and cosmopolitan reason reached in the history of its employments, religion and theology can appear as resources of critique and commitment to a greater solidarity than a 'derailing' modernity is still able to provide. A new stage of cooperation is called. I shall investigate the third phase of Habermas's engagement with religion in my two final chapters, by focusing on two major themes from his works since 2000 (Chapter 7), and by discussing the theological responses to the open questions they pose (Chapter 8).

The Rediscovery of Religion in the Genealogy of Reason and the Foundation of a Species Ethics

The rediscovery of religion as a vital contemporary factor, not only as a historical intellectual force that has shaped cultural self-understandings, leads to new developments in two areas: the genealogical reflection on the origins of Western thought is connected to the new requirement of cooperative translations (1); and current controversies on genetic engineering are met with the demand of a species ethics for which Kierkegaard's religiously founded concept of being able to be a self becomes the basis (2).

1. Genealogy and Translation

For Habermas, in contemporary culture, reason is being encroached by two opposite forms of fundamentalism: one scientistic, the other religious. In one of his most recent summaries of the relationship of postmetaphysical thinking to religious traditions, he goes back to the period in which the modern concept of reason emerged and distinguishes the factual alliances it found itself in from the philosophical intentions of its two main authors, Kant and Hegel. In conjunction with the

> two innovations of the age: an experimental and
> mathematized natural science and the bureaucratic power
> of the secular state . . . its emancipation from theology
> and metaphysics gave rise to a scientific and secular

111

self-understanding . . . Philosophy aligned itself with the sciences which it has to leave to its own course; at the same time, with its critical distance to religion and metaphysics, it bids farewell to its own past.[2]

Yet, in contrast to the Enlightenment critics of religion, Kant and Hegel took religion seriously as a formation of the human spirit. Rather than look for error and illusion as a 'truth *about* it', as the encyclopaedists did, they looked for 'truth contents *within* it'.[3] In the individual summaries of the three recent articles selected for the study edition which follow this general outline, Habermas maps a path that rejects the observer's perspective and recognizes religion as an intellectual formation with which reason shares its origin and which still contains motifs not appropriated or contained by it. On both counts, just turning one's back on religion is no longer sufficient. Instead of alignment or rejection, a reflective mode is necessary:

> a secularist reason, *exclusively* critical of religion and
> taking the side of a scientistic understanding of science
> (*Wissenschaft*), transforms itself into a mode of reflection
> that defends its autonomy towards either side – against the
> vortex (*Sog*) of being assimilated to the theory formation
> of the natural sciences just as much as against religious
> fundamentalism.[4]

It traces and probes this development as part of its own history of formation. In contrast to the sociological perspective adopted in *Theory of Communicative Action*, the evolution of reason is now depicted as based on a shared origin 'in the revolution in world-views of the axial age' when the major world religions and the great philosophical systems emerged. Religion as one constitutive source is still alive, and two decisive factors of this revolution cannot be superseded: the break with magical and mythological worldviews, and the concept of individuality.[5]

> Viewed from the perspective of the cognitive advance from
> *mythos* to *logos*, metaphysics can be situated at the same
> level as all of the worldviews which emerged at that time,

including Mosaic monotheism. Each of them made it possible to take a synoptic view of the world as whole from a transcendent point of view and to distinguish the flood of phenomena from the underlying essences. Moreover, reflection on the place of the individual in the world gave rise to a new awareness of historical contingency and of the responsibility of the acting subject. However, if religious and metaphysical worldviews prompted similar learning processes, then both modes, faith and knowledge, together with their traditions based respectively in Jerusalem and Athens, belong to the history of the origins of the secular reason which today provides the medium in which the sons and daughters of modernity communicate concerning their place in the world. This modern reason will learn to understand itself only when it clarifies its relation to a contemporary religious consciousness which has become reflexive by grasping the shared origin of the two complementary intellectual formations in the cognitive advance of the Axial Age.[6]

While the turns and milestones of this path will need to be investigated, the overall direction offers a new vista of engagement, beyond the set stage of two abstemiously coexisting players, each involved in their own pursuits. The emergence of a multicultural and postsecular world society sets a mediating task for a post-metaphysical philosophy and for political ethics: 'Intercultural discourse on human rights and conceptions of justice does not only have to overcome the dispute between religious world views, but also the oppositions between religious parties on the one hand, and secularists on the other hand'.[7] Here, philosophy's role towards the world religions is no longer one of an 'inspector who examines the truth content of religious traditions . . . A fruitful dialogical relationship can only take place between an agnostic but receptive (*lernbereit*) philosophy and a religion that has itself become reflexive'. In this encounter, both parties know that dialogue 'excludes the instrumentalization of the other. What one side wins, does not have to be lost for the other'.[8]

Despite these more than marginal shifts in assessing the challenge of religion to reason, Habermas stresses the continuity of his thinking since his contribution to the Chicago conference of 1988, 'Transcendence from within, transcendence in this world'; it is republished in the study edition as the final text under the heading, 'Conversations on Religion' (*Religionsgespräche*). He identifies the core insight maintained since then as recognizing the 'specific boundary (*Sperre*)' between the two forms of the human spirit; it motivates the demand 'not to soften up discursive thinking by borrowing promising connotations from religious language'. This boundary is due to the fact that religion is not only an intellectual and practical tradition but also one expressed in ritual: 'Religion itself cannot survive without being enrooted in ritual praxis. This circumstance is what separates religion – even more stringently (*unerbittlicher*) than the authority of revelation – from all secular formations (*Gestalten*) of the spirit'.[9]

Thus, both sides are different enough to make a translation necessary that respects the integrity of each. It is an interest internal to philosophy that motivates this joint enterprise. It has to delve back into its own past to reconnect with the origins it shares with post-axial religion. Yet, it is also clear that their difference is not only that of languages on the same level. There is a core part that will resist complete translatability.

An enlightening comment on the connection between genealogy and translation is made by Friedo Ricken at the 2007 discussion in Munich. He indicates how the sought-for motivational power for a reason that is in danger of becoming defeatist needs a change of register from abstract concepts to their original contexts of experience, expressed in awareness- and response-provoking narratives. A religious framework of reference contributes heuristic and praxis-oriented pointers that can be recaptured at the abstract levels of philosophical anthropology and moral theory:

> But how can a changed perspective on the genealogy of reason make good the motivational deficit of practical reason and awaken a consciousness of the worldwide violation of solidarity? The return to the prehistory of the emergence of reason (*Entstehungsgeschichte*) can be understood as the reverse process to that of translation. Translation leads to abstract concepts, the study of

genealogy leads us back to the lifeworld context, to the anthropological phenomena, on which this abstraction is based. Religions perform a maieutic function in the sense that they enable us to see these phenomena, force us to confront them, and trigger our responses.[10]

Ricken gives the example of the experience of guilt arising from the insight of having been able to act otherwise. It gives rise to a transcendental concept of freedom that distinguishes between the formal condition of the possibility of agency and its empirical realization:

> Thus, the abstract concept of transcendental freedom, for example, has its origins in the concept of guilt, and what guilt means in lifeworld terms and how we experience it are shown by the corresponding religious narratives. Only through the encounter with the latter, therefore, can an 'awareness of what is missing, of what cries out to heaven' be awakened and kept awake.[11]

Placing the interaction of religion and reason under the term 'translation' does not entail that there is a one-to-one relationship between semantic units, as in natural languages. The project of returning to the origin of the two complementary forms and of finding adequate translations reaches beyond the semantic to the pragmatic level, as the example of translating the monotheistic concept of *imago Dei* into the key concept of a universalistic morality, human dignity, shows.

From the perspective of theology, the new-found interest which finally reciprocates its own relationship to philosophy is a great step forward. Yet for understanding and exchange to succeed, the target language of the translation has to be suitable. Which competency and receptivity are assigned to postmetaphysical reason, and where does its resonance fade? It has already become clear that philosophy of religion is seen as an exercise from the side of theology, not as philosophy, and not as something for post-metaphysical reason to engage in. Does this not reduce its scope? Once more, the treatment of Kant will be a significant test case not only for a concept of morality that is unconditional but also for the link between moral theory and philosophy of religion. How far is Habermas willing to follow his steps of reflection in the analysis of practical reason? His lecture on Kant's ethics and his philosophy of religion, 'The limit between faith and knowledge', held in 2004, the year of the 200th anniversary of Kant's death, rejects his postulates of practical reason as 'effusive' (*schwärmerisch*). What can solidarity – which religion is supposed to be able to strengthen – mean if the only reason that the 'highest good' cannot be realized is that it would require a collective, rather than individual, enterprise? Does Habermas ignore Kant's analysis of the paradox of the just person suffering and being deprived of the flourishing they would deserve for their virtue? Are moral aspirations reduced and religious terms, such as kingdom of God, left underdetermined? The other major area of theological debate emerging for Chapter 8 concerns the identity of religion. If religion stands for an awareness of what is missing, how is this deficit specified? And what presuppositions are implicit in linking its unspent potential to its 'opacity' and 'awkwardness' for reason? Before analyzing the theological responses to these points in the final chapter, first, a concrete example of using the resources of religious reasoning in secular contexts will be examined: the concept of being a self.

2. Genetics and the Ability to be a Self

One example for the cooperative effort of translating religious intuitions into the generally accessible language of philosophy arises from the context of current public debate on genetic engineering. It recaptures the foundational concept of theological anthropology, being made in the image of God, in the moral and legal claim of human dignity. Habermas's intervention in the controversy on the desirability and moral permissibility of genetic enhancement represents at the same time a surprising move in the basic parameters of his own theory. After having subordinated 'subjectivity' to 'interaction' in a programmatic theory decision that lasted for decades, the normative status of singularity is finally considered in the debate of future possibilities of offering genetic enhancements. A new understanding of what recognition implies, namely as relating to selves as authentic and irreplaceable individuals, emerges here; not in the encounter with rival philosophical approaches but with new technologies that can alter the presuppositions of argumentation in an unprecedented way (a). A turn which is equally interesting for theology's contribution to debate in the public sphere is his suggestion of a 'species ethics' which is not a worldview but an ethical self-understanding in which morality is embedded. The moral commitment to create and uphold relationships of symmetry between parents and children, present and future generations receives its motivation from it (b). The key term chosen to anchor species ethics, being able to be a self, with its decidedly religious foundation by Kierkegaard, is reinterpretated in an immanent way. Before moving to the theological debate of these new themes in Chapter 8, I shall discuss comments in philosophy (c).

a. Subjectivity Rediscovered in Disputes on Genetic Intervention

The current debates on biomedical technology have a radius of significance far beyond their domain-specific sphere circumscribed by concepts of illness, health and wellness, prevention and therapy. Habermas discovers in them forces that can change future conditions of the lifeworld by affecting the primary relations in which the capability for self-determined agency is nurtured. Not only do genetic enhancement proposals have profound consequences for future relations of symmetry between parents, children and all subsequent generations of offspring, but what is at stake is the sense of authorship of one's life needed for the functioning of democracy, as well as the unity of the species.[12] With great clarity, he restates the principles of symmetry on which discourse ethics is based in this new field of public concern and defends the right of a child to be respected for its own unmanipulated self. It is a theme that forces him to specify previously implicit assumptions on which the approach of discourse ethics depends and which are in danger of being eroded. This is why a moral argumentation is no longer deemed sufficient, and a new prior level, species ethics, is introduced.

What is remarkable in his argumentation is the new emphasis on the self; the realm of the ethical in its diversity of aims within personal and communal lives had been discovered before:

> The universalism of equal respect for all and of solidarity with everything that bears the mark (*Antlitz*) of humanity is first put to the test by radical freedom in the choice (*Freisetzung*) of individual life histories and particular forms of life.[13]

Yet it is only now that the sources of individual authorship in the course of one's life seem threatened that Habermas comes to its principled defence, not for the sake of respecting natural givens, but in the name of selfhood. In a climate in which the wish of adults to enhance their child's genetic inheritance is portrayed as an expression of parental love, he points out the irreversible and interminable character of the imposition of parental power. It breaches the symmetry demanded by the norm of repression-free communication. The argument is not that natural givens are sacred, as it has been read by a Christian ethicist accusing him of Scholasticism,[14] but that this 'choice' is unilateral and thus constitutes domination. The demand that everyone should be able to be 'the undivided author of his own life' and 'persons of equal birth (*ebenbürtig*)'[15] in relationship to the previous generation is put forward as the fundamental precondition of rights that are constitutive of liberal society.

> The person whose genetic composition has been prenatally altered may, upon learning of the design for her genetic makeup, experience difficulties in understanding herself as an autonomous and equal member of an association of free and equal persons . . . the potential harm lies not at the level of a deprivation of the rights of a legal person, but rather in the uncertain status of a person as a bearer of potential rights . . . the genetically programmed persons might no longer regard themselves as the sole authors of their own life history; and second . . . they might no longer regard themselves as unconditionally equal-born persons in relation to previous generations . . . Intervention into the

prenatal distribution of genetic resources means a
redefinition of those naturally fixed ranges of opportunities
and scopes for possible decision within which the future
person will one day use her freedom to give her own life
an ethical shape.[16]

Habermas's critique arises from his acute awareness of the possible
conflict between the choosers and the recipients, between
parental power and children's entitlement to be themselves.
The principle of discourse ethics that the mutual recognition as
equals is constitutive for argumentation rules out measures that
defy reciprocity:

> Eugenic interventions aiming at enhancement reduce
> ethical freedom insofar as they tie down the person
> concerned to rejected, but irreversible intentions of third
> parties barring him from the spontaneous self-perception
> of being the undivided author of his own life . . . The
> conviction that all actors, as persons, obtain the same
> normative status and are held to deal with one another
> in mutual and symmetrical recognition rests on the
> assumption that there is, in principle, a reversibility to
> interpersonal relationships.[17]

Which philosophical approaches inform the opposition between
'authorship of one's own life', and germ-line interventions that
are intended as benevolent parental measures to provide children
with new qualities for which they hope they may be grateful? His
formulations combine a Kantian understanding of autonomy in
terms of the principle of non-instrumentalization of the humanity
in oneself and in others, concluding in the definition of dignity as
not being at one's disposal, with Kierkegaard's concept of 'being
able to be oneself' (*Selbstseinkönnen*) which rules out any gradual
view of enhancement as only improving what is already given.
The concept of *Selbstseinkönnen*[18] serves as the critical standard
from which 'the grown and the made' can be distinguished as
the un-manipulated and the imposed.[19] The very possibility of
making the givenness of one's life into the project of one's own
freedom and assuming responsibility for it is taken away if not just

a person's existence is brought into being, but also her specificity.[20] Thus, the moral understanding of irreplaceability implicit in Kant's idea of autonomy as authorship of one's moral acts finds its complement and further elaboration in Kierkegaard's analysis of human subjectivity with its 'absolute choice' of the self in its contingency. Habermas's acceptance at a colloquium at New York University in 2001 that 'the connection between the contingency of a life's beginning that is not at our disposal and the freedom to give one's life an ethical shape' is to be further analyzed,[21] combines the key concepts of both thinkers: Kant's idea that the pricelessness of dignity excludes an attitude towards human life that treats it as being at our disposal,[22] and Kierkegaard's location of the ethical task between the polarities of the human constitution, such as freedom and necessity, eternal value and temporality, infinite possibilities and their finite realization. Whatever synthesis can be achieved, it has to be a personal one that is true to one's authenticity. The heritage of these reflections forms the background to Habermas's argumentation for respecting the uniqueness of each person in her task to decide how to deal with her talents and limitations in her life history and thus become 'an irreplaceable individual'.[23]

From these philosophical parameters, it is clear that the question of enhancement is not seen as being about pushing back limitations which mar potential opportunities. By distinguishing the level of 'opportunities' from that of the 'freedom' of giving one's life an ethical orientation, Habermas is subscribing to a different concept of autonomy than the one that identifies it with 'choice' or the empirical ability to select between goods and features on offer. What is in danger of being undermined is the precondition of autonomy not as empirical choice, but in the Kantian understanding of the 'capability to be moral'. The sense of responsibility for one's own life is compromised by being able to blame the intrusion of another into the core of one's physical being, and consequently, of one's self-understanding:

> As the designer makes himself the co-author of the life of another, he intrudes – from the interior, one could say – into the other's consciousness of her own autonomy. The programmed person, being no longer certain about the

contingency of the natural roots of her life history, may feel the lack of a mental precondition for coping with the moral expectation to take, even if only in retrospect, the sole responsibility for her own life.[24]

From the recognition of the sense of selfhood developed so far, the issue is not simply the feeling of being determined, which could equally arise from the anonymous natural forces of inherited genes. Nor does the argumentation imply that Habermas subscribes to the simple assumption that genes equal features. The nub of the problem for him is that what should be marked as a reciprocal relationship from its very beginning has cut off the possibility of response. It is the intention, not the outcome of the gene selection that hurts the sense of self-ownership which is the presupposition to holding oneself accountable:

> Being at odds with the genetically fixed intentions of a third person is hopeless. The genetic programme is a mute and, in a sense, unanswerable fact; for unlike persons born naturally, someone who is at odds with genetically fixed intentions, is barred from developing . . . an attitude toward her talents (and handicaps) which implies a revised self-understanding and allows for a productive response to the initial situation . . . the only thing that counts for the psychical resonance of the person concerned is the intention associated with the programming enterprise.[25]

While a child growing up can negotiate, dispute and distance herself from the offers and impositions of her upbringing, the inclusion of parental intentions into her genes does not allow her to come to terms with it discursively. Educational determinations can be counteracted and revised by the child; yet the fact that her original genetic inheritance and that of her descendants have been regarded by her parents as a matter at their disposition, and altered accordingly, cannot be undone.[26] What makes 'genetically fixed intentions of a third party' an insurmountable obstacle to taking responsibility for one's own life, can be shown to be based on three features: their empirical irreversibility, the transcendental, 'condition-of-the-possibility' level of the effect of intervention and lastly, the intention to design instead of accepting the child in his or her contingent singularity.

A final point in the defence of an unmanipulated set of genes is the stance taken to natural limitations, from personal impediments to general human finitude. The awareness of the human designer's finitude and fallibility is a third reason for resisting those who advocate the tailoring of genes to their conceptions of a flourishing life, besides respect for individuality, and the willingness to prize the incalculability of freedom over the desire to control.

The insinuation that limitations are something unacceptable finds a counter-position in the insight developed from the Romantic Age to Kierkegaard that the very concept of individuality implies that no person can be everything. This is why for Kierkegaard (against the aesthetic mode of reflection in some Romantics), 'self-choice' as the condition of an 'ethically resolute conduct of life'[27] becomes necessary. Limitations as well as possibilities are to be made one's own.

While Habermas specifies that his critique pertains to measures of enhancement and not of therapy, he makes it equally clear that he does not want to subscribe to the view that an optimal life is only possible on the basis of optimal genes. The role of finitude comes into play again in admitting that no one is able to predict what is beneficial to a particular child. Against a newly emerging perfectionism, Habermas explicitly states that this lack of fore-knowledge includes physical imperfections and how they will be dealt with.

> Even in the best of cases, our finite spirit doesn't possess the kind of prognostic knowledge that enables us to judge the consequences of genetic interventions within the context of a future life history of another human being . . . Irrevocable decisions over the genetic design of an unborn person are always presumptuous . . . Since we can have no objective knowledge of values beyond moral insight, and since a first person perspective is inscribed in all of our ethical know-ledge, we overtax the finite constitution of the human spirit by expecting that we can determine which sort of genetic inheritance will be 'the best' for the lives of our children.[28]

Habermas's critique is informed by a marked appreciation of human finitude and an ideology-critical insistence on human fallibility. Finitude plays a crucial role in deciding what is permissible practice. It is denied in proposals of enhancement that pretend to be able to know what specifications upon a child's natural make-up are in his or her best interest, while the cognitive capacity of finite human beings does not avail of such objective knowledge. This is one more reason to reject genetic enhancement and selection which constitutes the victory of parents' projections over the otherness of the child. In co-creating the specificities of his or her embodied being – sex, bodily features, character predispositions – the singularity that is based on an unmanipulated originality is put into question.

b. Species Ethics as a New Level of Explicating Human Self-understanding

The need to defend the principles of symmetry and autonomous authorship against the new cultural trends towards unilateral control and perfection exemplified by liberal eugenics leads to the proposal of a new level of reflection: a 'species ethics' to undergird the conduct of universalizing practical discourses that establish which norms are legitimated. This move bridges the gap uncovered in Hille Haker's comparison of his approach with those of Hans Krämer, Charles Taylor, and Paul Ricoeur which thematized the link of moral obligation to the self with its biographical evidences and convictions. It now fulfils what her analysis found lacking: the need to connect morality to people's ethical self-understanding. Previously, Habermas had found the question of why to be moral to be unanswerable, as well as not in need of an answer for 'communicatively socialized individuals' since they learnt moral intuitions at 'home, not in school'.[29] Now that resources that could be taken for granted in the lifeworld are being challenged, for example the ideals guiding parent-child relationships, the need for spelling out the presuppositions at work in the contexts of recognition becomes compelling. It is not only a response to the question of motivation for a lifestyle of solidarity that is being endangered by the infiltration of economic imperatives even into the foundations of social and cultural reproduction;

more profoundly, a previously unproblematized understanding of the unity of humanity and the dignity of its members has been challenged and has made it necessary to explicate the ethical basis in which the moral commitment to humans in their dignity is embedded.

Two points have to be clarified: first, regarding the intersection between morality and ethics, what makes 'self-understanding', or 'the other's consciousness of her own autonomy' into which the genetic programmer intrudes such a crucial factor? Secondly, at the level of institutions, how are species ethics to be distinguished from particular worldviews towards which the state has to keep its neutrality? Habermas finds the solution in a rediscovery that philosophical commentators such as Thomas Schmidt and Georg Lohmann see as 'astonishing':[30] the concept on which his critique of liberal eugenics is based, Kierkegaard's idea of being able to be a self, combines formality and relevance for biographies. In contrast to approaches that identify specific goods and virtues to be pursued in a life, 'Selbstseinkönnen' is a formal qualifier for every life project. Kierkegaard's ethics establishes a foundational level that does not undermine modernity's distinction between the good and the right. I shall first discuss the connection which Habermas establishes between morality and this prior level, and secondly examine how human dignity is seen as the core species ethical concept which orients law in a way that grounds the legitimacy of the state and keeps this task apart from the question of its stability.

In his interpretation of the steps of argumentation in *The Future of Human Nature*, Thomas Schmidt points out the 'significant enlargement' in the division of tasks between morality and ethics that Habermas undertakes by identifying the 'species ethical framework conditions of a discourse theory of morality. He treats, so to speak, the weak metaphysical presuppositions of a postmetaphysical morality . . . since the self-understanding of the human species as a whole is at stake . . . in the face of the bioscientific revolution'.[31] The investigation is about nothing less than the '*conditions* under which the practical self-understanding of modernity may be *preserved*'.[32] What Habermas discovers in the controversy about genetic programming is that autonomy has to be accompanied by the self-understanding of being autonomous.

It is not that enhancement destroys autonomy directly, but that it violates the conditions of anticipated interaction with a person who can say No. This is why being endowed with new genetic qualities is inherently contradictory for the child whose own consent is deemed irrelevant. Educational measures decided on by parents are taken in anticipation of the ability to confirm, select, or reject these paths, which protects the source of becoming a self, each person's most basic resource of acting *sua sponte* with which the child will give its life its own direction. In his answer to Ronald Dworkin's question, Habermas insists on the respect for the ability to say No as the marker of a relationship to another person as a 'you', as someone in the role of the second person, who is not being objectified by the attitude of the speaker as someone to whom he relates in the third person and over whom he can dispose.[33] Thomas Schmidt points out the sequence of prior conditions in which autonomy is anchored.[34] The ability to say No, respected in educational interactions, presupposes that the person 'be at home, so to speak, in her own body'[35] by deciding herself which properties she will develop. Habermas draws on Hannah Arendt's idea of natality as 'a beginning that eludes human disposal' (*unverfügbarer Anfang*)[36] to explain the importance of this given starting point for the practical self-understanding of a responsible agent: 'In the case of 'natural' birth . . . . it is left to the individual which of its properties (*Eigenschaften*) it will regard as merely given determinants, and which it will interpret as an expression of its own identity conscious of itself (*selbstbewusste Identität*)'.[37] Such unsubstitutible (*unvertretbar*) individuality is the condition of being able to say No, and critically select, reject, appropriate, and own one's possibilities and limitations in one's life history. It is a self-understanding from which action may follow, in contrast to normative reasoning which remains at the 'cognitive' level but needs to connect with the motivation to act.

It is at this level that Habermas seeks to renew intuitions and practices operative in the lifeworld that could hitherto be taken for granted: the symmetry which expresses the recognition of everyone's basic equality, and respect for each one's individuality or 'authorship' of their lives. Having experienced them oneself, one can extend them to others. These two conditions are put into question by genetic manipulation and have to be regained by understanding 'ourselves anthropologically as members of the species'.[38]

Individuals' striving towards becoming a self is set in the horizon of the species and includes the wish for a 'flourishing life of the human species as a whole'. Since 'species ethics contains questions about general human self-understanding into which the moral life form shared by all reasonable persons is embedded', Kierkegaard's concept has a 'lynchpin function between existentialist individual ethics of authenticity, and species ethical embedding of a universal rational morality of equal respect'.[39]

The argumentation explored so far already makes it clear why genetic interventions are not a matter of the private rights of parents, but of constitutional relevance. This leads over to the second question, the role of the state in disputes at the level of ethical self-understandings which it would normally leave to public debate between the groups that constitute civil society. They still have to bring to the public forum what their convictions contribute to species ethics, but the state has to safeguard the conditions of its legitimate functioning at present although it cannot foresee what the actual shifts in self-understanding might be if liberal eugenics were permitted. Thomas Schmidt emphasizes Habermas's argument of a pluralistic democracy, while Walter Schweidler explicates the pragmatic and prohibitive function of the concept that legitimates all law-giving of the state, human dignity. Schmidt explains why the 'procedural rationality of the constitutional state is overtaxed' by this question for which according to Habermas the 'political consensus required would be either too strong or too weak'.[40] It belongs to the core of modernity to leave the option of the good to the individual person. In this 'determination of collective goods', the heart of modern pluralism is at stake if citizens are allowed to cast their vote on 'generally obligatory targets of positive eugenics'. It 'would intervene too far into the ethical autonomy of individual citizens'.[41] On the other hand, the consensus is 'too weak' in view of the radical reversal of the relationships between the generations and towards the species if parents were allowed to devise targets of eugenic interventions that undermine their child's self-interpretation and the basic structure of its social relations. Thus, his 'skeptical conclusion' is: 'in the context (*Rahmen*) of a democratically constituted pluralistic society where every citizen has an equal right to an autonomous conduct of life, practices of enhancing eugenics cannot be "normalized" in a legitimate way'.[42]

Walter Schweidler completes this argument with a principled reflection on why this question cannot be left to 'biopolitics', that is, changing outcomes of majority votes in which the different worldview constituencies engage themselves politically. It belongs to the legitimacy of the state to suspend conceptions of comprehensive orientation which originate from worldviews and religions. Yet species ethics does not operate at their level of particularity but secures the very legitimacy of the state through the ethical idea of human dignity.

> Habermas identifies a decisive sphere when political conflicts that require political regulation and that cannot be decided at the level of world views need to be mediated: the sphere of the legitimation of the neutrality of the state towards worldviews which is itself ethical – thus, not ethically neutral. The '"priority of the just over the good" must not blind us to the fact that the abstract morality of reason proper to subjects of human rights is itself sustained by a prior *ethical self-understanding of the species*, which is shared by all *moral persons*'.[43]

With this idea, Habermas has moved the debate from the presumed rights of parents as individual agents over against the state, to the conditions which the state has to guarantee if it is not to lose its legitimacy. The state does not have to submit to the least demanding position held within society's plural conceptions of values; it has a position to defend from which it receives its legitimacy. This ethical 'source towards which the state is not neutral because its legitimation comes from it' is human dignity:

> Questions of practices that do not violate human dignity are not conceptions of meaning owed to worldviews, but implications of universal normativity. With the concepts of

human dignity and law, the state does not designate an indefinite space for arbitrary wills which it – for instance as the agent of unfettered private interests – would have to keep clear of worldview-generated options of meaning; it designates precisely the option of meaning which it opposes to them as the only one at its disposition, and the one on which it founds its monopoly of force.[44]

While it has to maintain an equal distance to religions and worldviews, it can assert 'an ethical self-understanding of the species which is crucial for our capacity . . . to recognize one another as autonomous persons'.[45]

Schweidler points out the difference between an approach that bases the legitimacy of the modern state of law on the connection of the concept of dignity to a species ethical foundation, to the model devised by John Rawls. In the proposal put forward in *Political Liberalism*[46], he conceives of the 'difference between a neutrality regarding worldviews, and ethical commitment through the dichotomy between "comprehensive doctrines" and "public conceptions" of the just by which citizens submit to the ethical claim that the conditions of preserving the democratic state place on them.' What Schweidler rejects in this model is that the ultimate content towards which citizens are to be ethically committed is exactly the preservation and stability of the order which was to receive its legitimation by this commitment. He judges that here 'the transformation from conditions of legitimation into conditions of acceptance is made programmatic'.[47] Citizens commit themselves to the stability of their state, but to nothing beyond it which would justify the state, such as the protection of human dignity. Against the strategy of moving 'principles of dignity and the right of humans into the corner of worldviews, especially religiously loaded ones', Schweidler recognizes in them 'the ethical conditions of the sovereignty of modern statehood'.[48]

While these critically appreciative observations show the fertility of Habermas's contribution both to biomedical and to political ethics, the question remaining for theologians is how he deals with the religious foundations of Kierkegaard's concept.

c. 'Being Able to be a Self' without 'the Ground That Posited it': Reading Kierkegaard in Postmetaphysical Immanence

If 'being able to be a self' is to be advanced as the formal core term of an ethics of the species, it has to allow for being read independently of its monotheistic horizon and target point. The aim is to find 'secular (reasons) which in a society with a pluralistic outlook may reasonably be expected to meet with a rather general acceptance'.[49] As Georg Lohmann points out, two elements in this concept make it suitable for a level of ethics dedicated to express the self-understanding of the human species. The responsibility of taking over one's own biography which was mentioned already in *Theory of Communicative Action* is now interpreted in a post-metaphysical way through the formal and negative concept of an 'unfailed' (*nicht verfehlt*) life; and a dimension of otherness on which the self is dependent is constitutive for this relation.[50] For Kierkegaard, this absolute power is God which Habermas replaces by the immanent concept of the 'transsubjective power of intersubjectivity'. Yet can this 'weak proceduralistic reading' take the place of the relationship of a transcendent and unconditioned God towards all finite individuals whose use of reason makes them conscious of their contingency? It is remarkable that also here, not just in the context of practical reason, resort is taken to joint human 'effort':

> the 'right' ethical self-understanding is neither revealed nor 'given' in some other way. It can only be won in a common endeavour (*in gemeinsamer Anstrengung*). From this perspective what makes our being-ourselves possible appears more as a transsubjective power than an absolute one.[51]

This solution stays below the level of Kierkegaard's analysis of the absolute contingency of the self. The anxiety arising from the insight into its facticity cannot be quenched by seeking support in other, equally ungrounded fellow-humans. The fact that the other person is just as unnecessary as I am is not an adequate response to the depth of the question. It seems that Habermas mines the concept of being able to be a self for the element of irreplaceability but then entrusts the 'grounding' that should remain beyond assimilation to secular reason, to a 'transsubjective power'. As Thomas Schmidt points out, in 'Kierkegaard, the individual finds its final ground and thus the guarantee of its ability to be a self not in itself but in God'.[52] It is through the affirmation of each person's singularity by God and God's wish for each individual to be a unique self that the contingency question is answered. This is not an element that can be made immanent and granted by other equally finite and contingent fellow-humans. In this regard, the 'transsubjective' dimension remains bound to the 'bad infinity' of the species. For Kierkegaard, the two forms of despair – not wanting in despair to be oneself, and wanting in despair to be oneself – are forms of authentic existence. The leap from the moral to the religious level is not necessary for authenticity. But even if living at the level of the two existential forms of morality may be called 'unfailed' (*unverfehlt*) since it is authentic, it is far from a flourishing life of recognized identity. Thus, rather than transfer this task of fulfilment to the species, it would be more in keeping with the radical nature of Kierkegaard's questioning to indicate that there is a problem that will remain unanswered outside the theistic framework which is the only one in which everyone's irreplaceable individuality can be 'grounded'.[53] Habermas quotes these lines only to propose a 'deflationary interpretation of the "totally other"' in terms of the prior existence of the 'linguistically structured lifeworld'. The 'transcending power of communication forms' may be an answer if the problem is only that the 'finite spirit is dependent on enabling conditions which are outside its control', but it does not capture why Kierkegaard concludes with the alternative between despair and faith.

To summarize the new phase opening up in Habermas's treatment of religion since the year 2000:[54] postmetaphysical reason now takes religion seriously as an intellectual formation with which philosophy shares its genealogy. It can therefore translate between these two contemporary formations of the human spirit to make its semantic and pragmatic potential fruitful for current challenges. His discussion of liberal eugenics marks a breakthrough in two respects: by including the ethical level of self-understanding from which the motivation to act morally arises, he accepts the self's striving for an unfailed life in its significance for a universalist morality. This extension provides a structural parallel to the combination of Aristotle and Kant in Paul Ricoeur's approach which defines the 'ethical intention' as 'aiming for the "good life" with and for others, in just institutions'.[55] While it cannot be developed any further here, it is a significant departure for a proceduralist moral theory which previously always drew the line at questions it considered to be a matter of the lifeworld, such as motivation, or 'existential' concerns, among them the irretrievable suffering of victims. The second new development is the previously unexpressed regard for the protection of singularity. Especially his differentiated response at the discussion at New York University in 2001 explicates its unsubstitutible role. Ronald Dworkin had objected that only certain features, not the morally relevant identity of the person, would be affected by enhancement and that only an intervention which 'reduces the range of her future life choices' (Lebensentwürfe)[56] should be ruled out. Habermas insists that precisely the knowledge of what would be restrictive presupposes that the person advising has already got to know the person to benefit from enhancement as a being individuated through her life history.[57] No objectifying judgement a priori is possible, singularity has the last and only word. It is taken seriously as a matter of principle, not of gradation.

The new directions into which Habermas has taken his theory project provide open invitations for theological questioning, from the concept of creation, through religious resources of democracy, to the key term chosen for this exchange: translation.

Chapter 8

Religious Resources for the Project of Modernity in Theological Debate

The new openings towards the unexhausted potential of religion bring with them challenges to be further examined, such as the discontinuation of philosophy of religion as a branch of philosophy, and the combination of the call for cooperative translations with the designation of religious contents as 'awkward', 'opaque', 'dogmatically encapsulated', and 'discursively exterritorial'.[1] Habermas's own lucid interpretation of the concept of creation, however, shows that these features do not always apply (1). Against the 'proviso' conceded by John Rawls, his defence of the right of religious fellow-citizens to use their own religious language in public debate seems to speak for a genuinely two-sided cooperation in postsecular society. There is no need to supply 'in due course . . . proper political reasons . . . that are sufficient to support whatever the comprehensive doctrines introduced are said to support'.[2] Yet which approach to the relation between religion and reason does this position imply (2)? A core question for theology is the parameters of cooperation since they may lead to religious resources being appropriated in a restrictive way, cutting off some of their potential also for secular reason. Does it capture the difference between an origin that can only be expressed in religious terms, and one generated by reason if the task is described as translating contents with opaque kernels into generally accessible language? I shall assess the theological critiques of this point and put forward a framework in which commitment to the categories and the normative achievements of modernity can be justified from the core of the Christian message (3).

1. Freedom as the Ability to Say No: Creation versus Emanation

For the task of safeguarding both the radical equality of all members of the species, and the singularity of each, the monotheistic idea of creation offers an unambiguous and consistent framework. Keeping both equality and recognized diversity together, it shows its heuristic potential at a time when multiple successors to the unity of the human race are argued for as desirable results of enhancement. In his Peace Prize speech in 2001, Habermas makes use of the heritage of monotheism by uncovering the critical standard which the concept of God's creation of free humans has set for the development of European thought. He offers a perceptive interpretation of the theological doctrine of *imago Dei* as the human counterpart whom God has called into being in a free decision to create. Decisive in the biblical account is the distinction between creator and creature which, unlike the thought form of emanation, sets the creature free from her originator. This alternative philosophical tradition, renewed by Neoplatonism, entails a participative continuity between the origin and the originated. In the controversy about parents wishing to enhance their children's genetic make-up, the biblical concept of 'creation' immediately reveals its critical significance: it enables us to envisage a relationship that sets the creature free and does not keep it tied to its creator. Thus, the religious understanding of each human being as made in the image of God contains a still unexhausted potential of resistance:

> One knows that there can be no love without recognition
> of the self in the other, no freedom without mutual
> recognition. So, the other who has human form (*Gegenüber
> in Menschengestalt*) must himself be free in order to be able
> to return God's affection (*Zuwendung*). In spite of his
> likeness to God, however, this other is also imagined as
> being God's creature. Regarding his origin, he cannot be
> of equal birth with God. This *creatural nature* of the image
> (*Ebenbild*) expresses an intuition which in the present
> context may even speak to those who are tone-deaf
> to religious connotations. Hegel had a feeling for this

difference between divine 'creation' and mere 'coming from' (*Hervorgehen aus*) God. God remains a 'God of free men' (*Menschen*) only as long as we do not level out the absolute difference that exists between the creator and the creature. Only then, the fact that God gives form to human life does not imply a determination (*Determinierung*) interfering with man's self-determination (*Selbstbestimmung*).[3]

Having first examined Habermas's explicit rejection of Hegel's integration and dissolution of the Christian belief in the incarnation of God into the philosophical idea of the 'identity of the divine and the human', the systematic theologian Magnus Striet points out how much his interpretation captures 'the intention of the Christian theology of creation and anthropology': a 'free recognition of the human being by God, founded on the original and lasting difference between God and human, which is granted in mercy and to which the creature is to respond and correspond in her own freedom'.[4] The interpretation of *imago Dei* from the side of philosophy is unique in his work; in it, Habermas displays a theological literacy unmatched by his liberal fellow-theorist, John Rawls. His perception of an argument from within a religious tradition that might persuade religious citizens to accept the demands of transforming their 'comprehensive doctrines' into 'reasonable political conceptions of justice' is contained in the line, 'such are the limits that God sets on our liberty'.[5]

God's respect for human freedom includes the ability of the created counterpart to say No. The sequence in the Book of Genesis, from the two accounts of creation in Chapters 1 and 2, to Chapter 3 on the Fall, exemplifies the incalculable relationship between freedoms and the risk God takes in respecting the autonomy of the creature; it sets an example for interaction and non-paternalistic initiatives between humans by offering the relationship of a covenant which can only be concluded in free response. Thus, creation is not determination of individual specificity but opening up the space of freedom through which humans are the image of God. Individuality is not pre-set but worked out in each historical personal response to the creator. The idea of the chance of becoming a self in response to God's call into being, thus 'grounding the self transparently in the power that established it', belongs to this heritage.

The Peace Prize speech shows that the interest in religion does not merely arise for the functional reasons of motivating or stabilizing democratic society but for reasons of a content which only religion can provide. The biblical and theological concept of *imago Dei* which has inspired, but cannot be dissolved into, the idea of human dignity[6] is a successful example of what is intended with the call to mutual translation. Yet, there must be other examples of theological conceptualizations of religious contents that remain opaque. When Habermas refers to 'the archaic elements' of 'the experiential world of rituals' or to the 'collectively exercised cult praxis of the world religions' with their 'peculiar form of communication'[7] it becomes clearer why he continues to speak of the 'discursive exterritoriality' of religion. How theology has responded to the problems indicated by the range of his assessments will be the subject of the chapter's third and final section on translation. First, however, the consequence of his appreciation of the contribution of monotheism to Western ethics will be analyzed. In keeping with a citizen-oriented concept of public reason and aware of the need for 'mentalities of solidarity'[8] in contemporary society, he argues against John Rawls's understanding of democratic legitimation. Habermas's civil society understanding of public reason admits all the resources of motivation and meaning available in the lifeworld to public discourse on which democratic procedures depend for their legitimacy.

2. Religious Resources in Postsecular Democracy

While religions are not alone in their ability to renew the motivation of citizens, they are recognized as contributing to the species ethical foundations by embedding values that support democracy in the lifeworld (b). Yet they are also seen as one of two polarized sides which have to engage in dialogue if the achievements of modernity are not to be lost in mutual incomprehension that could lead to culture wars within established democracies. The precondition for this dialogue is the recognition that despite the fundamentalisms into which both scientific rationality and religion can descend, it is not a priori irrational to be a believer (a). Although Habermas identifies the language of 'secularity' as 'accessible to all', he is doubtful of the ability of 'common sense' to be critical enough against the increasing tendencies towards self-objectification and submission to economic priorities (c).[9]

a. The Rationality of Religious Belief from a Postmetaphysical Standpoint

Ever since the status, tasks and method of philosophy have been revised to the new designation as stand-in for universalistic questions and as interpreter between expert cultures and the lifeworld, has its cognitive claim been declared as 'fallible'. Against the rise of scientism Habermas now insists again on its distinct rationality of self-reflection which is coupled with the new task for modern reason to relate to its own tradition of origin. For religion, the consequence of this new set of motives is that the position espoused in *Theory of Communicative Action*, of communicative reason taking over the function of religion, which paralleled the secularization theory of the time that envisaged the disappearance of religion, is now critiqued and rescinded. The fallibility of time-bound insights is expressed by no longer being able to predict whether the two formations of the human spirit will continue to exist side by side, or whether religion, and possibly also enlightened reason, will be exhausted by the pressures of a modernity no longer retained by the universalistic ethos of its origin. For Habermas, this is an 'open empirical question' for future enquiries.[10] At present, society is postsecular in the sense that 'religious communities continue to exist in a context of ongoing secularization'.[11] At the conceptual level, he argues for disconnecting the theory of modernity from secularization theory.[12] Regarding the epistemic status of religion, he requires secular knowledge (*Weltwissen*) to be self-critical and to accord religious convictions 'an epistemic status as not simply (*schlechthin*) "irrational"'. This judgment is the basis for distinguishing between the secularity of the neutral state, and a secularist 'worldview' which is claiming too much ground if exclusively secular contributions are accepted in public debate.

This appreciation also motivates the demand that efforts to 'translate' should be mutual:

> 'The guarantee of equal ethical liberties calls for the secularization of state power, but it forbids the political overgeneralization of the secularized world view. Insofar as they act in their role as citizens, secularized citizens may neither fundamentally deny that religious convictions may be true nor reject the right of their devout (*gläubig*) fellow-citizens to couch their contributions to public discussions in religious language. A liberal political culture can even expect its secularized citizens to participate in efforts to translate relevant contributions from religious language into a publicly accessible language'.[13]

Thus, there is a fine line which separates the legitimate task of finding a common language that is able to devise shared policy goals in a pluralist society, from a 'political overgeneralization of the secularized worldview'.[14] The expectation towards secular citizens to enquire about the intended meaning of religious expressions also shows that they are to some degree accessible. If the content of religions was merely opaque, the invitation could not be issued. Before investigating what is implied in the task of translation – for instance, should those who carry it out, be they philosophers, theologians or citizens, be 'bilingual'?[15] – I shall analyze the reasons for this inclusion: equal access for all citizens to public debate, and the power of religion to generate motivation and a mindset that offers some resistance to encroachments by instrumental reason.

b. Equal Participation and Mentalities of Solidarity against the Pathologies of Modernity

For the author who first made the 'public sphere' – its origins in modernity, its subsequent transformations and the normative standard it poses as the citizens' forum of discourse located between the state and the market – a theme of enquiry in philosophy and the humanities since 1961,[16] the question of access is a matter both of its heuristic potential and of its inclusiveness. Already his first response to political liberalism had shown the difference between his participative concept of democratic opinion and will formation and Rawls's institution-oriented interpretation of 'public reason'.[17] In the new debate on the conditions and limits for religious citizens to participate in civic debate, Habermas not only argues for the democratic need to hear their voices, but also appreciates their objections to political proposals as an early warning system.[18] Their right to have and to express their particular identities as believers is put forward as a matter of fairness – the concern which Rawls has made the central theme of his work, first with regard to the basic structures of justice, then with regard to pluralism. Habermas bases his comment on his normative understanding of the foundations of democracy which guarantees freedom of religion. Rather than take those reasons that constitute the intersecting, or 'overlapping' segment between different positions as a justified consensus, he seeks legitimation through reasons that fulfil the discourse criterion of validity by testing their universalizability, such as an equal distribution of burdens. The way to achieve a genuinely universal acceptability is to actively engage with the position of the other side and, by listening to what they have a right to express, pacify the conflict arising from unequal chances of being heard:

> The other side of religious freedom is in fact a pacification of the pluralism of world views that distribute burdens unequally. To date, only citizens committed to religious beliefs are required to split up their identities, as it were, into their public and private elements. They are the ones who have to translate their religious beliefs into a secular language before their arguments have any chance of gaining majority support . . . But only if the secular side, too, remains sensitive to the force of articulation inherent in religious languages will the search for reasons that aim at universal acceptability not lead to an unfair exclusion of religions from the public sphere, nor sever secular society from important resources of meaning. In any event, the boundaries between secular and religious reasons are fluid. Determining these disputed boundaries should therefore be seen as a cooperative task which requires *both* sides to take on the perspective of the other one.[19]

Thus, the reasons for the rehabilitation of religious convictions in the public realm are the concerns for fairness in the sense of access to political exchange, a new emphasis on the openness to learn in the exercise of mutual perspective taking, and the desire to include all available resources of meaning that can resist new pathologies in the structures and the common sense of society: such as the reduction to the imperatives of a market that 'cannot be democratized',[20] the loss of civic agency and practical reason succumbing to defeatism. Remarkably, the pathologies of modernity also include fundamentalism which is therefore not only seen as an extreme form of religion. Habermas observes that fundamentalism, in spite of its 'religious language, . . . is an exclusively modern phenomenon, and, therefore, not only a problem of others'. Western secularity needs to become more self-critical regarding the self-understanding it portrays: 'We do not want to be perceived as crusaders of a competing religion or as salespeople of instrumental reason and destructive secularization'.[21]

Habermas is not concerned with pluralism as a problem for stability but with modernity's own destructive tendencies. Rather than make it a virtue of citizens to promote the stability of the state by renouncing to the articulation of their convictions, he welcomes the store of experience, reflections and mentalities which religious traditions in their coherence provide as a resource to be appropriated by their members, and valued by reflective fellow-citizens. His concept of public reason counters the liberal prioritization of individual rights with the diagnosis that mentalities of solidarity are sorely lacking. In this analysis, he agrees with the famous 1960s statement of the German constitutional lawyer and later Supreme Court judge, Ernst-Wolfgang Böckenförde, that the liberal state lives off presuppositions it cannot guarantee itself. It is the theme of his debate in 2004 with Joseph Ratzinger, then Cardinal, on the 'pre-political foundations of democracy'.[22] The vitality of religious traditions alongside different humanisms is needed for the horizon of meaning they provide, for their hope in a fulfillment of moral intentions beyond human powers, and for their trust in the eschatological power of God, even if this confidence – indeed, as Habermas assumes, pre-modern certainty – is beyond secular fellow-citizens.

Where does this appreciation of what religions can offer leave the non-religious contemporaries who, after all, supply the benchmark of what is acceptable, not in civic debate, but beyond the 'institutional threshold' of parliament and courts? Habermas's comments on the concept suggested by John Rawls for this shared level, 'common sense', shows that his idea of a generally acceptable language for civic consensus is based on a different understanding of what goes into this foundation.

c. Secularity and 'Democratic Common Sense'

On the one hand, the target language of the translations that are to be 'accessible' to all citizens is identified as a 'secular' one. On the other hand, Habermas mistrusts the currency of 'common sense' which Rawls has foreseen as the level beyond which no acceptable proposals for an overlapping consensus can be made. In political liberalism, it thus acquires a limiting function for the arguments admitted in public moral disputes.[23]

> 'Considering the religious origins of its moral foundation, the liberal state should be aware of the possibility that Hegel's "culture of common sense" ('*Kultur des gemeinen Menschenverstands*') may, in view of entirely novel challenges, fail to be up to the level of articulation which characterized its own origins. Today, the all-pervasive language of the market puts all interpersonal relations under the constraint of an egocentric orientation towards one's own preferences. The social bond, however, being made up of mutual recognition, cannot be spelled out in the concept of contract, rational choice, and maximal benefit alone'.[24]

Rather than seek a consensus on a minimal level, his normative notion of the public sphere requires 'democratic common sense' to aim for a more strenuous, but also more enriching process of encouraging debate between worldviews on different concepts of the human, including those inspired by religious sources.

As seen before, the resistance they may offer to current policies is taken seriously:

> liberal politics must abstain from externalizing the perpetual dispute over the secular self-awareness of society, that is, from relegating it only to the religious segment of the population. Democratic common sense is not singular, it describes the mental state of a *many-voiced* public. Secular majorities must not reach decisions in such questions before the objections of opponents who feel that these decisions violate their beliefs have been heard, they have to consider these objections as a kind of dilatory plea (*aufschiebendes Veto*) in order to examine what may be learnt from them'.[25]

Thus, a pluralist civic sphere has to be able to draw on all existing resources to stem the various reductive tendencies at work in liberal societies; such as the sense of forming a polity being reduced to individual self-interest, of individual self-understanding to a market-led orientation towards one's body and mind as assets, or the division of universal human rights into urgent rights and constitutional rights of established democracies.

At the same time, unlike Rawls, Habermas does not see 'the secular' as constituting a worldview; this only happens if it is 'over-generalized' politically. As the sociologist Jens Greve points out, the 'secular attitude is not the expression of a particular worldview, but makes it possible to keep a cognitive distance to different worldviews (*Weltbilder*)' and life forms.[26] The crucial difference for Habermas is between 'learning process', which should be open to consider other truth claims, and 'outcome', which should not be religiously biased in order to be 'acceptable not just for the members of *one* religious community'.[27]

Yet are the terms in which Habermas distinguishes 'secular' from 'religious', regarding contents, language and adherents, not too clear-cut? Can 'learning process' (mutual, via cooperative translations) and 'outcome' (secular) be distinguished so clearly, especially if one takes into account that also secular contributions to public debate have the status of convictions in which universal norms are already mediated with subjectively appropriating interpretations? In view of the abiding otherness of the discourse partners, could they not equally contain an element that remains 'opaque'? Habermas has admitted that 'the boundaries between secular and religious reasons are fluid'.[28] Can these conflicting descriptions be resolved by examining the task of translation?

3. Translation as a Cooperative Task

Against Rawls, Habermas has insisted on the admission also of religiously grounded positions into public debate without the need for prior translation, or, in Rawls's terminology, for trans-formation into 'political conceptions' agreeable to public reason. In this defence of the contributions of religious fellow-citizens he partly endorses the critiques of Nicholas Wolterstorff and Paul Weithman, as well as his own understanding of the public sphere as owned by citizens reviewing and shaping democratic politics guided by their own interpretations of universalistic standards. There is a danger, however, in describing the mindset of the 'devout (*fromm*) person' as conducting 'her daily existence *on the basis of* her faith', which if 'genuine', is 'not merely a doctrine, something believed (*geglaubter Inhalt*), but is also a source of energy that the person of faith taps into performatively to nurture her whole life'. Unsurprisingly, he identifies this understanding of faith as 'totalizing' and, since it 'permeates the very pores of daily life' as resisting, 'so the objection goes, any nimble switchover of religiously rooted political convictions onto a *different* cognitive basis'.[29] Does a type of faith that fits this description not deny a core assumption of Habermas's reconstruction of linguistically mediated intersubjectivity, namely, the capability for mutual perspective-taking? And how can it be distinguished from identity formations that reject any outreach and critical self-examination in authoritarian, ideological or fundamentalist ways? As the systematic theologians Knut Wenzel and Gesche Linde point out, believers can equally draw on the secular consciousness they have as bearers of reason, and are well able to translate, depending on what this term stands for.[30] Wenzel is concerned that Habermas's position is more aligned to an integralist Christian position hostile to secularity than to one open to pluralism.[31] He subjects a similarly enclosed formulation, 'infallible revealed truths',[32] to a helpful theological analysis which dissolves the conglomeration of theological epistemology, dogmatics and ecclesiology through the necessary distinctions:

> The coupling of theology of revelation with infallibility . . .
> does not represent a continuous Christian consensus
> on these questions . . . According to the Second Vatican
> Council's Constitution on Revelation, *Dei Verbum*, the core
> of revelation does not consist in the divine communication
> of propositions . . . but in the self-giving of God which
> creates a relationship. Infallible statements which the
> church makes through its *Magisterium* are related back
> to this revelation which in its substance is not the giving
> of information but God's self-communication. The
> truth of these statements does not depend on their
> infallibility; declaring them infallible celebrates their
> truth, but does not make them 'truer'. Thus, their truth
> has to be able to be shown in a principally different
> way, namely corresponding to the discursive means of
> 'natural reason'.[33]

In his projections about religion from a secular perspective, a concern comes true that Habermas has expressed in view of the opposite example, namely radically demythologizing theologies: that believers will not find themselves represented.[34] A better understanding of the religious counterpart than these descriptions insinuate may be found in the history of translations that have brought forth the syntheses of European culture (a). What has to be examined subsequently is what the opposite side, the 'secular', stands for. Is it autonomous morality, or the neutrality of the state, or the guiding premise of a shared human capacity for universal, yet fallible, reason? The test case here will be the reception of the philosopher whom Habermas regards as having provided 'salvaging', rather than 'destructive' transformations, Kant (b). Once the two partners in the translation project have been identified more closely, the final section can further specify what translation consists in (c).

a. Translating Biblical Monotheism

Habermas's interest in the as yet unexhausted potential of religion has been consistently expressed in his debates with theologians, but has grown stronger in view of the self-destructive turns of a modernity dissociating itself from the normative framework of equality and self-determination which it announced. Translation serves the double task of making religious motives available to secular reason in its normative orientation, and to retrace the development of its own self-understanding from its shared foundations with religion. Already in his response to the polarization between 'Jerusalem' and 'Athens' which Johann Baptist Metz undertook in the effort to uncover the dimension of memory within critical reason, did Habermas recognize the mediating and justifying achievements since Antiquity of translating biblical monotheism into the cultural frameworks of subsequent eras. As referred to before, in Chapter 1, he is aware that religions can maintain and articulate their vitality only by mediating their original revelation to the problems posed within a culture which is itself understood as 'an ensemble of enabling conditions for problem-solving activities'. It is the task of the religious tradition to engage in this reinterpretation: 'A tradition must be able to develop its cognitive potential in such a way that the addressees are convinced that this tradition is really worth pursuing'.[35]

The internal task of religions to translate and justify their message in new cultural contexts differs from the use postmetaphysical reason makes of it. The mediating tasks religious traditions perform in their inculturation and apologetics cannot be judged by philosophy. The following description, dating already from his debate with Metz, elucidates the genealogical significance of the monotheistic transformation of Greek concepts and mentions some universalizing translations:

> The Greek *logos* has transformed itself on its path from the intellectual contemplation of the cosmos, via the self-reflection of the knowing subject, to a linguistically embodied reason . . . the idea of a covenant which promises justice to the people of God, and to everyone who belongs to this people, a justice which extends through and beyond a history

of suffering, has been taken up in the idea of a community tied by a special bond. The thought of such a community, which would entwine freedom and solidarity within the horizon of an undamaged intersubjectivity, has unfolded its explosive force even in philosophy. Argumentative reason has become receptive to the practical experiences of threatened identity suffered by those who exist historically.[36]

Thus, 'covenant' is translated into a connection between the freedom presupposed in those who are invited to conclude it and the solidarity it generates with those who suffer. In view of this heritage, Habermas explains the core concepts of modernity which would have been unthinkable without the biblical idea of a God who, unlike the different conceptions of God in Greek metaphysics, 'calling into life communicates within a morally sensitive universe'.[37] Subjective freedom, autonomy, mutual recognition and liberation are retraced to these roots before they are reconfigured in the language of postmetaphysical thinking as 'socialized' and 'individualized subjects'.

Without this subversion of Greek metaphysics by notions of authentically Jewish and Christian origin, we could not have developed that network of specifically modern notions which come together in the thought of a reason that is both communicative and historically situated. I am referring to the concept of subjective freedom and the demand for equal respect for all – and specifically for the stranger in her distinctiveness and otherness. I am referring to the concept of autonomy, of a self-binding of the will based on moral insight, which depends on relations of mutual recognition. I am referring to the concept of socialized subjects, who are individuated by their life histories, and are simultaneously irreplaceable individuals and members of a community; such subjects can only lead a life that is genuinely their own through sharing in a common life with others. I am referring to the concept of liberation – both as an emancipation from degrading conditions and as the utopian project of a harmonious form of life. Finally, the irruption of historical thought into philosophy has fostered insight into the limited span of human life . . . This awareness includes a sense of the fallibility of the human mind, and of the contingent conditions under which even our unconditional claims are raised.[38]

The heritage of epoch-making translations which created European culture is there to be critical appropriated:

Can postmetaphysical thinking which has lost Hegel's strong concept of theory exclude that religious traditions carry semantic potentials with themselves which unfold an inspiring power for *all of* society, when they offer (*preisgeben*) *profane* contents of truth? Without detriment to its secular self-understanding, postmetaphysical thinking can relate to religion in a way that is *at the same time* agnostic and ready to learn. Faith retains something opaque for knowledge which can neither be denied nor just ignored. Secular reason insists on the difference between certainties of faith and publicly criticizable validity claims, yet abstains from a theory which judges the rationality or irrationality (*Vernunft oder Unvernunft*) of religion as a whole.[39]

The journey of a postmetaphysical reason willing to learn from religion thus ends with the guiding dichotomy of 'certainties' over against 'criticizable validity claims'. The culture-hermeneutical and interpretive achievements of the paradigm changes in which the articulation of the 'identity' of the Christian faith took place through different upheavals and encounters are ultimately taken to be only reassertions of certainties. There is no sense of the struggles implied in the attempt to faithfully express the meaning of a salvation to which the Bible testifies but which predates and exceeds the words of Scripture. As Knut Wenzel points out, 'the "identity" of these religious traditions . . . cannot be abstracted from the ongoing controversy about the adequate formulation of this identity'.[40]

Habermas seems interested above all in the finished product, the religious motive or theological concept which can be appropriated by reason. The productivity aspect, that is, the fact that there has been reason at work in creating these concepts in the quest to relate the core of the biblical message to the emerging cultural constellations co-created by these reinterpretations, is not part of the analysis. This process is better captured by Herta Nagl-Docekal:

> Habermas's way of referring to 'dogmatic authority' seems over-simplified. What hermeneutic research on 'tradition' has found in general, does apply to religious traditions: They can only persist through centuries if the believers manage – over and over again – to re-interpret the core convictions of their faith in a way that renders them accessible, and convincing, in view of their respective contemporary condition.[41]

Oppositions such as 'certain' and 'discursively exterritorial' over against 'public and criticizable' are misconceived. The controversies that led to the prototype of all Councils, the Council of Nicaea, are a case in point. The process which Habermas refers to, of the transformation of the 'Greek *logos* . . . on its path from the intellectual contemplation of the cosmos, via the self-reflection of the knowing subject, to a linguistically embodied reason' is owed to Nicaea. With its core term, *homoousios*, it insisted, against Arius's Neo-Platonic cosmological interpretation of the *Logos* as the instrument of creation, on Jesus Christ's equal standing and 'one being' with God.[42] The Council still lacked the distinction developed subsequently by the three Cappadocians between *ousia* and *hypostasis*, being and actualization, which prepared the way to the 'self-reflection of the knowing subject' through a conceptual creativity which sought to safeguard both the complete humanity and the equal divinity of the saviour, Jesus Christ, without which salvation could not happen. As Gesche Linde summarizes, these translations have been 'the genuine work of theology . . . This makes theology – who would have thought it –, so-to-speak, the avant-garde of the postsecular society proposed by Habermas.'[43]

b. The Target Language of the 'Secular'

If the process of transmission, explication and renewal of a faith tradition is marked by the use of reason, making it less 'encapsulated' than Habermas's metaphor suggests, does this not even speed up its avant-gardist dissolution into reason? Is he not doing religious faith a favour by insisting on a core untranslatable into secular thought, while remaining open, receptive and willing to learn from the elements it can assimilate? It is true that there should be no theological objections to contemporary culture drawing on a religious heritage it no longer shares but still finds inspirational. But misleading descriptions of either side of the translation process will not promote successful conditions for keeping this heritage alive within faith communities or in late modern culture. Thus, the question is not only to theology whether its approaches do justice to the revelation it is entrusted with transmitting, but also to the side of reason whether it draws boundaries of its own that prevent it from grasping what the message is about. I shall examine the reasons for this question, and the answer Habermas gives to it, which has been asked of him repeatedly by theologians, here by Josef Schmidt: 'Secular reason must face the question of where it has drawn its own rational boundaries too hastily, so that the latter do not match its real scope'.[44] While the 'opportunity' for critique applies to both sides, and reason also gives religion the chance to 'expose itself to criticism to its own advantage', Josef Schmidt specifies the objection that the boundaries of postmetaphysical reason are too restrictive. This affects both practical reason (1) and the theory of subjectivity implied by it (2).

b.1. The Limits of Practical Reason

Josef Schmidt questions the foundation of ethics on the 'inescapable' presuppositions of discourse since they offer a 'merely factual explanation' rather than a 'reflexive justification', just a 'higher form of facticity' that can 'ultimately be explicated in naturalistic terms'.[45] A similar critique from Karl-Otto Apel against Habermas's avoidance of a transcendental justification was explained in Chapter 4. Josef Schmidt's fellow-Jesuit Friedo Ricken reminds Habermas of the outreach of Kant's concept of practical reason by fully supporting his critique of Pope Benedict XVI's interpretation of Kant in his Regensburg speech in 2006. He first points out the objection Habermas and the Pope 'share . . . against a narrow scientistic concept of reason'. Yet against the Pope's critique of "'the modern self-limitation of reason, classically expressed in Kant's 'Critiques', but in the meantime further radicalized by the impact of the natural sciences"', Ricken states that this does not

> even begin() to do justice to the Kantian concept of reason. Reason enquires into the unconditioned; the critique of theoretical reason leaves this question open and practical philosophy, taking as its point of departure the apodictic law of practical reason, answers it through rational faith. It is difficult to understand how Kant could be depicted as the father of a scientistic–naturalistic worldview. His hypothesis of the primacy of practical reason represents a resolute rejection of naturalism; it states that the primary interest of reason consists in our understanding of ourselves as free, morally acting beings. Habermas rightly objects to Benedict XVI's interpretation of Kant that 'Kant's transcendental turn leads not only to a critique of the proofs of God's existence but also to the concept of autonomy which first made possible our modern European understanding of law and democracy'.[46]

Having defended Kant against being cast as having facilitated the advent of scientistic reason, Ricken concludes with questions to Habermas:

> Which concept of reason does Habermas contrast with this? . . . What means does postmetaphysical reason have at its disposal if it is to perform a translation rather than an assimilation (*Angleichung*), a translation in which parts of the religious traditions are transposed into another language without detriment to their semantic content? . . . Does the moral consciousness which has not been fully undermined by scientism supply postmetaphysical reason with the necessary categories for its task of translation?[47]

The concern that postmetaphysical thinking undersells the side of philosophy is echoed also in several contributions of philosophers and theologians at the Vienna Symposium with Habermas in 2005. His speech there in 2004 on 'The boundary between faith and knowledge: On the reception and contemporary importance of Kant's philosophy of religion'[48] rejected his concept of the highest good with its insistence on the fulfilment of a happiness proportionate to moral effort. The antinomy can only be resolved through a rational faith in the existence of God as a postulate of practical reason. In Habermas's disputed reading, this need only arises from making the realization of the highest good a duty: 'The doctrine of the postulates rests on introducing a problematic duty that drives the ought so far beyond human capabilities that this asymmetry must be rectified by extending knowledge through faith'.[49]

What is at stake in his critique that Kant has overstepped the boundaries of philosophy by allowing his *Critique of Practical Reason* to include the idea of God as the author of a world which cannot be totally indifferent to moral endeavour? The disagreement with his philosophical colleagues on the status of the 'highest good' relates both to the scope of moral obligation and to the place of hope: does it belong to morality, that is, to the realm of the 'right' which Habermas's discourse ethics speaks for, and where postmetaphysical reason has the cognitive claim to justify what can be demanded; or does hope belong to the 'ethical' or 'teleological', which it can leave to individual self-interpretations? His philosophical interlocutors, Rudolf Langthaler and Herta Nagl-Docekal, each clarify that the moral ought is independent of the desire for happiness, however justified the latter may be. Thus, the autonomous foundation of moral obligation is not in doubt. What they disagree about with Habermas is whether moral agency is itself oriented towards a hope for meaning, and whether the problems arising here are questions for practical reason itself which philosophy has to face up to, as Kant does with his doctrine of the postulates of practical reason. It is a debate about what is within and what is beyond the limits of philosophy. Is it, as described by Friedo Ricken, 'practical philosophy, taking as its point of departure the apodictic law of practical reason', that 'answers it through rational faith', or has Kant changed register and left the theory of morality behind for a philosophy of religion that is speculative and unwarranted? For Habermas, the problem is one of theory design which leads to overboarding (*überschwänglich*) answers:

> The objection is evident: The problem how the realization
> of the highest good can be thought as possible speaks

less *for* the postulate of God than *against* the prior and completely unjustified step of assuming a problematic duty which through its effusive (*überschwänglich*) aim only generates the problem.[50]

For Langthaler and Nagl-Docekal, it is a problem of actual moral action under the conditions of the real world: 'What needs to be clarified is from where humans – as finite beings – can (or *de facto* do) take the courage and the strength for public engagement in moral effort'.[51] Thus, the 'asymmetry' between 'the ought' and 'human capabilities' which Habermas refers to is not Kant's invention; it is a reflection on the discrepancy between the unconditionality of the good will to act morally and its conditions: finite, and already marked by a propensity towards evil which is not as original as the human disposition towards the good, but which continues to create antagonisms that thwart the realization of the good intention to follow the moral law of reason. According to Habermas, 'Langthaler extends the moral-practical question, 'What ought I do'? in such a way that it *includes* the question treated in his philosophy or religion, 'What may I hope for'?[52] For his two philosophical colleagues, it indicates both Kant's insistence on the unconditional character of moral obligation, and his deliberate inclusion of a 'trans-moral dimension of meaning'.[53] Habermas reduces both to the scale of what is likely to be achieved by human efforts. In an earlier publication, he has critiqued Kant's idea of the good will in its unconditionality as striving for 'omnipotence':

> Kant confused the autonomous will with an omnipotent will and had to transpose it into the intelligible realm in order to conceive of it as absolutely determinative. But in the world as we experience it, the autonomous will is efficacious only to the extent that it can ensure that the motivational force of good reasons outweighs the power of other motives.[54]

Equally, the postulate of God's existence is rejected for a reason that is already familiar from his critique of Helmut Peukert: 'Kant's own answer to the question, "What may we hope for"? obscures (*verwischt*) despite all diligence (*Vorsicht*) the boundary between hope and confidence (*Zuversicht*)'.[55] Thus, a philosophical argumentation that recognizes the antinomy which practical reason encounters and suggests a perspective of 'morally justified meaning'[56], is assimilated to the 'certitudes' and confident assurances Habermas associates with religion. This, however, misconceives the epistemological status of a postulate:

> 'Postulates' never have an 'ascertainable' status – that is, they
> do not open up knowledge which can be secured but
> only outline logical spaces of what can be thought (and
> believed) – this is left out in Habermas's (*prima facie* plausible)
> attack on 'compensatory' metaphysical constructions.[57]

The debates in Vienna with his philosophical colleagues, and with theologians in Vienna and Munich have posed the question whether reason remains below its potential when hope in the realization of the highest good – against the defeats which the moral actions of finite humans face and their risk of making morality absurd – is given up as an inalienable part of reason. Yet besides practical reason, there is a separate point of argumentation important for determining the relationship between faith and reason: independently from its inspiring potential for morality, the rationality of religion itself needs to be shown.

b.2. The Need to Determine the Concept of Religion in an Analysis of Subjectivity

Taking as his basis culturally given particular religions, especially Jewish and Christian monotheism, Habermas does not engage with the question of what constitutes religion and where it is located within the human spirit. He distances his enterprise from this task:

> The interest that motivates me to engage with *questions* of
> philosophy of religion is not an enquiry of philosophy of
> religion in the strict sense. My point is not to conceptualize
> (*auf den Begriff zu bringen*) in a philosophically adequate
> way religious speech and experience.[58]

Herta Nagl-Docekal and the systematic theologian Saskia Wendel both point out the philosophical need to clarify this link:

> The question about the origin of the phenomenon of 'religion' which transcends both cultures and eras remains virulent, that is, the question: is there a place for religion in the individual to which the multiple confessions that have developed historically can be connected?[59]

For Wendel, the relationship between knowledge and faith as well as the criteria for identifying successful, 'salvaging' translations can only be dealt with if two central problems are no longer bracketed: first, the question about the conditions of the possibility of the emergence of religion; secondly, the issue of its *differentia specifica* from other phenomena of the human spirit.[60] Without this type of reflection, it can only be accessed as a conventional feature of the lifeworld, as a fact with a specific historical origin, for example, a prophetic founder. This is what Habermas does when he refers to the 'prophetic origin and the positivity of transmitted doctrines, that is, the *proprium* of lived faith' which reason has no competence to judge 'since it overdraws the account of postmetaphysical reason and pretends to know more about religion than it can claim'.[61] For Wendel, this position claims too little, and puts religion in the contradictory situation that it is asked to translate and justify its faith-based convictions to the public sphere, yet is denied the philosophical means to do so. The reason for avoiding the type of reflection needed to enquire into the foundation and determination of religion are the strictures imposed by post-metaphysical thinking. It remains doubtful for her whether the aim of preventing modernity from destroying its own basis of normativity can be achieved

> with the means he makes available, or whether a different thought form is needed . . . Perhaps, greater trust in reason and in philosophy regarding religion is needed than Habermas shows when one asks for justification and translation, and objects at the same time to 'Wittgensteinian fideism', to 'reformed epistemology' as well as pragmatism . . . Habermas contradicts himself

when, on the one hand, in line with postmetapysical thinking, he restricts the terrain of philosophy and does not want to extend the foundational reflection to the question for the reasons of the emergence and the determination of religion, yet on the other hand, demands the effort to justify the validity claims of religious convictions; he breaks off this justification effort almost dogmatically when it threatens to become 'metaphysical' . . . , when it enters a forbidden field and breaks a self-imposed taboo.[62]

The alternative philosophical method proposed by Wendel is a transcendental analysis of human subjectivity, critically modelled on Schleiermacher's 'Introduction' to *The Christian Faith* which traces the emergence of religion in self-reflection to the feeling of absolute dependence. In critical reference to Dieter Henrich's position, Wendel proposes that the *differentia specifica* of religion consists in the consciousness of owing one's existence to the unconditioned. Despite recently distinguishing transcendental from metaphysical thinking, Habermas steers clear of it because its foundational claims are stronger than he is willing to accept.

Can this critique be confirmed in Habermas's argumentation? I see the response he gives to Josef Schmidt as an indication that her suspicion about 'what Habermas does not dare to think' is correct. His answer to the question 'where (secular reason) has drawn its own rational boundaries too hastily', begins with elucidating the 'correct kind of self-limitation' by repeating the restrictive view of philosophy as 'stand-in' and 'interpreter':

A finite reason which is embodied in historical time and in the social space of cultural forms of life cannot determine these limits at its own discretion. It must understand itself from out of a constellation as a cognitive undertaking which finds itself in predefined relations to science and religion.[63]

Having ruled out the earlier 'self-confidence' of a reason claiming to know what is true and what is false in religions, he explains the horizon of an 'inclusive community' referred to by Schmidt, as 'uneluctible . . . communicative presuppositions', in which '(s)ober postmetaphysical thinking, however, identifies . . . only the "unconditionality" of a factually unavoidable claim of reason.' Thus, the opening towards a stronger moral foundation which Schmidt had suggested against the danger of such a factual basis succumbing to naturalism does not take place. Reason remains in its postmetaphysical confinement. Having responded to the questioning of these restrictions by toning down reason one more time, the only glimpse of an enlargement then belongs to religion. He warns that while the sciences, autonomous morality and law have to be accepted by religious believers, the

> same forms of reflection which we owe to the scientific-technical, procedural-legal, and social achievements of modernity can also lead us into the dead end of a dialectic of enlightenment. The encounter with theology can remind a self-forgetful, secular reason of its distant origins in the revolution in worldviews of the Axial Age. Since the Judeo-Christian and Arabian traditions are no less part of the inheritance of postmetaphysical thinking than Greek metaphysics, biblical motifs can remind us . . . of dimen-sions of a reasonable personal self-understanding which have been abandoned too hastily.[64]

Indeed! Where do these sobering responses leave the task to translate?

c. Opacity, or Given Truth of God's Self-revelation?

On the one hand, Habermas appreciates the perceptiveness and the resources of meaning for an undamaged life which religions still make available; on the other, he criticizes Kant's idea of the highest good, of the fulfilment of the striving for meaning, and reduces the scope of the 'ought' to what can be delivered empirically. What are the heuristic sensitivity, the attentiveness to social pathologies, and the unexhausted potential of transcendence-related religions good for?

Before exploring further the work of translation at the intersection of religion and reason, it is helpful to see how

Habermas distinguishes between theological and postmetaphysical appropriations:

> From its beginnings and into the early modern period,
> Christian theology drew upon the conceptual apparatus of
> Greek metaphysics to make explicit the contents of the
> faith and to subject them to discursive treatment. This labor
> of dogmatization must not destroy the core of faith . . .
> Here the internal rationalization of the transmitted
> doctrines (*Lehre*) serves the need to justify a religion to
> itself and to the world. Something completely different is
> meant when secular reason tries to use the means of
> postmetaphysical thinking to assimilate contents from the
> Christian tradition in accordance with its own standards . . .
> Philosophical concepts such as those of the person,
> freedom, and individuation, history and emancipation,
> community and solidarity, are infused with experiences and
> connotations which stem from the biblical teaching and its
> tradition . . . What counts on the philosophical side is the
> persuasiveness which philosophical translations acquire for
> the secular environment.[65]

The goal of making unspent religious potential available to secular society is not problematic in itself for theology; the only reservation concerns the unforeseeable dynamics of such social and political fruitfulness. Habermas is aware of this double face: 'Who, apart from the churches and religious communities can set free (*freisetzen*) motives out of which people can act in solidarity? And as we know, when religious motives become effective politically, it is often a dubious blessing'.[66] The problem arising for religion is the discrepancy between the task and the properties assigned to it. Thomas Schmidt agrees that there is a 'conceptual tension':

> How can a philosophy that remains 'agnostic' in view of the
> principally hidden core of religious experience make its
> semantic contents generally accessible in the course of a
> salvaging translation? The idea of an 'opaque core of
> religious experience' overemphasizes the difference between

religious faith and rational knowledge and separates the area
of the religious artificially from the continuum and
the plurality of forms of human experience and their
conceptual interpretations . . . In addition, it appears as a
one-sided radicalization of such a postmetaphysical understanding to see authentic faithful existence precisely in the
independence from general grounds of reason.[67]

The more the 'cognitively unacceptable imposition' of the source
of revelation[68] is stressed, the less likely the chance of reconstructing
the shared genealogical origin. The stark contrast between faith
and reason is reinforced when Kierkegaard is preferred to
Schleiermacher.[69] While Habermas notes Kierkegaard's downgrading of tradition over against the contemporaneity of each
individual believer with Christ, he esteems him for being a religious thinker who is nonetheless postmetaphysical.[70] Over against
Kierkegaard's commitment to explicating the encounter of the
infinite and the finite in terms of a paradox, Schleiermacher's
alternative would have matched Habermas's emphasis on the joint
genealogical origin of reason and religion much better. Yet his
metaphor for the relationship between religion as 'feeling', and
'reason', expressed in his 1818 letter to F. H. Jacobi, the 'galvanic
column' formed by the one waterstream of a fountain that divides
at its top into two arcs, is not of interest.[71] This insistence on the
otherness of religion to reason makes translation, mediation and
justification impossible tasks. The fruits of monotheism can be
harvested once, but it is doubtful whether the fertility needed for
them to re-grow and help regenerate a culture can be maintained
if religion is seen as cut off from reason.

A more productive and less predictable route could be taken
if the cooperative venture allowed each side to develop their
integrity together with their capability for self-reflection.
The concrete religious self-understandings of believers and communities would not be taken as the ultimate manifestation of
religion but themselves be measured by God's self-revelatory
action who has called them and to whom they are responsible in
freely shaping their lives (2). Since the irrepressible questions
of reason in its general accessibility express the openness of the
human spirit for being fulfilled by the unconditioned, no talk

about God can renounce to reason. Yet it cannot assume the role of a self-sufficient target language into which the foreign language of religion has to be translated (1).

c.1. Reason in the Mode of Receptivity

By relating the integrity of a religious existence to the *fides qua*,[72] Habermas has already gone beyond an instruction theoretical understanding of revelation and should have left behind the reification of dogmatic propositions into unquestionable statements of authority. The decisive difference to autonomous reason then does not have to be sought in various 'infallible truths of revelation' but in the singular truth of one constitutive revelation. Foundational is the given character of the truth of God's self-communication which cannot be transformed into reason, yet can be interpreted by it. What can be expected from reason is the readiness to understand itself also as receptive. While philosophy should be able to agree to this point, it may disagree with theology on whether the universal faculty of human reason is still reason when it is open to the claim of a faith tradition and accepts that it responds to a prior offer which to initiate was not in its power. Theology will insist that reason, if is not encapsulated in itself, has to keep open the possibility of being addressed from beyond its own sovereignty. As a spirit aware of its limits it can discover through God's initiative its receptiveness as a capability. The event of God's self-communication to which Christianity testifies is a gift which reason can explicate in its logic and reconstruct *post festum*, but cannot originally produce. The insight of reason into its own need for the fulfillment of its hope for meaning does not take away from its authority.

How the human hope for meaning, the content of revelation as God's love, and God's respect for human freedom interrelate, can be shown by reflecting on the correspondence of form and content of God's self-revelation. Here, its origin in God, which cannot be appropriated by reason, and its ability to be mediated come together. If the content of revelation is God's love, rather than divine propositions, then this can only be revealed in concrete human experience through the encounter with a fellow-human, in the person and history of Jesus Christ.[73] The content of love can, as Habermas has succeeded in showing with regard to being created as *imago Dei*, only be expressed in categories of freedom in which the capability to freely respond is recognized. The vulnerable form God's self-manifestation chose in its exposal to human freedom requests subsequent mediations to continue to respect its free responsiveness. This includes the legitimate reception of the cultural idiom and thought forms in which the self-understanding and longings of an era are expressed, and in which the message of salvation is determined anew.

c.2. Given Nature and Inculturation of the Truth of Faith

If translations are not something alien but even requested as new interpretations faithful to the spirit of Jesus Christ (Jn 14.26), and if according to Schleiermacher, the faith tradition of Christianity has been marked by a 'capability to create language' (*sprachbildende Kraft*), then the crucial problem cannot be that the state forces believers to undertake an 'artificial division'[74] between their religious and civil existences. The task is then to judge which of the unavoidable and necessary syntheses express the core of the message of salvation in the contemporary cultural situation most adequately. It is a work of hermeneutics which goes beyond comparing individual terms (for example, the different concepts of God, or of justice, in Greek philosophy with those of biblical thinking); it implies the reconstruction 'of the whole situation in which the question of salvation arises'.[75] The categories of freedom which were anticipated by Duns Scotus but have come into their own in modernity, offer a paradigm which has been able to overcome previous theological stalemates, for example, between divinity and humanity in Christ, and between 'nature' and 'grace' in theological anthropology, where substance onto-logical thinking had reached a dead end. It is this shared ground which makes the mediation between reason and faith possible without sacrificing the 'provocativeness'[76] of what remains God's invitation. This type of translation keeps the inviting character alive which gets lost in the language of paradox. Unlike the secular appropriations of solidarity Habermas argues for, these contents cannot be had without their foundation in the prevenient love of God. This is where speaking of religious 'heterogeneity'[77] and of an unexhausted cognitive content makes sense.

The course of the enquiry began with the theological reception of a philosophical enterprise which was at first still wedded to a linear conception of the loss of significance of religion as the result of modern rationalization (Part 1). It went on to examine the major Continental philosophical critiques which have retained their importance throughout Habermas's work (Part 2). Its final part has debated his recent estimation of religion as a factor in keeping the project of modernity on track against structures and justifications which reduce the universal scope of its deontology. Its key term, mutual recognition, is oriented towards a genesis of selves whose authorship over the script of their lives is anticipated in all the stages of asymmetry and advocacy. It thus continues to re-enact the model of God's anticipation of the free response of humans created to become '*alios condiligentes*'[78]: a pre-modern designation well able to inspire modernity's cultural renewal.

Conclusion

Christian theology and ethics owe more to Habermas's project than the critical discussions of his theory decisions indicate. Not only has he responded to these questions, often in an exasperatingly restrictive way, he has given reasons for his reticence in his understanding of what the postmetaphysical stage of philosophy entails. He has also changed his mind on specific concerns, such as the contribution of religion not only to the legitimation, but also to the critique of power structures, and most significantly so on the role of religion in contemporary 'postsecular' European, and possibly global, societies. In the last five decades, by elaborating the capacity of reason against different counterproposals, and by connecting it critically with the work of the sciences, he has created a space shared by those philosophies and theologies which continue to see their theory efforts as relating to the hopes of humanity for universal reason to become practical in the recognition of all of its members both as equal and diverse.

His own work and the network of theories it has inspired and accompanied have put into action the decision to opt for the human capacity to cooperate. While his action theory needs to be complemented by a more encompassing and structured approach that relates the different levels of ethics to each other and understands agency from the aspirations of the self, such as Paul Ricoeur's, he has unfolded his core concerns, including his defence of singularity, in an interdisciplinary body of work. It has anchored the 'presuppositions of argumentation', increasingly undermined by a market-led rationality, in the public sphere where new social movements, among them those inspired by religion, work out core commitments of monotheism and modernity.

It is an approach he has had to spell out against the unexpected renaissance of Nietzsche in the 1980s and the unbroken tendency to explain human action together with natural processes solely in terms of power. Christian theology and ethics owe to his indefatigable struggle their chance to appeal to a paradigm of recognition to mediate their message of redemption, rather than a vitalist paradigm of survival against the violent assault of the neighbour. In the alternative between basing one's theory either on the power analyses of Machiavelli, Hobbes, and Nietzsche, or on those of philosophies of recognition, he has made the case for reason in its communicative, identity-building capacities.

After several decades of theological engagement which met with his own interest in the roots of critical theory not only in Marx but also in intuitions from Jewish monotheism, a stage has been reached in which the attention is being requited. Religion, with its obstinate 'encapsulation' of contents closed to reason, now appears to have resources at hand which reason, depleted by pathologies, lacks. I have based my enquiry on a different understanding of the heterogeneity of the Christian message. Not opaque, but given as a truth that can be reconstructed, yet not created by reason, through its origin in God's self-revelation it remains a counterpart with which reason continues to wrestle. Rather than emphasize how 'awkward' (*sperrig*) this heritage is for contemporary thinking, and against new attempts of Christian integralism to denounce the critical light of human reason, Christian theology will expose the inviting character of its message of salvation in which autonomy is presupposed and respected.

Notes

Introduction

1 Habermas, 'Mit Heidegger gegen Heidegger denken. Zur Veröffentlichung von Vorlesungen aus dem Jahr aus 1935', in *Politisch-philosophische Profile* (Frankfurt: Suhrkamp, 1987), 65–71. It is not part of the ET, *Political-philosophical Profiles*, trans. F. Lawrence (Cambridge/Mass.: MIT Press, 1983). Cf. Brunkhorst, H./Müller-Doohm, S., 'Intellektuelle Biographie', in H. Brunkhorst/R. Kreide/C. Lafont (eds), *Habermas-Handbuch. Leben – Werk – Wirkung* (Stuttgart: J.B. Metzler'sche Verlagsbuchhandlung/ C.E. Poeschel Verlag und Darmstadt: Wissenschaftliche Buchgesellschaft, 2009), 1–14, 3.

2 Horkheimer, M./Adorno, Th. W., *Dialectics of Enlightenment*, trans. J. Cumming (New York: Seabury Press, 1975), xi.

3 Graumann, S., 'Experts on Philosophical Reflection in Public Discourse – the German Sloterdijk Debate', in *Biomedical Ethics* 5 (2000) 27–33.

4 Outhwaite, W., *Habermas. A Critical Introduction*, 2nd ed. (Series: Key Contemporary Thinkers) (Cambridge: Polity Press, 2009), and Thomassen, L., *Habermas. A Guide for the Perplexed* (London/New York: Continuum, 2010), are two recent assessments of his philosophy in English. The studies by D. Ingram, *Habermas: Introduction and Analysis* (Ithaca, N.Y.: Cornell University Press, 2010) and by J. G. Finlayson, *Habermas: A Very Short Introduction* (Oxford: OUP, 2010) appeared when the manuscript had already been completed.

Chapter 1

1 The designation of theology as *scientia practica* goes back to Duns Scotus. Cf. the comment on his *Lectura, Prologus* §164, in A. Vos et al. (ed.), *Duns Scotus on Divine Love* (Aldershot: Ashgate, 2003), 24–27, and Mette, N., *Theorie der Praxis. Wissenschaftsgeschichtliche und methodologische Untersuchungen zur Theorie-Praxis-Problematik innerhalb der praktischen Theologie* (Düsseldorf: Patmos, 1978), 257–259.

2 Forms of worship in the public sphere were created, such as a 'Political Night Prayer' in which Dorothee Sölle, Fulbert Steffensky and Jürgen Moltmann protested against the Vietnam War, the nuclear arms race and apartheid at

Notes

a time when new forms of political organization emerged, some of them inspired by religion: Sölle, D./Steffensky, F. (ed.), *Politisches Nachtgebet* (Mainz: Grünewald/Stuttgart/Berlin: Kreuz, 1969).

3 Cf. Moltmann, J., 'A living theology', in D. C. Marks (ed.), *Shaping a Theological Mind* (Aldershot: Ashgate, 2002), 87–96. Ashley, J. M., 'Johann Baptist Metz', in P. Scott/W.T. Cavanaugh (ed.), *The Blackwell Companion to Political Theology* (Oxford: Blackwell, 2004), 241–255. Peukert, H., 'Nachwort zur 3. Auflage 2009', in *Wissenschaftstheorie – Handlungstheorie – Fundamentale Theologie. Analysen zu Ansatz und Status theologischer Theoriebildung* (Frankfurt: Suhrkamp, 3rd ed. 2009), 357–394, 359–361.

4 Cf. Peukert's summary of Horkheimer's 1937 essay in the context of the 'positivism dispute' first between Adorno and Karl Popper, then between Habermas and Hans Albert, in *Science, Action, and Fundamental Theology: Toward a Theology of Communicative Action*, trans. J. Bohman (Cambridge/Mass.: MIT Press, 1984), 117–18 (ET of German original 1976 (see previous fn.).

5 Peukert, 'Enlightenment and theology as unfinished projects', trans. E. Crump/ P. Kenny, in D.S. Browing/F. Schüssler Fiorenza (ed.), *Habermas, Modernity, and Public Theology* (New York: Crossroad, 1992), 43–65, 48. The quote is from Adorno's *Negative Dialectics*, trans. E. B. Ashton (New York: Seabury Press, 1973), 320.

6 Regarding theoretical reason, Habermas has since developed a different understanding: 'Rightness versus truth: On the sense of normative validity in moral judgments and norms' (1999), in *Truth and Justification* (Cambridge: Polity Press, 2003), 237–275.

7 Moltmann, *The Crucified God. The Cross of Christ as the Foundation and Criticism of Christian Theology*, trans. R. A. Wilson/J. Bowden (London: SCM Press, 1974); *Theology of Hope* (London: SCM Press, 1967).

8 Sölle, D., *Die Hinreise* (Stuttgart: KreuzVerlag, 1975). ET: *The Inward Road and the Way Back* (Eugene/Or.: Wipf & Stock, 2003).

9 Metz, 'Redemption and Emancipation' (1972), in *Faith in History and Society*, trans. David Smith (NewYork: Crossroad, 1980), 119–135, 119–122.

10 The main texts in Metz, *Faith in History and Society*, are the following: Ch. 6, 'The future in the memory of suffering' (100–118), Ch. 11, 'Memory' (184–199), and 'Dogma as a dangerous memory' (200–204). 'Memory' is the adapted version of his article, 'Erinnerung', in H. Krings/H. M. Baumgartner/ C. Wild (ed.), *Handbuch philosophischer Grundbegriffe*, Vol. 2 (München: Kösel, 1973), 386–396. For a recent account, see his contribution, 'In memory of the other's suffering. Theological reflections on the future of faith and culture', in A. Pierce/G. Smyth OP (ed.), *The Critical Spirit. Theology at the Crossroads of Faith and Culture. Essays in Honour of Gabriel Daly OSA* (Dublin: Columba Press, 2003), 179–188. Recent overviews of his approach are given by J. M. Ashley (see fn. 3), and by E. Regan, *Theology and the Boundary Discourse of Human Rights* (Washington, DC: Georgetown University Press, 2010), 114–142.

Notes

11 Metz, 'Art. Erinnerung', in *Handbuch philosophischer Grundbegriffe*, Vol. II, 386–396, 392. Any translations from titles in German are my own.

12 Quoted from Habermas, *Erkenntnis und Interesse* (Frankfurt: Suhrkamp, 1968), 31, in *Faith in History and Society*, 194.

13 Metz, *Faith in History and Society*, 194.

14 Metz, *Faith in History and Society*, 195.

15 Metz, 'Art. Erinnerung', in *Handbuch philosophischer Grundbegriffe*, Vol. II, 393.

16 Metz, 'Art. Erinnerung', in *Handbuch philosophischer Grundbegriffe*, Vol. II, 393.

17 Metz, 'In memory of the other's suffering', 179–80. As Matthew Ashley points out, this hope presupposes not a triumphant ecclesiology but a God for whom 'not even the past is concluded'. Ashley, J.M., 'Johann Baptist Metz', in *Blackwell Companion to Political Theology*, 241–255, 252.

18 Metz, 'Anamnestic reason', in A. Honneth et al. (ed.), *Cultural-Political Interventions in the Unfinished Project of Enlightenment* (Cambridge/Mass. and London: MIT Press, 1992), 189–194.

19 Habermas, 'Israel or Athens: Where does anamnestic reason belong?' Trans. P. Dews, republ. in *Religion and Rationality. Essays on Reason, God, and Modernity*, ed. and introduced E. Mendieta (Cambridge: Polity Press, 2002), 129–138, 130.

20 Habermas, 'Israel or Athens', in *Religion and Rationality*, 131.

21 Habermas, 'Israel or Athens', in *Religion and Rationality*, 131.

22 Habermas, 'Israel or Athens', in *Religion and Rationality*, 131.

23 The ninth of Walter Benjamin's 'Theses on the philosophy of history' (*Illuminations*, 257–8) interprets a drawing of a figure with frightened eyes and upstretched wings by Paul Klee as follows:

> A Klee painting names 'Angelus Novus' shows an angel looking
> as though he is about to move away from something he is fixedly
> contemplating. His eyes are staring, his mouth is open, his wings are
> spread. This is how one pictures the angel of history. His face is turned
> toward the past. Where we perceive a chain of events, he sees one single
> catastrophe which keeps piling wreckage upon wreckage and hurls it in
> front of his feet. The angel would like to stay, awaken the dead and make
> whole what has been smashed. But a storm is blowing from paradise; it
> has got caught in his wings with such violence that the angel can no
> longer close them. This storm irresistibly propels him into the future to
> which his back is turned, while the pile of debris before him grows
> skyward. This storm is what we call progress.

24 Peukert, *Science, Action, and Fundamental Theology*, 201–210. The term 'anamnestic solidarity' is owed to an article by the Habermas translator Christian Lenhardt on the Frankfurt School entitled, 'Anamnestic solidarity: The proletariat and its *manes*', *Telos* 25 (1975) 133–55.

25 Peukert, 'Nachwort', in *Wissenschaftstheorie*, 3rd ed., 386.

26 '(H)umanity as a whole has become the *object* of our political decisions and of our economic activity, yet . . . it is not yet the *subject* of its activity'.

Peukert, 'Enlightenment and theology', in Browing/Schüssler Fiorenza (eds), *Habermas, Modernity, and Public Theology*, 43.

27 Peukert, 'Nachwort', in *Wissenschaftstheorie*, 3rd ed., 392–93.

28 Peukert, 'Enlightenment and theology', in Browing/Schüssler Fiorenza (eds), *Habermas, Modernity, and Public Theology*, 57.

29 Peukert, 'Enlightenment and theology', in Browing/Schüssler Fiorenza (eds), *Habermas, Modernity, and Public Theology*, 58.

30 Peukert, 'Enlightenment and theology', in Browing/Schüssler Fiorenza (eds), *Habermas, Modernity, and Public Theology*, 60.

31 Kant distinguishes two components in the 'highest good' that action can aspire to: the 'virtue' of having followed the Categorical Imperative of treating every human being as an end in themselves, and 'happiness'. The only perspective of reconciling the two in the face of frequent failures of our best intentions is the hope in a God who has created a world which is not closed to our moral endeavours. Otherwise, the moral principle of unconditional respect turns into the despair of practical reason: 'If . . . the highest good is impossible according to practical rules, then the moral law which commands that it must be furthered must be fantastic, directed to empty imaginary ends and consequently inherently false.' Kant, I., *Critique of Practical Reason*, trans. L. W. Beck (Indianapolis: Bobbs Merrill, 1956), 118.

32 Peukert, 'Enlightenment and theology', in Browing/Schüssler Fiorenza (eds), *Habermas, Modernity, and Public Theology*, 60.

33 Peukert, 'Enlightenment and theology', in Browing/Schüssler Fiorenza (eds), *Habermas, Modernity, and Public Theology*, 60.

34 Peukert, 'Enlightenment and theology', in Browing/Schüssler Fiorenza (eds), *Habermas, Modernity, and Public Theology*, 61.

35 Henke, T., *Seelsorge und Lebenswelt. Auf dem Weg zu einer Seelsorgetheorie in Auseinandersetzung mit soziologischen und sozialphilosophischen Lebensweltkonzeptionen* (Würzburg: Echter, 1994), 299.

36 Striet, M., 'Wissenschaftstheorie – Handlungstheorie – Fundamentale Theologie. Analysen zu Ansatz und Status theologischer Theoriebildung, Helmut Peukert (Düsseldorf: Patmos, 1976)', in M. Eckert et al. (eds), *Lexikon der theologischen Werke* (Stuttgart: Kröner, 2003), 812–813, 813.

37 Part of the problem is that it is not clear what is to be superseded. For the Protestant theologian Joachim von Soosten one major deficit is the lack of a consistent concept of religion: 'It operates with the most diverse partial functions without coming to a systematically clarified picture: dealing with the extra-ordinary (*Ausseralltägliches*); social integration, symbolization of experiences of community, possibility of solidarity; rationalization of morality and law; coping with suffering, guilt and death; cosmification of the world'. Von Soosten, J., 'Zur theologischen Rezeption von Jürgen Habermas' Theorie des kommunikativen Handelns', *Zeitschrift für Evangelische Ethik* 34 (1990) 129–143, 131.

38 Cf. Habermas, 'The German Idealism of the Jewish philosophers' (1961), and his portraits, e.g., of E. Bloch, Th. W. Adorno, W. Benjamin, H. Marcuse, and G. Sholem, in *Philosophical-Political Profiles*, 21–43.

Notes

39 Forrester, D., *Christian Justice and Public Policy* (Cambridge: CUP, 1997), 188–192,190. He ends his treatment of Habermas by summarizing Peukert's position through the following questions (192):

> This principled universal solidarity . . . raises four questions for which theology offers distinctive resources. What of the dead, of the victims of injustice and oppression, of those who in the past have been excluded and forgotten and on whose past suffering our present flourishing depends? Is there a hope for future generations and for the victims of today who will die without having done more than greet justice and community from afar? Can a hope for justice be sustained when it appears to be denied by experience and empirical evidence at every turn, unless it is based upon a faith which is embodied in an actual community which encompasses past and future generations as well as people of today? . . . the theologians who are attracted to his (cf. Habermas's) position believe that it is not fully coherent unless it is placed within a theological horizon.

40 An overview of the theory debates and a helpful analysis of the different approaches can be found in F. Schweitzer/J. Van der Ven (eds), *Practical Theology – International Perspectives* (Frankfurt: P. Lang, 1999) (repr. of 1993).

41 Henke, *Seelsorge und Lebenswelt*, 320.

42 Henke, *Seelsorge und Lebenswelt*, 21, Fn. 22.

43 Henke, *Seelsorge und Lebenswelt*, 319–20.

44 Henke, *Seelsorge und Lebenswelt*, 320.

45 In Roman Catholicism, the theological rediscovery of the parish had been prepared by Karl Rahner's reappraisal in 1956 of the local church as the unique and irreplaceable site where the 'event' of the Eucharist is celebrated which is foundational for the whole church. Rahner, K., 'Zur Theologie der Pfarre', in H. Rahner (ed.), *Die Pfarre. Von der Theologie zur Praxis* (Freiburg: Herder, 1956), 27–39. His position that the 'particular church' is more than just an 'agency' of the world church was confirmed in *Lumen gentium*, nn. 26, 27 and 37, which restate the constitutive role of the particular churches. Cf. Dogmatic Constitution on the Church, *Lumen gentium*, in *Vatican Council II. The Conciliar and Post Conciliar Documents*, ed. A.Flannery O.P. (Dublin: Dominican Publ./Talbot Press, 1975), 350–432.

46 Kuhnke, U., *Koinonia. Zur theologischen Rekonstruktion der Identität christlicher Gemeinde* (Düsseldorf: Patmos, 1992), 95–96.

47 Kuhnke summarizes Peukert's critique as follows: 'With this elementary situation as pointed to by H. Peukert in which the reality of God . . . becomes identifiable, a radically different talk of God is introduced than what J. Habermas is ready to concede to theology. For Habermas, at the end of social evolution God signifies "hardly more than a structure of communication which obliges the participants to elevate themselves on the basis of mutual recognition of their identities beyond the contingency of a merely external existence". Viewed from the history of humanity, religion appears as superseded; nothing remains of it apart from the "core substance of

Notes

a universalistic morality". However, exactly the normative core of communicative action has uncovered an experience which seems to dissolve communicative praxis into self-contradiction and absurdity if it is not possible to indicate a reality which can only be named, or better, "invoked", in the context of religion'. Kuhnke, *Koinonia*, 94–95.

48 Joas, H. (ed.), *Was sind religiöse Überzeugungen?* (Göttingen: Wallstein Verlag, 2003). Arens, E., *Bezeugen und Bekennen. Elementare Handlungen des Glaubens* (Düsseldorf: Patmos, 1989). A philosophical framework in which the categories 'conviction', 'attestation' and 'testimony' are related to a differentiated concept of self, has been developed by Paul Ricoeur.

49 Schüssler Fiorenza, F., 'Introduction: A critical reception for a practical public theology', in Browning/Schüssler Fiorenza (eds), *Habermas, Modernity, and Public Theology*, 3.

50 Mette, *Theorie der Praxis*, 345. For a recent account with references to subsequent receptions in practical theology, see his 'Kommunikation des Evangeliums – zur handlungstheoretischen Grundlegung der Praktischen Theologie', in *International Journal of Practical Theology* 13 (2009) 183–198.

51 Mette, 'Identität ohne Religion? Eine religionspädagogische Herausforderung', in E. Arens (ed.), *Habermas und die Theologie. Beiträge zur theologischen Rezeption, Diskussion und Kritik der Theorie kommunikativen Handelns* (Düsseldorf: Patmos, 1989, 2nd ed.), 160–178, 163–64.

52 Kierkegaard, S., *The Sickness unto Death*, trans. A. Hannay (Harmondsworth: Penguin, 1989)

53 Mette, 'Identität', in Arens (ed.), *Habermas und die Theologie*, 165.

54 Peukert, H., 'Kontingenzerfahrung und Identitätsbildung', in J. Blank/ G. Hasenhüttl (eds), *Erfahrung, Glaube und Moral* (Düsseldorf: Patmos, 1982), 76–102, 99, quoted by Mette, 'Identität', in Arens (ed.), *Habermas und die Theologie*, 163–64.

55 Mette, *Theorie der Praxis*, 355.

56 This is a concern that also affects theological ethics. Cf. Haker, H., *Moralische Identität* (Tübingen: Francke, 1999), 67.

57 Habermas, *Theory of Communicative Action*, Vol. II, trans. T. McCarthy (Boston: Beacon Press, 1987), 77–111.

58 Tomberg, M., *Religionsunterricht als Praxis der Freiheit. Überlegungen zu einer religionsdidaktisch orientierten Theorie gläubigen Handelns* (Berlin/New York: De Gruyter, 2010), 40.

59 Tomberg, M., *Religionsunterricht*, 42.

60 Tomberg, M., *Religionsunterricht*, 162, Fn. 121.

61 Tomberg, M., *Religionsunterricht*, 268.

62 In this recent article, Norbert Mette discusses two different approaches to moral and to religious development, one from theory of interaction (L. Krappmann), the other structural genetic (F. Oser/P. Gmünder), and argues that the religious contents are reconstructed newly at each reflective stage: 'Identität aus Gratuität. Freiheit als Prinzip von religiöser Erziehung

Notes

und Bildung', in M. Böhnke et al. (eds), *Freiheit Gottes und der Menschen* (*Festschrift* T. Pröpper) (Regensburg: Pustet, 2006), 433–451, 448.

63 Cf. the systematic theologian Georg Essen on this argument on which the move of the Second Vatican Council to recognize the neutrality of the state as the reverse side of the freedom of religion is based: *Sinnstiftende Unruhe im System des Rechts* (Götttingen: Wallstein Verlag, 2004), 21.

64 Habermas, 'Equal treatment of cultures and the limits of postmodern liberalism', in *Between Naturalism and Religion*, trans. C. Cronin (Cambridge: Polity, 2008), 271–311, 302–03, quoted in Mette, N., 'Identität aus Gratuität', in M. Böhnke et al. (eds), *Freiheit Gottes*, 451.

65 Siller, H. P., 'Art. Autonomie III. Religionspädagogisch', in *Lexikon für Theologie und Kirche* I (1993, 3rd ed.), 1297, quoted in Mette, N., 'Identität aus Gratuität', in M. Böhnke et al. (eds), *Freiheit Gottes*, 451.

66 Lob-Hüdepohl, A., *Kommunikative Vernunft und theologische Ethik* (Studien zur theologischen Ethik 47) (Freiburg i. Ue./Freiburg i. Br.: Universitätsverlag, 1993), 264.

67 Lob-Hüdepohl, *Kommunikative Vernunft* , 265–66.

68 Lob-Hüdepohl, *Kommunikative Vernunft*, 266, with reference to Peukert's analyses.

69 Habermas, 'Transcendence from within, transcendence in this world', in Browning/Schüssler Fiorenza (eds), *Habermas, Modernity and Public Theology*, 226–248, 239.

70 Haker, *Moralische Identität*, 28, and 28, Fn. 47.

71 Haker, *Moralische Identität*, 28.

72 Cf. Haker, *Moralische Identität*, 15.

73 Haker, *Moralische Identität*, 26.

74 Haker, *Moralische Identität*, 27.

75 Haker, 'Kommunitaristische Kritik an der Diskursethik', in *Ethik und Unterricht* 5 (1994) 12–18, 18. The Aristotelian question of the good life was put back on the agenda earlier in English-speaking philosophical ethics. Haker points out that its reception via translation and discussion happened through ethicists connected with the Frankfurt School, such as Axel Honneth, Micha Brumlik, Hauke Brunkhorst and Wolfgang Kuhlmann. The only communitarian author to have engaged at this stage with Habermas is Charles Taylor (12).

76 Haker, 'Kommunitaristische Kritik', in *Ethik und Unterricht* 5 (1994) 18.

77 Habermas, 'On the pragmatic, the ethical and the moral employments of practical reason', in *Justification and Application. Remarks on Discourse Ethics*, trans. C. Cronin (Cambridge/Mass.: MIT Press, 1993), 1–18, 12.

78 Haker, *Moralische Identität*, 67.

79 Metz, J.B., 'Monotheismus und Demokratie. Über Religion und Politik auf dem Boden der Moderne', in J. Manemann (ed.), *Demokratiefähigkeit (Jahrbuch Politische Theologie I)* (Münster: LIT Verlag, 1996), 39–52, 50–52.

80 Ricoeur, P., *Hermeneutics and the Human Sciences. Essays on Language, Action, and Interpretation*, ed. and trans. J. B. Thompson (Cambridge/Mass:

Notes

MIT Press, 1981), 99–100. See also *Oneself as Another*, trans. K. Blamey (Chicago: University of Chicago Press, 1992), 286 and 287, Fn. 79.

81 'Our Western self-understanding of modernity has arisen from engaging with its own traditions. The same dialectic between modernity and tradition is repeated today in other parts of the world'. Habermas/Mendieta, E., 'Ein neues Interesse der Philosophie an der Religion?' in *Deutsche Zeitschrift für Philosophie* 58 (2010) 3–16, 4.

82 Schüssler Fiorenza, F., 'The church as a community of interpretation: Political theology between discourse ethics and hermeneutical reconstruction', in Browing/Schüssler Fiorenza (eds), *Habermas, Modernity, and Public Theology*, 66–91. In his contribution to the same conference, David Tracy has pointed out that in Habermas's references to utopian thinking the horizon is extended to the realm of the 'good': 'As Habermas's own formal account of morality itself shows, there is great room for further contextual arguments about different substantive proposals for the "good life" and "happiness". In his recent work, moreover, he makes more substantive use of utopian theory for further rational suggestions for the "good" society'. Tracy, D., 'Theology, critical social theory, and the public realm', in Browning/ Schüssler Fiorenza (eds), *Habermas, Modernity and Public Theology*, 19–42, 33.

83 Habermas, 'Revitalisierung der Weltreligionen', in *Studienausgabe* Vol. 5, *Kritik der Vernunft* (Frankfurt: Suhrkamp, 2009), 392–93.

84 A theological assessment that comes to opposite conclusions is offered by Nicholas Adams in *Habermas and Theology* (Cambridge: CUP, 2006), 199: 'To the extent that theologians are willing to adopt and rely on a theory of communicative action, they abandon their own Christian tradition. Habermas makes this claim, and I think that it is persuasive'. The perspective from which he develops his critique of Habermas's work is expressed in the judgement that Habermas 'wastes valuable energy searching for universal rules' (21).

Chapter 2

1 For an analysis of formative philosophical approaches, their combination and transformation, see Honneth, A., 'Geschichtsphilosophie, Anthropologie und Marxismus', and 'Frankfurter Schule', in Brunkhorst et al. (eds), *Habermas-Handbuch,* 15–17. 17–20.

2 Cf. Lafont, C., 'Hermeneutik und *linguistic turn*', in Brunkhorst et al. (eds), *Habermas-Handbuch*, 29–34.

3 Habermas, 'The entwinement of myth and enlightenment: Max Horkheimer and Theodor Adorno', in *The Philosophical Discourse of Modernity. Twelve Lectures*, trans. F. Lawrence (Cambridge/Mass.: MIT Press, 1987), 106–130, 106.

4 Habermas, 'Appendix. Knowledge and human interests: A general perspective', in *Knowledge and Human Interests*, trans. J. J. Shapiro (Boston: Beacon Press, 1971), 301–317, 314.

5 Habermas summarizes the original insight of Fichte which Henrich had treated in his 1967 book, *Fichtes ursprüngliche Einsicht*, as a reason to leave the philosophy of consciousness behind: 'The subject that relates itself to itself *cognitively* comes across the self, which it grasps as an object, under this category as something derived, and not as it-itself in its originality, as the author of spontaneous self-relation'. 'Metaphysics after Kant', in *Postmetaphysical Thinking. Philosophical Essays*, trans W.M. Hohengarten (Cambridge/Mass.: MIT Press, 1992), 10–27, 24. This article is his contribution to the 1987 *Festschrift* for Dieter Henrich and responds to his critique of Habermas's approach.

6 Henrich, D., 'What is metaphysics – what modernity?', in P. Dews (ed.), *Habermas: A Critical Reader*, (Oxford: Blackwell, 1999), 291–319, 307.

7 Henrich points out that since Habermas agrees that the paradigm of language was 'already available' in early classic modernity, he should explain why these authors who 'were concerned to illuminate the fundamental tendencies of the life of rational beings' (307) did not use it.

8 Habermas, 'Metaphysics after Kant', in *Postmetaphysical Thinking*, 23.

9 In his introduction to Dieter Henrich's defense of metaphysics within modern thinking, Peter Dews summarizes the doubts about the ability of the two approaches to be combined as follows: Habermas's 'readiness to draw on both the resources of the phenomenological tradition – for example, in making crucial use of the concept of the "lifeworld" – and the analytical tradition in the philosophy of language reveals this. For it suggests that Habermas would like the ideological benefits of naturalism, without paying the philosophical price which analytical thinkers are in many cases more than willing to pay'. Dews (ed.), *Habermas – A Critical Reader*, 291–92.

10 Habermas, 'Themes', in *Postmetaphysical Thinking*, 28–53, 43.

11 Cf. the analysis of the late Tübingen philosopher Walter Schulz on how these two opposite approaches are combined, in *Grundprobleme der Ethik* (Pfullingen: Neske, 1989), 239–40.

12 Habermas, *Theory of Communicative Action*, trans. T. McCarthy (Boston: Beacon Press, 1987), Vol. II, 145.

13 Wimmer, R., *Universalisierung in der Ethik. Analyse, Kritik und Rekonstruktion ethischer Rationalitätsansprüche* (Frankfurt: Suhrkamp, 1980), 196–97.

14 Ricoeur, P., *The Just*, trans. D. Pellauer (Chicago: University of Chicago Press, 2000), 118. He sees value in the move to actual discourses, but judges it as being in continuity with Kant's own recognition of plurality: 'Kant had already taken into account the plurality of moral subjects in his second formulation of the categorical imperative, requiring us to treat humanity, in our own person and in that of others, as an end in itself and not simply as a means. But it is in the idea . . . of argumentation, as presented by Habermas, that we can see the dialogical or conversational implications of this second formulation of the categorical imperative fully unfolded in the figure of the mutual respect people must have for one another'. (151)

15 Two systematic theologians draw attention to Fichte's *Grundlagen des Naturrechts* (1796) (Foundations of Natural Law), esp. Chapter 3: 'The human

Notes

being becomes human only among humans', quoted from WW III, 39 by T. Pröpper in *Erlösungsglaube und Freiheitsgeschichte. Eine Skizze zur Soteriologie (München: Kösel*, 3rd ed.1991), 186–87. Hansjürgen Verweyen characterizes Fichte as having been the 'first to show transcendentally the intersubjective constitution of the "I think"'. He summarizes Fichte's Ch. 3 as demonstrating that 'self-consciousness cannot arise without the act of another freedom'. *Gottes letztes Wort, Grundriss der Fundamentaltheologie* (Düsseldorf: Patmos, 1991), 191, Fn. 30. 259–60.

16 Henrich, D., 'What is metaphysics – what modernity?', in Dews (ed.), *Habermas – A Critical Reader*, 310–11.

17 Habermas, 'Individuation through socialization: On George Herbert Mead's theory of subjectivity', in *Postmetaphysical Thinking*, 149–204, 177. The English translation leaves out an elucidating phrase after '*innewohnendes*' (inherent): '*ihm zur Disposition stehendes... Phänomen*'.The complete version is thus, 'not a phenomenon inherent in and at the disposition of the subject'.

18 Henrich, 'What is metaphysics – what modernity?', in Dews (ed.), *Habermas – A Critical Reader*, 311.

19 Cf. Schleiermacher, F., *Hermeneutics and Criticism*, ed. A. Bowie (Cambridge: CUP, 1998), 233–235.

20 The original German text in Henrich, 'Was ist Metaphysik – was Moderne? Zwölf Thesen gegen Jürgen Habermas', in *Konzepte. Essays zur Philosophie in der Zeit*, Frankfurt: Suhrkamp, 1987, 11–43, 35) is: '*Gelernt werden (cf. höhere sprachliche Funktionen) wohl, aber nicht schrittweise, sondern, zwar im Blick auf ein Vorbild, aber aus spontanen Versuchen, in denen sich schließlich auch das Verstehen in einem mit dem Können spontan einstellt*'. Above, I have given my retranslation instead of its version in Dews, *Habermas: A Critical Reader*, 312: 'They (cf. higher linguistic achievements) are indeed learned, not step by step, but through spontaneous strivings, oriented towards an example, which eventually result in the spontaneous and simultaneous emergence of a form of knowledge and a capacity'.

21 Henrich, 'What is metaphysics – what modernity?', 312.

22 Henrich, 'What is metaphysics – what modernity?', 311.

23 Theunissen, M., 'Society and History: a critique of Critical Theory', trans. G. Finlayson/P. Dews, in Dews (ed.), *Habermas: A Critical Reader*, 241–271, 242. 254.

24 Theunissen, 'Society and History', 251.

25 Theunissen, 'Society and History', 252.

26 Theunissen, 'Society and History', 253.The quotes are taken from Habermas, *Technik und Wissenschaft als Ideologie* (=TWI) (Frankfurt: Suhrkamp, 1968), here 161.

27 Theunissen, 'Society and History', 268, Fn. 68, with reference to TWI 160.

28 Theunissen, 'Society and History', 253.

29 Theunissen, 'Society and History', 254:'But mere transcendence is powerless to free human beings from the grasp of nature. The very negativity of the concept, which is supposed to indicate something more than mere nature, testifies to nature as the positive moment beneath it'.

30 Theunissen, 'Society and History', 254.

31 Theunissen, 'Society and History', 254, with reference to TWI, 55ff.

32 Theunissen, 'Society and History', 262.

33 In Dews' summary of Theunissen, 'Habermas's quasi-transcendental grounding strategy results in a "naturalization" and immobilization of structures
which are then mistakenly assumed to be immune to historicity. The result
is a danger of falling prey to ideological illusion, and a limiting of the
possibilities of real historical transformation'. Dews (ed.), *Habermas: A Critical
Reader*, 241.

34 Henrich, 'What is metaphysics – what modernity?', 298–99.

35 Henrich, 'What is metaphysics – what modernity?', 309.

36 Henrich, 'What is metaphysics – what modernity?', 299. The original
sentence is: '*Wer reflektiert, der hat auch verstanden, dass er nicht nur in einer
Welt beheimatet ist und dass er nicht ohne Bruch in sie hineinwachsen kann*'
('Metaphysik', 19).

37 Henrich, 'What is metaphysics – what modernity?', 297–98.

38 Henrich, 'What is metaphysics – what modernity?', 296–97.

39 Theunissen investigates the parallels between the first and the third phase of
critical theory: 'Failing to fulfil its intention, Critical Theory threatens to collapse back into what it originally sought to overcome, into an ontology of
nature which is now indeed unquestionably objectivistic. At the very least, it
threatens to collapse back into a kind of thinking that prioritizes nature over
history, and which inflates the former into an absolute origin. Furthermore,
it is easy to show that this apotheosis of nature lies at the end of an avenue
of thought which begins with a certain overburdening of the empirical
subject – or more precisely, of the human species as the totality of empirical
subjects'. (Theunissen, 'Society and History', 248–49). Habermas contributes
to this through his 'enormous overestimation of the truth value of intersubjectivity . . . The expansion of subjectivity into intersubjectivity . . . is a false
absolute . . . indicated by its catastrophic reversal into the equally false
absolute of nature. The suspicion here is that nature functions as a surrogate
for an historical absolute, whose tasks cannot be carried out by the individuals
who have been mystified into the "overarching subject" of the human
species' (259).

Chapter 3

1 Habermas, 'Themes in postmetaphysical thinking', in *Postmetaphysical
Thinking*, 29–34.

2 Habermas, 'Themes', in *Postmetaphysical Thinking*, 33.

3 Habermas, 'Themes', in *Postmetaphysical Thinking*, 33–34.

4 In 'Rückkehr zur Metaphik? Eine Sammelrezension', repr. in *Nachmetaphysisches Denken*, 267–279, 271, one of the books reviewed critically is by Dieter
Henrich who was Gadamer's assistant and wrote his PhD and his *Habilitation*
theses with him. In his mapping of the contemporary background to the

return of metaphysics, Habermas links it to representatives of the right-Hegelian *Richter School*: 'This type of philosopher does not just want to rely on his arguments, he allows himself to be called into duty by the institutions of the state and the church also as a philosophical expert. He travels around the country as an intellectual guardian of the constitution, delivers his dossiers on the spiritual-moral state of the nation to the state chancellery or assembles a group of crisis counsellors for the Pope. In short, the period of reaction of the last decade has helped the time diagnostic forces of right-wing Hegelianism to enjoy a surprising neo-conservative late bloom. A favourable climate developed from this for expectations which are directed towards a renewal of metaphysical thinking. But a favourable climate does not create a changed situation of argumentation'.

5 Habermas, 'Metaphysics after Kant', in *Postmetaphysical Thinking*, 10–27, 13.
6 Habermas, 'Metaphysics after Kant', in *Postmetaphysical Thinking*, 10–27, 12.
7 Habermas, 'Metaphysics after Kant', in *Postmetaphysical Thinking*, 10–27, 17.
8 Habermas, 'Themes', in *Postmetaphysical Thinking*, 32.
9 Habermas, 'Themes', in *Postmetaphysical Thinking*, 44.
10 Habermas, 'Themes', in *Postmetaphysical Thinking*, 48.
11 Schnädelbach, H., 'Metaphysik und Religion heute', in *Zur Rehabilitierung des animal rationale. Vorträge und Abhandlungen 2* (Frankfurt: Suhrkamp, 1992), 137–157, 137–38.
12 Henrich, 'What is metaphysics – what modernity?', 306
13 Henrich, 'What is metaphysics – what modernity?', 292.
14 Cf. Henrich, 'What is metaphysics – what modernity?', 306.
15 Henrich, 'What is metaphysics – what modernity?', 294.
16 Schnädelbach, 'Metaphysik und Religion heute', in *Zur Rehabilitierung*, 144.
17 Schnädelbach, 'Metaphysik und Religion heute', in *Zur Rehabilitierung*, 140.
18 Schnädelbach, 'Metaphysik und Religion heute', in *Zur Rehabilitierung*, 137.
19 Schnädelbach, 'Metaphysik und Religion heute', in *Zur Rehabilitierung*, 138.
20 Schnädelbach, 'Metaphysik und Religion heute', in *Zur Rehabilitierung*, 138–39.
21 Schnädelbach, 'Metaphysik und Religion heute', in *Zur Rehabilitierung,* 149.
22 In 'Leben wir in einem postmetaphysischen Zeitalter?', in *Stimmen der Zeit* 228 (2010) 241–252, 243, E. Runggaldier, S.J., explains its 'function of integrating different areas of life'. He speaks of 'the need for a reasonable (*vernünftig*) and viable (*tragbar*) unifying view of the different areas of life and knowledge, for example, the personal-subjective and the objective-scientific' which was one of the 'main tasks of traditional metaphysics . . . it was to clarify how subjective forms of access to reality (the first person perspective) relate to objective knowledge; how personal or integrative explanations connect with scientific prognostic ones; whether also life experiences play a role for knowing (*Erkenntnis*), or only repeatable experiences which are typical for experiments. Finally, metaphysics was and is about the unity of reason, that is, the connection between theoretical and practical reason, between the question what is the case, and what is to be done – while avoiding naturalistic fallacies'.

Notes

23 Schnädelbach, 'Metaphysik und Religion heute', in *Zur Rehabilitierung*, 151.

24 Schnädelbach, 'Metaphysik und Religion heute', in *Zur Rehabilitierung*, 149–50.

25 Cf. Schnädelbach's review of the revival of Aristotelianism, 'Was ist Neoaristotelismus?', in the same book, *Zur Rehabilitierung des animal rationale*, 205–230.

26 Habermas, 'Themes', in *Postmetaphysical Thinking*, 38–39.

27 Cf. Lohmann, G., 'Nachmetaphysisches Denken', in *Habermas-Handbuch*, 356–58, 357.

28 Habermas, 'An awareness of what is missing', in Habermas et al., *An Awareness of What is Missing. Faith and Reason in a Postsecular Age*, trans. C. Cronin (Cambridge: Polity Press, 2010), 15–23, 18.

29 Schnädelbach, H., 'Der fromme Atheist', in M. Striet (ed.), *Wiederkehr des Atheismus. Fluch oder Segen für die Theologie?* (Freiburg: Herder, 2008), 11–20.

30 Schnädelbach, 'Was ist Neoaristotelismus?', in *Zur Rehabilitierung*, 157.

31 Schnädelbach, 'Metaphysik und Religion heute', in *Zur Rehabilitierung*, 155.

32 David Tracy identifies the 'fit between Kant and Weber' regarding the three spheres of science, morality and art as the background to this reduction. He agrees that 'these three Weberian sociological autonomous spheres parallel the distinct cognitive interests of Kant's three critiques'. The problem is that in this sociological division, the possibility of posing overarching questions is lost, and with it, the level to which religion responds: 'Indeed, the basic character of religious claims (namely to speak validly of the "whole" of reality) renders them exceptionally difficult to analyse in modern critical terms. Furthermore, the fact that any religion's claim to construe the nature of ultimate reality (and not any one part of it) makes it logically impossible to fit religion as simply another autonomous sphere alongside science, ethics and aesthetics'. Tracy, D., 'Theology, critical social theory, and the public realm', in Browning/Schüssler Fiorenza (eds), *Habermas, Modernity and Public Theology*, 32–33.37.

Chapter 4

1 Brunkhorst, 'Platzhalter und Interpret', in H. Brunkhorst et al. (eds), *Habermas-Handbuch*, 214–220, 215.

2 Cf., from his experience as president of the German research community, *Deutsche Forschungsgemeinschaft*, W. Frühwald, 'Von der Rationalität des Glaubens', in Th. Pröpper (ed.), *Bewusstes Leben in der Wissensgesellschaft. Wolfgang Frühwald und Dieter Henrich Ehrendoktoren der Katholisch-Theologischen Fakultät der Universität Münster* (Altenberge: Oros Verlag, 2000), 79–91, 87.

3 Brunkhorst, H., 'Platzhalter und Interpret', in *Habermas-Handbuch*, 214–15.

4 Habermas, 'Philosophy as stand-in and interpreter', in *Moral Consciousness and Communicative Action*, trans. C. Lenhardt and S. Weber Nicholsen (Cambridge/Mass.: MIT Press, 1990), 1–20, 3.

Notes

5 Habermas, 'Stand-in and interpreter', in *Moral Consciousness,* 2.

6 Habermas, 'Stand-in and interpreter', in *Moral Consciousness,* 4.

7 Habermas, 'Stand-in and interpreter', in *Moral Consciousness,* 15.

8 Habermas, 'Stand-in and interpreter', in *Moral Consciousness,* 16. Here, the English translation adopts an ironic style and inserts a word which is not part of the original sentence, 'venerable': 'Marked down in price, the venerable transcendental and dialectical modes of justification may still come in handy', for 'Dabei können die ermäßigten transzendentalen und dialektischen Begründungsweisen durchaus hilfreich sein' ('Platzhalter und Interpret', in *Moralbewusstsein und kommunikatives Handeln,* 23).

9 Habermas, 'Stand-in and interpreter', in *Moral Consciousness,* 16.

10 Habermas, 'Stand-in and interpreter', in *Moral Consciousness,* 15–16. Here, I have modified the English translation which renders *Rationalität* as an adjective: 'the presumably universal bases of rational experience and judgment, as well as action and linguistic communication'.

11 Habermas, 'Stand-in and interpreter', in *Moral Consciousness,* 16. I have left out the addition of the ET which is not in the original text: 'hoping instead that the success that has for so long eluded it might come . . .'.

12 Habermas, 'Stand-in and interpreter', in *Moral Consciousness,* 9–10.

13 Schulz, *Grundprobleme,* 14.17.

14 Schulz, *Grundprobleme,* 95. 299.

15 Apel, K. -O., 'Normatively grounding "critical theory" by recourse to the lifeworld? A transcendental-pragmatic attempt to think with Habermas against Habermas', in D.M. Rasmussen/J. Swindal (eds), *Jürgen Habermas,* Vols. I–IV (Sage Masters of Modern Thought) (London: Sage, 2002), Vol. III, 344–378, 344.

16 Habermas, 'Stand-in and interpreter', in *Moral Consciousness,* 13–14.

17 Habermas, 'Stand-in and interpreter', in *Moral Consciousness,* 11.

18 Apel, 'Normatively grounding "critical theory"', in Rasmussen/Swindal (eds), *Jürgen Habermas,* Vol. III, 363.

19 Habermas, 'Themes', in *Postmetaphysical Thinking,* 50.

20 Apel, 'Normatively grounding "critical theory"', in Rasmussen/Swindal (eds), *Jürgen Habermas,* Vol. III, 362.

21 Habermas, 'Stand-in and interpreter', in *Moral Consciousness,* 19–20.

22 Apel, 'Normatively grounding "critical theory"', in Rasmussen/Swindal (eds), *Jürgen Habermas,* Vol. III, 361.

23 Apel, 'Normatively grounding "critical theory"', in Rasmussen/Swindal (eds), *Jürgen Habermas,* Vol. III, 362.

24 Apel, 'Normatively grounding "critical theory"', in Rasmussen/Swindal (eds), *Jürgen Habermas,* Vol. III, 362.

25 Habermas, 'Metaphysics after Kant', in *Postmetaphysical Thinking,* 17. 14.

26 Cf. Habermas, 'Stand-in and interpreter', in *Moral Consciousness,* 2. The ET translates '*Herrschaftsfunktionen*' with 'arrogating authority to itself'.

27 Habermas, 'Stand-in and interpreter', in *Moral Consciousness,* 3.2.

28 Habermas, 'Stand-in and interpreter', in *Moral Consciousness,* 2–3.

Notes

29 Habermas, 'Stand-in and interpreter', in *Moral Consciousness*, 19.

30 Habermas, 'Stand-in and interpreter', in *Moral Consciousness*, 16.18.

31 Habermas, 'Metaphysics after Kant', in *Postmetaphysical Thinking*, 21.

32 Habermas, 'Themes', in *Postmetaphysical Thinking*, 28.

33 Habermas, 'Stand-in and interpreter', in *Moral Consciousness*, 18. 'Yesteryear' translates '*in den Gründen und Abgründen der klassischen Vernunftphilosophie*': *Moralbewusstsein und kommunikatives Handeln* (Frankfurt: Suhrkamp, 1983), 26.

34 Habermas, 'Stand-in and interpreter', in *Moral Consciousness*, 18–19.

35 Habermas, 'Themes', in *Postmetaphysical Thinking*, 34.

36 Habermas, 'Themes', in *Postmetaphysical Thinking*, 32.

37 Habermas, 'Themes', in *Postmetaphysical Thinking*, 32.

38 Habermas, 'The unity of reason in the diversity of its voices', in *Postmetaphysical Thinking*, 115–148, 126. Here, he traces the turn from a teleological concept of reason to a capacity of the subject: 'By taking the totality of beings and making it dependent upon the synthetic accomplishments of the subject, Kant downgrades the cosmos into the object domain of the nomological natural sciences. The world of appearances is no longer a "whole organized according to ends"'.(125).

39 Habermas, 'Themes', in *Postmetaphysical Thinking*, 38–39.

40 Habermas, 'Metaphysics after Kant', in *Postmetaphysical Thinking*, 16–17.

41 The ET translates the plural 'Bedingungen' with 'structure' in the singular and thus obscures what Brunkhorst points out, that unconditionality is attributed to something that is 'contingent through and through', namely 'the historical and societal conditions of action oriented toward reaching understanding'. For him, it is integrating Kant and Hegel with Marx, 'preserving the heritage of Kantian universalism for political praxis by turning Kant from the philosophical head onto the historical-societal feet.' Brunkhorst, 'Platzhalter und Interpret', in Brunkhorst et al. (eds), *Habermas-Handbuch*, 220.

42 Apel, 'Normatively grounding "critical theory"', in Rasmussen/Swindal (eds), *Jürgen Habermas*, Vol. III, e.g., 363.

43 Theunissen, 'Society and History', in Dews (ed.), *Habermas: A Critical Reader*, 261.

44 Ricoeur, P., *Hermeneutics and the Human Sciences*, 245.

Chapter 5

1 Ott, K.,'Kommunikative Ethik', in J.-P. Wils/C. Hübenthal (eds)., *Lexikon der Ethik* (Paderborn: Schöningh, 2006), 186–194, 189.

2 Habermas, 'Morality and Ethical Life', in *Moral Consciousness,* 207–8.

3 Cf. the summary of this foundational article by Forst, R., 'Diskursethik der Moral. "Diskursethik – Notizen zu einem Begründungsprogramm" (1983)', in Brunkhorst et al. (eds), *Habermas-Handbuch*, 234–240, 234: Its 'most

important feature is the replacement of the reflexive testing of moral maxims, as in the precedent (*Vorgabe*) of the Categorical Imperative, through an argumentative vindication of the validity claims of moral norms in a practical discourse. Methodically, the transcendental self-reflection of practical reason in Kant's sense becomes a pragmatic reconstruction of the normative implications of communicative rationality'.

4 Habermas, 'Discourse Ethics', in *Moral Consciousness*, 43–115, 58.

5 Habermas, 'What is universal pragmatics'?', in *Communication and the Evolution of Society*, trans. T. McCarthy (Boston: Beacon Press, 1979), 1–68. Cf. the reconstruction of Anzenbacher, A., *Einführung in die Philosophie* (Freiburg: Herder, 2002, 8th ed.), 197–9.

6 Habermas, 'On the pragmatic, the ethical and the moral employments of practical reason', in *Justification and Application. Remarks on Discourse Ethics*, trans. C. Cronin (Cambridge/Mass.: MIT Press, 1993), 1–17, 9: '(W)e are concerned with the justification and application of norms that stipulate reciprocal rights and duties, and the terminus *ad quem* of a corresponding moral-practical discourse is an agreement concerning the just resolution of a conflict in the realm of norm-regulated action'.

7 Habermas, 'Morality and Ethical Life: Does Hegel's critique of Kant apply to discourse ethics'?', in *Moral Consciousness*, 195–215, 210–11. He identifies what he sees in 1986 as the four pressing global problems: 'In view of the four big moral-political liabilities of our time – hunger and poverty in the third world, torture and continuous violation of human dignity in autocratic regimes, increasing unemployment and disparities of social wealth in Western industrial nations, and finally the self-destructive risks of the nuclear arms race – my modest opinion about what philosophy can and cannot accomplish may come as a disappointment'.

8 Habermas, 'Discourse ethics', in *Moral Consciousness*, 94. With '*nicht in eigener Regie*' he is using a similar expression as in his redesign of the role of philosophy, implying that the moral theorist is not the stage director and receives the contents, perhaps also the criteria, from elsewhere. Cf. Habermas, 'Stand-in and interpreter', in *Moral Consciousness*, 16: As interpreter, philosophy 'no longer directs its own pieces' and has to 'operate under conditions of rationality that it has not chosen'.

9 Habermas, 'Vorwort', *Moralbewusstsein und kommunikatives Handeln*, 6–7.

10 Habermas, 'Discourse ethics', in *Moral Consciousness*, 44. 43.

11 Habermas, 'Discourse ethics', in *Moral Consciousness*, 88.

12 Habermas, 'Discourse ethics', in *Moral Consciousness*, 44.

13 Habermas, 'Discourse ethics', in *Moral Consciousness*, 89.

14 Habermas, 'Discourse ethics', in *Moral Consciousness*, 89–90. A further example is, 'Having excluded persons *A, B, C,* . . . from the discussion by silencing them or by foisting our interpretation on them, we were able to convince ourselves that *N* is justified'. (91)

15 Habermas, 'Discourse ethics', in *Moral Consciousness*, 92.

16 Habermas, 'Diskursethik', in *Moralbewusstsein und kommunikatives Handeln* (1st edn), 103.

Notes

17 Habermas, 'Discourse ethics', in *Moral Consciousness*, 92–93. He stresses the inclusion of consequences into the reflection process in 'Morality and Ethical Life', 206:

> 'Discourse ethics has a built-in procedure that ensures awareness of consequences. This comes out clearly in the formulation of the principle of universalization (U), which requires sensitivity to the results and consequences of the general observance of the norm for every individual'.

18 Habermas comments on his move to weaken the prior understanding of norm justification in 'Morality and Ethical Life', in *Moral Consciousness*, 212, n. 7: 'The concept of the justification of norms must not be too strong, otherwise the conclusion that justified norms must have the assent of all affected will already be contained in the premise. I committed such a *petitio principii* in the essay on "Discourse Ethics"'.

19 Forst, 'Diskursethik der Moral', in Brunkhorst et al. (eds), *Habermas-Handbuch*, 239. The quote is from Habermas, *Between Facts and Norms. Contributions to a Discourse Theory of Law and Democracy*, trans. W. Rehg (Cambridge: Polity Press, 1996), 4.

20 Forst, 'Diskursethik der Moral', in *Habermas-Handbuch*, 239.

21 Habermas, *Between Facts and Norms*, 4.

22 Wellmer also questions the linking of rationality and normativity in Apel's approach, although here the problem is not the restriction of recognition to the situation of argumentation, but the dependency of rationality on moral foundations. The three chapters of *Ethik und Dialog* (Frankfurt: Suhrkamp, 1986), without the appendix, have been translated as the fourth and final part of *The Persistence of Modernity*, trans. D. Midgley (Cambridge: Polity Press, 1991), 113–231.

23 Habermas, 'Discourse Ethics', in *Moral Consciousness*, 85–86.

24 Wellmer, *The Persistence of Modernity*, 184–85.

25 Habermas, 'Remarks on discourse ethics', in *Justification and Application*, 33.

26 Between these alternatives, Klaus Günther seems to take a middle position: they 'recognize each other as persons who speak from their own conviction and therefore stand up for their statements. Günther, 'Diskurs', in Brunkhorst et al. (eds), *Habermas-Handbuch*, 303–306, 305.

27 Habermas, 'Remarks on discourse ethics', in *Justification and Application*, 33.

28 Wimmer, *Universalisierung*, 48–49. Apel accuses him of 'reconstructivistic naturalism' resp. of a '*naturalistic* or *substantialistic fallacy*' in 'Normatively grounding critical theory' in Rasmussen/Swindal (eds), *Jürgen Habermas*, Vol. III, 364. 350.

29 A parallel debate is conducted today on the loss of the genuine competence of philosophy when it becomes subordinated to empirical cultural studies. Its genuine task and method of reflecting on the genesis and validity claims of products of the human spirit is levelled down in their comparatistic perspective. See especially Birgit Recki's contributions to the discussion on "Die kulturwissenschaftliche Wende" with Thomas Goeller, Ralf Konersmann and Oswald Schwemmer in *Information Philosophie* 33 (2005) 20–32.

30 Ricoeur, *Oneself as Another*, 286–87, besides other definitions, such as 'ethics of discussion' (283), and 'morality of communication' (281). The same precision can be found in the theological ethicist Arno Anzenbacher's reconstruction of the argumentation of universal pragmatics. In his *Einführung in die Philosophie*, 197–9, he identifies the need over against the strategic attitude to 'presuppose the orientation towards intersubjective recognition of validity claims' (198). This is not the same, but has often been identified with recognition of persons. Also in Rainer Forst's account, the summary of the main feature of discourse ethics, quoted at the beginning, is accurate and can now, after treating the critiques of more demanding Kantians, be read in a new light as pointing to a reduction: Its 'most important feature is the replacement of the reflexive testing of moral maxims, as in the precedent (*Vorgabe*) of the Categorical Imperative, through an argumentative vindication of the validity claims of moral norms in a practical discourse. Methodically, the transcendental self-reflection of practical reason in Kant's sense becomes a pragmatic reconstruction of the normative implications of communicative rationality'. Forst, 'Diskursethik der Moral', in Brunkhorst et al. (eds), *Habermas-Handbuch*, 234.

Chapter 6

1 In his article on 'Diskurs', in Brunkhorst et al. (eds), *Habermas-Handbuch*, 303–306, Klaus Günther maps the misunderstandings and misrepresentations of this key concept, and explains its designation as 'repression-free'.

2 Habermas, 'Discourse Ethics', in *Moral Consciousness*, 106.

3 Habermas, 'Remarks on discourse ethics', in *Justification and Application*, 33–34.

4 Kant, *Critique of Practical Reason*, trans. L.W. Beck, 118.

5 Tracy, D., 'Theology, critical social theory, and the public realm', in Browning/Schüssler Fiorenza (eds), *Habermas, Modernity and Public Theology*, 37. Tracy observes: 'Even in Habermas's own intellectual tradition, it is somewhat strange to find him silent on the role of religious questions as limit-questions in Kant'.(36).

6 Habermas, 'Transcendence from within', in Browning/Schüssler Fiorenza (eds), *Habermas, Modernity, and Public Theology*, 226–250, 239.

7 Habermas, 'Transcendence from within', in Browning/Schüssler Fiorenza (eds), *Habermas, Modernity, and Public Theology*, 239.

8 Apel, 'Normatively grounding critical theory?', in Rasmussen/Swindal (eds), *Jürgen Habermas*, Vol. III, 367: 'For this person, who . . . poses the question "Why ought I be moral at all"? – a question that means, among other things, why ought I accept co-responsibility for the consequences of the industrial society's collective activities and not rather live by the motto . . . "After me the deluge"! – for such a person the reference to the unavoidable ethical lifeworld is not a relevant answer at all. For our . . . questioner can also comfortably make do with this ethical lifeworld, conceived as it is without

the incisive standard of postconventional morality, should he not be up to answering the above decisive question about the rational grounding of morality'.

9 Habermas, 'Remarks on discourse ethics', in *Justification and Application*, 34–35.
10 Nagl-Docekal, H., 'Moral und Religion aus der Optik der heutigen rechtsphilosophischen Debatte', in *Deutsche Zeitschrift für Philosophie* 56 (2008) 843–855, 847.
11 Habermas, 'Remarks on discourse ethics', in *Justification and Application*, 75.
12 Habermas, 'Prepolitical Foundations of the Constitutional State?', in *Between Naturalism and Religion*, trans. C. Cronin (Cambridge: Polity Press, 2008), 101–13, 105.
13 Habermas, 'Discourse Ethics', in *Moral Consciousness*, 44. He specifies that 'discourse ethics takes its orientation for an intersubjective interpretation of the categorical imperative from Hegel's theory of recognition but without incurring the cost of a historical *dissolution* of morality in ethical life. Like Hegel it insists, though in a Kantian spirit, on the internal relation between justice and solidarity'. ('Employments of practical reason', in *Justification and Application*, 1).
14 Habermas, 'Discourse ethics', in *Moral Consciousness*, 104.
15 One such link could be found in the validity claims which include sincerity, as David Tracy points out perceptively: there 'is further need to see how ethical discussions of the "good" (the good life and happiness) might be related to (because already implied by) Habermas's formal analysis of the validity claims entailed by a morality of "right". Tracy, 'Theology, critical social theory, and the public realm', in Browning/Schüssler Fiorenza (eds), *Habermas, Modernity and Public Theology*, 34.
16 Habermas, 'Discourse Ethics', in *Moral Consciousness*, 104.
17 In *Moralische Identität*, 63–64, Hille Haker points out a parallel between Ricoeur's characterization of the self by the ethical dimension of conviction, and the role of ethical self-clarification and reassurance of identity in Habermas (cf., e.g., 'Employments of practical reason', 5); she regrets that he does not explore it any further but only develops its intersubjective and cultural conditions.
18 Peukert, 'Beyond the present state of affairs: *Bildung* and the search for orientation in rapidly transforming societies', in *Journal of Philosophy of Education* 36 (2002) 421–435, 431.
19 Habermas, 'Morality and ethical life', in *Moral Consciousness*, 210.
20 Habermas, 'Replik auf Einwände, Reaktion auf Anregungen', in Langthaler/ Nagl-Docekal (eds), *Glauben und Wissen*, 366–414, 407.
21 Habermas, 'Transcendence from within', in Browning//Schüssler Fiorenza (eds), *Habermas, Modernity and Public Theology*, 237.
22 In his discussion of the same text, the Vienna philosopher Ludwig Nagl points out that Peirce's philosophy of religion pursues a different intention:

'Here, Habermas's reference to Peirce is not fully justified. For in the *locus classicus* of Peirce's philosophy of religion, "A neglected argument

for the reality of God", the argument developed is not a communal-
"humanistic" one, but a cosmological-semiotic one. It is an argument
that does not aim at sublating "religious belief" through reinterpretation,
but at supporting it with the means of thinking'. Nagl, L., 'Das verhüllte
Absolute. Religionsphilosophische Motive bei Habermas und Adorno',
in *Das verhüllte Absolute. Essays zur zeitgenössischen Religionsphilosophie*
(Frankfurt/Berlin/Bern/Bruxelles/New York/Oxford/Wien: Peter Lang,
2010), 13–38, 24, Fn. 32.

23 Habermas, 'Transcendence from within', in Browning/ Schüssler Fiorenza
(eds), *Habermas, Modernity and Public Theology*, 240.
24 Habermas, 'Replik auf Einwände', in Langthaler/Nagl-Docekal (eds),
Glauben und Wissen, 405.

Chapter 7

1 Habermas, 'Einleitung', *Studienausgabe*, vol. V, *Kritik der Vernunft* (Frankfurt:
Suhrkamp, 2009), 9–32, 31.
2 Habermas, 'Einleitung', *Studienausgabe*, vol V, 27.
3 Habermas, 'Einleitung', *Studienausgabe*, vol. V, 27.
4 Habermas, 'Einleitung', *Studienausgabe*, vol. V, 31. This 'reflective mode'
safeguarding the autonomy of philosophy is practiced in the contribution
which forms the third text included into the study edition. It is the basis of
the discussion held in 2007 at the Jesuit School of Philosophy in Munich
with a title taken from the introduction to *Between Naturalism and Religion*,
and alluding to a quote from Adorno, *An Awareness of What is Missing*.
5 Cf. the short summary of Greve, J., *Jürgen Habermas. Eine Einführung*
(UTB 3227) (Konstanz: UVK Verlagsgesellschaft, 2009) 163, and Nagl,
'Religionsphilosophie bei Habermas und Adorno', in *Das verhüllte Absolute*,
22, on the crucial role of religion for the concept of the 'ineffability' of
individuality.
6 Habermas, 'An awareness of what is missing', in Habermas et al., *An
Awareness*, 17–18.
7 Habermas, 'Einleitung', *Studienausgabe*, vol.V, 30.
8 Habermas, 'Einleitung', *Studienausgabe*, vol.V, 30.
9 Habermas, 'Einleitung', *Studienausgabe*, vol.V, 32.
10 Ricken S.J., F., 'Postmetaphysical Reason and Religion', in Habermas et al.,
An Awareness, 51–58, 52–53.
11 Ricken, 'Postmetaphysical Reason and Religion', in Habermas et al., *An
Awareness*, 53.
12 As mentioned in the Introduction, the controversy on 'elective breeding'
begun by the philosopher Peter Sloterdijk's welcome for future genetic
technologies as fulfilling the dreams of Plato and Nietzsche was the starting
point of a debate in German political culture, in advance of the stage of
its technical feasibility. For an early review, see Graumann, S., 'Experts on

Notes

Philosophical Reflection in Public Discourse – the German Sloterdijk Debate', in *Biomedical Ethics* 5 (2000) 27–33.

13 Habermas, 'Employments of practical reason', in *Justification and Application*, 15.

14 Tanner, K., 'Das Ende der Enthaltsamkeit? Die Geburt einer "Gattungsethik" aus dem Geist der Diskursethik', in *Zeitschrift für Evangelische Ethik* 46 (2002) 144–150, 150. Habermas has already referred to concerns about a 'rather dubious sanctification (*fragwürdige Resakralisierung*) of human nature': *The Future of Human Nature*, trans. W. Rehg/M. Pensky/H. Beister (Cambridge: Polity Press, 2003), 25. For postmetaphysical reason, the attempt to identify features of human nature in an objectivist and essentialist way clearly belongs to the pre-critical stage and is one of the typical traits of metaphysics which it sets out to replace.

15 Habermas, *The Future of Human Nature*, 63–64.

16 Habermas, *The Future of Human Nature*, 77–79.

17 Habermas, *The Future of Human Nature*, 63. In this section, I am drawing on quotes and interpretations from 'Genetic Enhancement as Care or as Domination? The Ethics of Asymmetrical Relationships in the Upbringing of Children', in *Journal of Philosophy of Education* 24 (2005) 1–12. In it, I compare Habermas's position to the one taken by Alan Buchanan, Daniel Brock, Norman Daniels and Dan Wikler in *From Chance to Choice. Genetics and Justice* (Cambridge: CUP, 2000); he comments on this book in footnotes (e.g., Habermas, *The Future of Human Nature*, 118–19, n. 13).

18 Habermas, *The Future of Human Nature*, 5–15. 63.

19 Habermas, *The Future of Human Nature*, 44–53.

20 *Die Zukunft der menschlichen Natur. Auf dem Weg zu einer liberalen Eugenik?* (Frankfurt, Suhrkamp, 2001), 111. In the English translation, '*Sosein*' is translated as 'essence' (ET, 64) rather than as 'specificity'.

21 Habermas, *Zukunft der menschlichen Natur*, 75.

22 In the debate held in the autumn of 2001 in New York University on *Die Zukunft der menschlichen Natur*, included in the English translation as a 'Postscript' (75–100), Habermas repeats the need in a pluralist society to 'distinguish the inviolability (*Unantastbarkeit*) of human dignity (*Menschenwürde*), as established in Article 1, Section 1 of the German Basic Law, from the non-disposability (*Unverfügbarkeit*) of pre-personal human life' (77). Not wanting to foreclose or unilaterally decide the debate on whether embryos are bearers of human dignity, he thus maintains a distinction between the *Unantastbarkeit* of dignity, the category with which the written constitution of Germany (1949) opens, and the *Unverfügbarkeit* of human life that pertains to all its stages. In the face of a technological trend toward 'shopping in the genetic supermarket' that changes 'the relation between generations' (75) he calls for a discussion which includes both discourse on universalizable norms, and its species ethical embedding.

23 Habermas, *The Future of Human Nature*, 6–7.

24 Habermas, *The Future of Human Nature*, 81–82.

25 Habermas, *The Future of Human Nature*, 62–63.

Notes

26 A different formulation of the major objection to this justice project in its unreflected 'paternalism' (Habermas, *The Future of Human Nature*, 64) is '*Zwangsbeglückung*', a forced submission to another person's idea of happiness. Cf. Siep, L., 'Moral und Gattungsethik', in *Deutsche Zeitschrift für Philosophie* 50 (2002) 111–120, 112. Andrew Edgar concludes his article on the key term of genetics as follows: 'The designer imposes the child's purpose and meaning upon it, rather than allowing it to discover that purpose for itself'. Edgar, A., 'Genetics', in *Habermas – The Key Concepts* (London/New York: Routledge, 2006), 52–58, 58.

27 Habermas, *The Future of Human Nature*, 6.

28 Habermas, *The Future of Human Nature*, 90.

29 Habermas, 'Transcendence from within', in Browning/Schüssler Fiorenza (eds), *Habermas, Modernity, and Public Theology*, 239.

30 Schmidt, T., 'Menschliche Natur und genetische Manipulation. *Die Zukunft der menschlichen Natur. Auf dem Weg zu einer liberalen Eugenik*'? (Frankfurt: Suhrkamp, 2002), in Brunkhorst et al. (ed.), *Habermas-Handbuch*, 282–291, 289 ('*überraschenderweise*'); Lohmann, G., 'Moral-Diskurse', in *Habermas-Handbuch*, 82–87, 86 ('*in einer erstaunlichen Interpretation*').

31 Schmidt, 'Menschliche Natur', in *Habermas-Handbuch*, 282–3.

32 Habermas, *The Future of Human Nature*, 26; cf. Schmidt, 'Menschliche Natur', in *Habermas-Handbuch*, 284.

33 Habermas, *The Future of Human Nature*, 62: 'With genetic enhancement, there is no communicative scope (*Spielraum*) for the projected child to be addressed as a second person and to be involved in a communication process (*Verständigungsprozess*). From the adolescent's perspective, an instrumental determination cannot, like a pathogenic socialization process, be revised by "critical reappraisal" (*Aneignung*)'.

34 Schmidt, 'Menschliche Natur', in *Habermas-Handbuch*, 285. 'It is exactly the indisposability of the natural history that makes the process of socialization appear as something able to be shaped and not just as something to be suffered'.

35 Habermas, *The Future of Human Nature*, 57.

36 Habermas, *The Future of Human Nature*, 58.

37 Schmidt, 'Menschliche Natur', in *Habermas-Handbuch*, 285.

38 Habermas, *The Future of Human Nature*, 29.

39 Schmidt, 'Menschliche Natur', in *Habermas-Handbuch*, 290.

40 Habermas, *The Future of Human Nature*, 66.

41 Schmidt, 'Menschliche Natur', in *Habermas-Handbuch*, 286.

42 Habermas, *The Future of Human Nature*, 66.

43 Schweidler, W., 'Biopolitik und Bioethik. Über Menschenwürde als ethisches Prinzip des modernen Rechtsstaates', in *Information Philosophie* 36 (2008) 18–25, 19–20. The quote is from *The Future of Human Nature*, 40.

44 Schweidler, 'Biopolitik und Bioethik', 20.

45 Schweidler, 'Biopolitik und Bioethik', 21, quoting Habermas, *The Future of Human Nature*, 25. It is in the context of this 'assertion of an ethical

self-understanding of the species' that '"moralizing human nature"' can be justified for Habermas.

46 Rawls, J., *Political Liberalism* (New York: Columbia University Press, 1993).

47 Schweidler, 'Biopolitik und Bioethik', 24.

48 Schweidler, 'Biopolitik und Bioethik', 25.

49 Habermas, *The Future of Human Nature*, 20.

50 Lohmann, 'Moral-Diskurse', in *Habermas-Handbuch*, 86.

51 Habermas, *The Future of Human Nature*, 11.

52 Schmidt, 'Menschliche Natur', in *Habermas-Handbuch*, 290.

53 Kierkegaard, S., *The Sickness unto Death*, trans. and intro. A. Hannay (Harmondsworth: Penguin, 1989), 43. His analysis of subjectivity concludes: 'This then is the formula which describes the state of the self when despair is completely eradicated: in relating to itself and in wanting to be itself, the self is grounded transparently in the power that established it'. (44).

54 Schmidt draws attention to the fact that the retrieval of Kierkegaard's ethics of being a self under the title of 'Reasoned abstention. Are there postmetaphysical answers to the question of the right life'?, the first essay in *The Future of Human Nature*, dates from a speech at the University of Zurich in September 2000. Also the second essay on species ethics as a response to liberal eugenics, which goes back to a lecture held at the University of Marburg in June 2001, predates the events of September 11, 2001. His speech on 'Faith and Knowledge', on receiving the Peace Prize of the German Booktrade in the Paulskirche in Frankfurt in October 2001, responds with a programmatic call for a new relationship of secular reason to religion with mutual commitment to 'translation'.

55 Ricoeur, P., *Oneself as Another* (Chicago: University of Chicago Press, 1992), 172.

56 Habermas, *The Future of Human Nature*, 85.

57 Habermas, The *Future of Human Nature*, 90.

Chapter 8

1 Cf., e.g., Habermas, 'Religion in the public sphere: Cognitive presuppositions for the "public use of reason" by religious and secular citizens', in *Between Naturalism and Religion*, 114–147, 129–130.

2 Rawls, J., 'The idea of public reason revisited', in *The Law of Peoples* (Cambridge/Mass.: Harvard University Press, 2001), 129–180, 152.

3 Habermas, 'Faith and Knowledge', in *The Future of Human Nature*, 101–115, 114–15. In the English translation, the decisive contrast does not come out as clearly since '"*Hervorgehen aus*" *Gott*' which refers to emanation is translated unspecifically as '"coming from" God'.

4 Striet, M., 'Grenzen der Übersetzbarkeit. Theologische Annäherungen an Jürgen Habermas', in Langthaler/Nagl-Docekal (eds), *Glauben und Wissen*, 259–282, 263. 269.

Notes

5 Rawls, 'Public reason revisited', in *The Law of Peoples,* 152. He agrees that this is an example of reasoning from 'what we believe, or conjecture, may be other people's basic doctrines . . . and seek to show them that, despite what they may think, they can still endorse a reasonable political conception of justice'. (152). Such 'reasoning from conjecture' does not speak for either the desire or the experience of testing such hypotheses in dialogue with religious citizens or colleagues.

6 E.g, Habermas, 'Prepolitical foundations', in *Between Naturalism and Religion*, 110.

7 Habermas/Mendieta, 'Ein neues Interesse der Philosophie an der Religion'?, in *Deutsche Zeitschrift für Philosophie* 58 (2010) 3–16, 8. This peculiar communication form is 'distinguished, on the one hand, by the *lack of world reference* (*Weltbezug*) of a self-referential collective praxis that circles in itself, and, on the other hand, by the *holistic content of meaning* of an undifferentiated use of various iconic symbols which have not yet been differentiated by propositions (such as dancing and singing, pantomime, decoration, body painting, etc.). I would like to maintain that today, only religious communities (*Gemeinden*) in their cultic practice keep the access to archaic experiences of this kind open' (12).

8 Cf. Habermas, 'Prepolitical foundations', in *Between Naturalism and Religion*, 107.

9 In keeping with the interest of this book to examine the development of Habermas's position regarding religion and his interactions with theology, I have prioritized issues relating to anthropology and theory of subjectivity, philosophy of religion, types of approaches to ethics, the foundations and limits of discourse and the relevance given to religious motives in current debates, e.g., on enhancement. I am treating his approach to political philosophy and to law from discourse ethical foundations in comparison to others, among them John Rawls and Paul Ricoeur, together with receptions and critiques they have found in 'public theology', in *Religion and Public Reason* (Berlin/New York: De Gruyter, 2011). The following subsection limits itself to offering an overview of the key points of Habermas's argument.

10 Habermas, 'Prepolitical foundations', in *Between Naturalism and Religion*, 108.

11 Habermas, 'Faith and knowledge', in *The Future of Human Nature*, 104.

12 Habermas/Mendieta, 'Ein neues Interesse der Philosophie an der Religion?' in *Deutsche Zeitschrift für Philosophie* 58 (2010) 3–16, 3.

13 Habermas, 'Equal treatment of cultures and the limits of postmodern liberalism', in *Between Naturalism and Religion*, 271–311, 310.

14 In 'Prepolitical foundations', Habermas speaks of a 'political generalization of a secularized worldview': *Between Naturalism and Religion*, 113.

15 Linde, G., '"Religiös" oder "säkular"? Zu einer problematischen Unterscheidung bei Jürgen Habermas', in Th. Schmidt/K. Wenzel (eds), *Moderne Religion? Theologische und religionsphilosophische Reaktionen auf Jürgen Habermas* (Freiburg: Herder, 2009), 153–202, 197.

16 Cf. Fraser, N., 'Theorie der Öffentlichkeit. *Strukturwandel der Öffentlichkeit* (1961)', in Brunkhorst et al. (eds), *Habermas-Handbuch*, 148–155, 148.

Notes

ET: *The Structural Transformation of the Public Sphere*, trans. T. Burger (Cambridge, Mass.: MIT Press, 1989).

17 Habermas, 'Reconciliation through the public use of reason' (1995), and '"Reasonable" versus "true", or the morality of worldviews' (1996), in *The Inclusion of the Other*, 49–74. 75–104. In 1984, publ. 1986 and republ. in *Erläuterungen zur Diskursethik* (Frankfurt: Suhrkamp, 1991), he referred to Rawls's *Theory of Justice* in the context of a debate on L. Kohlberg's stage theory of moral development, 'Gerechtigkeit und Solidarität. Zur Diskussion über Stufe 6', 49–76. For a comparison of both positions on the public sphere and on democratic participation, cf. McCarthy, T., 'Kantian Constructivism and Reconstructivism: Rawls and Habermas in Dialogue', in *Ethics* 105 (1994) 44–63.

18 They are given a 'delaying veto' (*aufschiebendes Veto*). The ET of this phrase from 'Faith and knowledge', in *The Future of Human Nature*, 109, chooses a weaker expression, 'dilatory plea'. For the context of this proposal, see below. I have treated Rawls' and Habermas's diverging conceptions of public reason in 'Between postsecular society and the neutral state: Religion as a resource for public reason', in N. Biggar/L. Hogan (eds), *Religious Voices in Public Places* (Oxford: OUP, 2009), 58–81.

19 Habermas, 'Faith and knowledge', in *The Future of Human Nature*, 109.

20 Habermas, 'Prepolitical foundations', in *Between Naturalism and Religion*, 107.

21 Habermas, 'Faith and knowledge', in *The Future of Human Nature*, 102–03.

22 For a closer analysis, see 'The Pre-Political Foundations of the State', in E. Borgman/M. Junker-Kenny/J. Martin-Soskice (eds), *The New Pontificate: A Time for Change?, Concilium* 2006/1 (London: SCM Press, 2006), 106–117.

23 In his quest for a 'public basis of justification', Rawls suggests that the viewpoints of the citizens should not have to be extended beyond what they presently hold. On matters of constitutional essentials and basic justice, 'the basic structure and its public policies are to be justifiable to all citizens, as the principle of political legitimacy requires. We add to this that in making these justifications we are to appeal only to presently accepted general beliefs and forms of reasoning found in common sense, and the methods and conclusions of science when these are not controversial . . . This means that in discussing constitutional essentials and matters of basic justice we are not to appeal to comprehensive religious and philosophical doctrines – to what we as individuals or members of associations see as the whole truth . . . As far as possible, the knowledge and ways of reasoning that ground our affirming the principles of justice and their application to constitutional essentials and basic justice are to rest on the plain truths now widely accepted, or available, to citizens generally. Otherwise, the political conception would not provide a public basis of justification'. Rawls, *Political Liberalism* (New York: Columbia University Press, 1993), 224–5.

24 Habermas, 'Faith and Knowledge', in *The Future of Human Nature*, 110–11.

25 Habermas, 'Faith and Knowledge', in *The Future of Human Nature*, 108–09.

26 Greve, *Jürgen Habermas. Eine Einführung*, 163.

27 Habermas, 'Faith and Knowledge', in *The Future of Human Nature*, 105. 108.

Notes

28 Habermas, 'Faith and Knowledge', in *The Future of Human Nature*, 109.

29 Habermas, 'Religion in the public sphere', in *Between Naturalism and Religion*, 127, with reference to Wolterstorff's and Weithman's objections which he finds 'compelling'. He does not, however, agree with eliminating the distinction between society's public sphere and the state which he wants to maintain its neutrality in view of 'competing worldviews' (132).

30 Linde enquires whether this term asks for the substitution of 'God-statements' and proposes an understanding of translation not as substitution but as explication. Linde, '"Religiös" oder "säkular"?, in Schmidt/Wenzel (eds), *Moderne Religion?*, 198–99.

31 Wenzel, K., 'Gott in der Moderne. Grund und Ansatz einer Theologie der Säkularität', in Schmidt/Wenzel (eds), *Moderne Religion?* 347–376, 352.

32 'Religiously rooted existential convictions, by dint of their if necessary rationally justified reference to the dogmatic authority of an inviolable core of infallible revealed truths, evade that kind of *unreserved* discursive examination to which other ethical orientations and worldviews, i.e., secular "conceptions of the good", are exposed'. Habermas, 'Religion in the public sphere', in *Between Naturalism and Religion*, 129.

33 Wenzel, 'Gott in der Moderne', in Schmidt/Wenzel (eds), *Moderne Religion?*, 353–54. '"Natural" reason' is a quote from Habermas, 'Religion in the public sphere', in *Between Naturalism and Religion*, 120.

34 Regarding Jens Glebe-Möller's *Political Dogmatics*, he remarks: 'But I ask myself *who* recognizes himself or herself in this interpretation'. Habermas, 'Transcendence from within', in Browning/Schüssler Fiorenza (eds), *Habermas, Modernity, and Public Theology*, 235.

35 Habermas, 'Equal treatment of cultures', in *Between Naturalism and Religion*, 302.

36 Habermas, 'Israel or Athens', in *Religion and Rationality*, 129–138, 132.

37 Habermas, 'Faith and Knowledge', in *Future of Human Nature*, 115.

38 Habermas, 'Israel or Athens', in *Religion and Rationality*, 132–33.

39 Habermas, 'Revitalisierung der Weltreligionen', in *Studienausgabe* vol. 5, 407.

40 Wenzel, 'Gott in der Moderne', in Schmidt/Wenzel (eds), *Moderne Religion?*, 355. He concludes: 'In this respect, articulations open to discourse of a religious tradition of conviction may be closer to its core identity than those versions of the same tradition which claim for themselves discursive exterritoriality'.

41 Nagl-Docekal, '"Many Forms of Nonpublic Reason"? Religious Diversity in Liberal Democracies', in H. Lenk (ed.), *Comparative and Intercultural Philosophy* (Berlin/Münster: LIT, 2009), 79–92, 85.

42 Cf., e.g., Kasper, W., *Jesus the Christ* (London: Burns & Oates/Mahwah/N.J.: Paulist Press, 1976), 175–179.

43 Linde, '"Religiös" oder "säkular"?, in Schmidt/Wenzel (eds), *Moderne Religion?*, 198.

44 Schmidt, S.J., J., 'A dialogue in which there can only be winners', in Habermas et al., *An Awareness*, 59–71, 66–67, and Habermas, 'A Reply', 72–83, 80.

45 Schmidt, J., 'A dialogue', in Habermas et al., *An Awareness*, 66. 70.

Notes

46 Ricken, 'Postmetaphysical reason and religion', in Habermas et al., *An Awareness*, 56.

47 Ricken, 'Postmetaphysical reason and religion', in Habermas et al., *An Awareness*, 56–57.

48 A revised version was published in *Between Naturalism and Religion*, 209–247.

49 Habermas, 'Boundary between faith and knowledge', in *Between Naturalism and Religion*, 227.

50 Habermas, 'Replik auf Einwände, Reaktion auf Anregungen', in Langthaler/Nagl-Docekal (eds), *Glauben und Wissen*, 366–414, 376. In 'The boundary between faith and knowledge', '*überschwänglich*' is translated as 'effusive' (*Between Naturalism and Religion,* 247).

51 Nagl-Docekal, 'Eine rettende Übersetzung? Jürgen Habermas interpretiert Kants Religionsphilosophie', in Langthaler/Nagl-Docekal (eds), *Glauben und Wissen*, 110.

52 Habermas, 'Replik', in Langthaler/Nagl-Docekal (eds), *Glauben und Wissen*, 377.

53 Langthaler, 'Zur Interpretation und Kritik der Kantischen Religionsphilosophie bei Jürgen Habermas', in Langthaler/Nagl-Docekal (eds), *Glauben und Wissen*, 32–92, 46. Cf. Habermas, 'Replik', 377.

54 'On the pragmatic, the ethical and the moral employments of practical reason', in *Justification and Application*, 10.

55 This statement is preceded by the line which is taken as the title of the interview: 'I have grown old, but not pious'. Habermas, 'Ich bin alt, aber nicht fromm geworden', in Funken, M. (ed.), *Über Habermas. Gespräche mit Zeitgenossen* (Darmstadt: Wissenschaftliche Buchgesellschaft, 2008), 181–190, 185.

56 Langthaler, 'Zur Interpretation', in Langthaler/Nagl-Docekal (eds), *Glauben und Wissen*, 46.

57 Nagl, *Das verhüllte Absolute*, 26.

58 Habermas, 'Replik', in Langthaler/Nagl-Docekal (eds), *Glauben und Wissen*, 367.

59 Nagl-Docekal, H., 'Eine rettende Übersetzung?', in Langthaler/Nagl-Docekal (eds), *Glauben und Wissen*,110.

60 Cf. Wendel, S., 'Die religiöse Selbst- und Weltdeutung des bewussten Daseins und ihre Bedeutung für eine "moderne Religion". Was der "Postmetaphysiker" Habermas über Religion nicht zu denken wagt', in Schmidt/Wenzel (eds), *Moderne Religion?*, 225–265, 227–30.

61 Habermas, 'Replik', in Langthaler/Nagl-Docekal (eds), *Glauben und Wissen*, 381, quoted in Wendel, 'Religiöse Selbst- und Weltdeutung', in Schmidt/Wenzel (eds), *Moderne Religion?*, 230.

62 Wendel, 'Religiöse Selbst- und Weltdeutung', in Schmidt/Wenzel (eds), *Moderne Religion?*, 232.230–31.

63 Habermas, 'A reply', in Habermas et al., *An Awareness*, 80.

64 Habermas, 'A reply', in Habermas et al., *An Awareness*, 81–82.

65 Habermas, 'A reply', in Habermas et al., *An Awareness*, 79–80.

66 Habermas, 'Ich bin alt, aber nicht fromm geworden', in Funken (ed.), *Über Habermas*, 183.

67 Schmidt, T., 'Nachmetaphysische Religionsphilosophie. Religion und Philosophie unter den Bedingungen diskursiver Vernunft', in Schmidt/ Wenzel (eds), *Moderne Religion?*, 10–32, 25–26.

68 Habermas, 'Boundary', in *Between Naturalism and Religion*, 242.

69 E.g., Habermas, 'Boundary', in *Between Naturalism and Religion*, 234–35: 'However, the Culture Protestantism of the late nineteenth and early twentieth centuries make clear the price Schleiermacher has to pay for this elegant reconciliation of religion and modernity, faith, and knowledge. The integration of faith into society and the privatization of faith rob the religious relation to transcendence of its disruptive power within the world … Kierkegaard's work stands in contrast to Schleiermacher's comforting analysis of the pious existence reconciled with modernity. He shares with his contemporary Marx the sense of crisis of a *restless* modernity'.

70 Cf. Habermas, *The Future of Human Nature*, 5.

71 This emphasis contrasts with the intellectual orientation of the theologians he quotes in footnotes – e.g., the Catholic systematic theologians Edmund Arens and Markus Knapp, the Protestant Hermann Düringer – whose works relate positively to modernity and contribute to a philosophically mediated theology. On the basis of Helmut Peukert's critical reception of the theory of communicative action, Arens has elaborated its fruitfulness in many fields of systematic theology. In *Between Naturalism and Religion*, 132, Fn. 37, Habermas refers to his work on biblical parables as innovative speech acts, *Kommunikative Handlungen* (Düsseldorf: Patmos, 1982), which, among others of his books, has been translated into English.

72 E.g., in his reference to Schleiermacher's analysis 'of what it means in a performative sense to have faith', in 'Boundary', in *Between Naturalism and Religion*, 232.

73 Cf. Pröpper, T., *Der Jesus der Philosophen und der Jesus des Glaubens* (Mainz: Grünewald, 1976), and *Evangelium und freie Vernunft* (Freiburg: Herder, 2001).

74 Habermas, 'Religion in the public sphere', in *Between Naturalism and Religion*, 127.

75 Pröpper, 'Exkurs 2: Ist das Identische der Tradition identifizierbar? Zur Aufgabe und Hauptschwierigkeit der Rekonstruktion der Überlieferungsgeschichte des christlichen Glaubens', in *Erlösungsglaube und Freiheitsgeschichte*, 230–236.

76 Ricken, 'Postmetaphysical reason', in Habermas et al., *An Awareness*, 58.

77 Habermas, 'Boundary', in *Between Naturalism and Religion*, 242.

78 In the unsurpassable formulation of Duns Scotus, the reason for creation is that God wanted to have counterparts in God's image to share God's love with: 'Vult habere alios condiligentes'. Duns Scotus, *Opus Oxoniense*, III d.32 q. 1 n. 6. Its significance is explored by Magnus Striet in 'Grenzen der Übersetzung'?, in Langthaler/Nagl-Docekal (eds), *Glauben und Wissen*, 266–270.

Bibliography

Works by Jürgen Habermas

Erkenntnis und Interesse (Frankfurt: Suhrkamp, 1968). ET *Knowledge and Human Interests*, trans. J. J. Shapiro (Boston, MA: Beacon Press, 1971).

Zur Rekonstruktion des Historischen Materialismus (Frankfurt: Suhrkamp, 1976). ET *Communication and the Evolution of Society*, trans. T. McCarthy (Boston, MA: Beacon Press, 1979).

Politisch-philosophische Profile (Frankfurt: Suhrkamp, 1971, extended eds 1981, 1987). ET *Political-philosophical Profiles*, trans. F. Lawrence (Cambridge, MA: MIT Press, 1983).

Vorstudien und Ergänzungen zur Theorie des kommunikativen Handelns (Frankfurt: Suhrkamp, 1984).

Theory of Communicative Action, vols I and II, trans. T. McCarthy (Boston, MA: Beacon Press, 1984, 1987).

Technik und Wissenschaft als Ideologie (Frankfurt: Suhrkamp, 1968). ET *Toward a Rational Society*, trans. J. J. Shapiro (Cambridge: Polity, 1986).

The Philosophical Discourse of Modernity. Twelve Lectures, trans. F. Lawrence (Cambridge, MA: MIT Press, 1987).

'Rückkehr zur Metaphik? Eine Sammelrezension', repr. in *Nachmetaphysisches Denken* (Frankfurt: Suhrkamp, 1988), pp 267–279.

Strukturwandel der Öffentlichkeit (Neuwied, Berlin: Luchterhand, 1961). ET *The Structural Transformation of the Public Sphere*, trans. Thomas Burger (Cambridge, MA: MIT Press, 1989).

Moralbewusstsein und kommunikatives Handeln (Frankfurt: Suhrkamp, 1983). ET *Moral Consciousness and Communicative Action*, trans. C. Lenhardt and S. Weber Nicholsen (Cambridge, MA: MIT Press, 1990).

Texte und Kontexte (Frankfurt: Suhrkamp, 1991).

Postmetaphysical Thinking. Philosophical Essays, trans. W. M. Hohengarten (Cambridge, MA: MIT Press, 1992).

Erläuterungen zur Diskursethik (Frankfurt: Suhrkamp, 1991). ET *Justification and Application. Remarks on Discourse Ethics*, trans. C. Cronin (Cambridge, MA: MIT Press, 1993).

Between Facts and Norms. Contributions to a Discourse Theory of Law and Democracy, trans. W. Rehg (Cambridge: Polity Press, 1996).

Die Einbeziehung des Anderen (Frankfurt: Suhrkamp, 1996). ET *The Inclusion of the Other. Studies in Political Theory*, Ciaran Cronin and Pablo De Greiff (ed.), trans. C. Cronin et al. (Cambridge: Polity Press, 1998).

Bibliography

Glauben und Wissen (Frankfurt: Suhrkamp, 2001).

'Replik auf Einwände, Reaktion auf Anregungen', in Langthaler and Nagl-Docekal (eds), *Glauben und Wissen* (Frankfurt: Suhrkamp, 2001), pp 366–414.

Religion and Rationality. Essays on Reason, God, and Modernity, ed. and intro. E. Mendieta (Cambridge: Polity Press, 2002).

Die Zukunft der menschlichen Natur. Auf dem Weg zu einer liberalen Eugenik? (Frankfurt, Suhrkamp, 2001). ET *The Future of Human Nature,* trans. W. Rehg, M. Pensky, H. Beister (Cambridge: Polity Press, 2003).

Wahrheit und Rechtfertigung (Frankfurt: Suhrkamp, 1999). ET *Truth and Justification, ed. and trans. B. Fultner* (Cambridge: Polity Press, 2003).

Between Naturalism and Religion, trans. C. Cronin (Cambridge: Polity, 2008).

Studienausgabe, vol. V, *Kritik der Vernunft* (Frankfurt: Suhrkamp, 2009).

Habermas, N. Brieskorn, S. J., M. Reder, F. Ricken, S. J., J. Schmidt, S. J., *An Awareness of What is Missing. Faith and Reason in a Postsecular Age,* trans. C. Cronin (Cambridge: Polity Press, 2010).

Habermas, and E. Mendieta, 'Ein neues Interesse der Philosophie an der Religion? Zur philosophischen Bewandtnis von postsäkularem Bewusstsein und multikultureller Weltgesellschaft', *Deutsche Zeitschrift für Philosophie* 58 (2010), pp 3–16.

Other Works

Abeldt, S., W. Bauer, et al. (eds), '. . . *was es bedeutet, verletzbarer Mensch zu sein', Erziehungswissenschaft im Gespräch mit Theologie, Philosophie und Gesellschaftstheorie. Festschrift H. Peukert* (Mainz: Grünewald, 2000).

Adams, N., *Habermas and Theology* (Cambridge: Cambridge University Press, 2006).

Adorno, Th. W., *Negative Dialectics,* trans. E. B. Ashton (New York: Seabury Press, 1973).

Anzenbacher, A., *Einführung in die Philosophie* (Freiburg: Herder, 8th edn, 2002).

Apel, K.-O., 'Normatively grounding "critical theory" by recourse to the lifeworld? A transcendental-pragmatic attempt to think with Habermas against Habermas', in Rasmussen and Swindal (eds), *Jürgen Habermas,* vol. III (London: Sage, 2002), pp 344–378.

Arens, E., *Kommunikative Handlungen* (Düsseldorf: Patmos, 1982).

—*Bezeugen und Bekennen. Elementare Handlungen des Glaubens* (Düsseldorf: Patmos, 1989).

Arens, E. (ed.), *Habermas und die Theologie. Beiträge zur theologischen Rezeption, Diskussion und Kritik der Theorie kommunikativen Handelns* (Düsseldorf: Patmos, 2nd edn, 1989).

Ashley, J. M., 'Johann Baptist Metz', in P. Scott and W. T. Cavanaugh (eds), *The Blackwell Companion to Political Theology* (Oxford: Blackwell, 2004), pp 241–255.

Bibliography

Benjamin, W., *Illuminations* (New York: Schocken, 1969).

Böhnke, M., M. Bongard, G. Essen, and J. Werbick (eds), *Freiheit Gottes und der Menschen. Festschrift T. Pröpper* (Regensburg: Pustet, 2006).

Browing, D. S., and F. Schüssler Fiorenza (eds), *Habermas, Modernity, and Public Theology* (New York: Crossroad, 1992).

Brunkhorst, H., 'Platzhalter und Interpret', in Brunkhorst et al. (eds), *Habermas-Handbuch* (Frankfurt: Suhrkamp, 2002), pp 214–220.

Brunkhorst, H., R. Kreide, and C. Lafont (eds), *Habermas-Handbuch. Leben – Werk – Wirkung* (Stuttgart: J. B. Metzler'sche Verlagsbuchhandlung, C. E. Poeschel Verlag and Darmstadt: Wissenschaftliche Buchgesellschaft, 2009).

Brunkhorst, H., and S. Müller-Doohm, 'Intellektuelle Biographie', in Brunkhorst et al. (eds), *Habermas-Handbuch* (Frankfurt: Suhrkamp, 2002), pp 1–14.

Buchanan, A., D. Brock, N. Daniels, and D. Wikler, *From Chance to Choice. Genetics and Justice* (Cambridge: Cambridge University Press, 2000).

Cooke, M., 'Säkulare Übersetzung oder postsäkulare Argumentation? Habermas über Religion in der demokratischen Öffentlichkeit', in Langthaler and Nagl-Docekal (eds), *Glauben und Wissen* (Frankfurt: Suhrkamp, 2001), pp 341–366.

Dews, P. (ed.), *Habermas – A Critical Reader* (Oxford: Blackwell, 1999).

Duns Scotus, *Opus Oxoniense*, in L. Vivès (ed.), *Opera omnia. Editio nova iuxta editionem Waddingi*, vol. XIV (Paris, 1891–1895). Facsimilie reprint Farnborough: Gregg, 1969.

Edgar, A., *Habermas – The Key Concepts* (London, New York: Routledge, 2006).

Essen, G., *Sinnstiftende Unruhe im System des Rechts. Religion im Beziehungsgeflecht von modernem Verfassungsstaat und säkularer Zivilgesellschaft* (Göttingen: Wallstein Verlag, 2004).

Fichte, J. G., *Grundlage des Naturrechts nach Principien der Wissenschaftslehre* (1796), *Werke*, vol. III, I. H. Fichte (ed.) (Berlin: De Gruyter, 1971).

Forrester, D., *Christian Justice and Public Policy* (Cambridge: Cambridge University Press, 1997).

Forst, R., 'Diskursethik der Moral. "Diskursethik – Notizen zu einem Begründungsprogramm" (1983)', in Brunkhorst et al. (eds), *Habermas-Handbuch* (Frankfurt: Suhrkamp, 2002), pp 234–240.

—*Das Recht auf Rechtfertigung. Elemente einer konstruktivistischen Theorie der Gerechtigkeit* (Frankfurt: Suhrkamp, 2007).

Fraser, N., 'Theorie der Öffentlichkeit. *Strukturwandel der Öffentlichkeit* (1961)', in Brunkhorst et al. (eds), *Habermas-Handbuch* (Frankfurt: Suhrkamp, 2002), pp 148–155.

Frühwald, W., 'Von der Rationalität des Glaubens', in Th. Pröpper (ed.), *Bewusstes Leben in der Wissensgesellschaft*. Wolfgang Frühwald und Dieter Henrich Ehrendoktoren der Katholisch-Theologischen Fakultät der Universität Münster (Altenberge: Oros Verlag, 2000), pp 79–91.

Bibliography

Funken, M. (ed.), *Über Habermas. Gespräche mit Zeitgenossen* (Darmstadt: Wissenschaftliche Buchgesellschaft, 2008).

Glebe-Möller, J., *Political Dogmatics* (Philadelphia, PA: Fortress, 1987).

Goeller, T., R. Konersmann, B. Recki, and O. Schwemmer, '*Die kulturwissenschaftliche Wende*', *Information Philosophie* 33 (2005), pp 20–32.

Graumann, S., 'Experts on Philosophical Reflection in Public Discourse – the German *Sloterdijk* Debate', *Biomedical Ethics* 5 (2000), pp 27–33.

Greve, J., *Jürgen Habermas. Eine Einführung* (UTB 3227) (Konstanz: UVK Verlagsgesellschaft, 2009).

Günther, K., 'Diskurs', in Brunkhorst et al. (eds), *Habermas-Handbuch* (Frankfurt: Suhrkamp, 2002), pp 303–306.

Haker, H., 'Kommunitaristische Kritik an der Diskursethik', *Ethik und Unterricht* 5 (1994), pp 12–18.

—*Moralische Identität. Literarische Lebensgeschichten als Medium ethischer Reflexion. Mit einer Interpretation der Jahrestage von Uwe Johnson* (Tübingen: Francke, 1999).

Henke, T., *Seelsorge und Lebenswelt. Auf dem Weg zu einer Seelsorgetheorie in Auseinandersetzung mit soziologischen und sozialphilosophischen Lebensweltkonzeptionen* (Würzburg: Echter, 1994).

Henrich, D., *Fichtes ursprüngliche Einsicht* (Frankfurt: Klostermann, 1967).

—'Was ist Metaphysik – was Moderne? Zwölf Thesen gegen Jürgen Habermas', in *Konzepte. Essays zur Philosophie in der Zeit* (Frankfurt: Suhrkamp, 1987), pp 11–43. ET 'What is metaphysics – what modernity?', in Dews (ed.), *Habermas: A Critical Reader* (Oxford: Blackwell, 1999), pp 291–319.

Honneth, A., 'Geschichtsphilosophie, Anthropologie und Marxismus', and 'Frankfurter Schule', in Brunkhorst et al. (eds), *Habermas-Handbuch* (Frankfurt: Suhrkamp, 2002), pp 15–17, 17–20.

Horkheimer, M., and Th. W. Adorno, *Dialectics of Enlightenment*, trans. J. Cumming (New York: Seabury Press, 1975).

Joas, H. (ed.), *Was sind religiöse Überzeugungen?* (Göttingen: Wallstein Verlag, 2003).

Junker-Kenny, M., 'Praxis gegenseitiger Anerkennung? Die Relevanz der philosophischen Kritik an Jürgen Habermas' Ansatz für die Entwicklung eines Begriffs christlicher Praxis', *International Journal for Practical Theology* 1 (1997), pp 41–82.

— *Argumentationsethik und christliche Praxis. Eine praktisch-theologische Auseinandersetzung mit der Handlungstheorie Jürgen Habermas'* (Stuttgart: Kohlhammer Verlag, 1998).

—'Kritische Theorie praktisch-theologisch', in H. D. Betz, D. S. Browning, B. Janowski, and E. Jüngel (eds), *Religion in Geschichte und Gegenwart,* vol. 4 (Tübingen: Mohr Siebeck, 4th edn, 2001), pp 1784–1785.

—'Das Risiko der Vorgabe. Zur Verletzbarkeit innovatorisch und advokatorisch handelnder Subjekte', in Abeldt, Bauer et al. (eds), '. . . was es bedeutet, verletzbarer Mensch zu sein' (Mainz: Grünewald, 2002), pp 61–72.

Bibliography

—'Moralisierung oder Abschied von der menschlichen Natur? Die Auseinandersetzung zwischen Habermas und der Rawls-Schule', *Der Mensch des Menschen. Jahrbuch für Bildung und Erziehungsphilosophie* 5 (2003), pp 125–155.

—'Genetic enhancement as care or as domination? The ethics of asymmetrical relationships in the upbringing of children', *Journal of Philosophy of Education* 24 (2005), pp 1–12.

—'Valuing the priceless: Christian Convictions in Public Debate as a Critical Resource and as "Delaying Veto" (J. Habermas)', *Studies in Christian Ethics* 18 (2005), pp 43–56.

—'The Pre-Political Foundations of the State', in E. Borgman, M. Junker-Kenny, and J. Martin-Soskice (eds), *The New Pontificate: A Time for Change?*, *Concilium* 2006/1 (London: SCM Press, 2006), pp 106–117.

—'Zwischen Integrität und Übersetzung. Christliche Überzeugungen in der Konstitution praktischer Freiheit im Bedingungsgefüge spätmoderner Gesellschaften', in Böhnke et al. (eds), *Freiheit Gottes und der Menschen* (Regensburg: Pustet, 2006), pp 359–380.

—'Between Postsecular Society and the Neutral State: Religion as a Resource for Public Reason', in N. Biggar and L. Hogan (eds), *Religious Voices in Public Places* (Oxford: Oxford University Press, 2009), pp 58–81.

—'Jenseits liberaler öffentlicher Vernunft: Religion und das Vermögen der Prinzipien', in Schmidt and Wenzel (eds), *Moderne Religion?* (Freiburg: Herder, 2009), pp 92–127.

—'Der Gipfel des Schöpferischen. Das Jesuszeugnis als Quelle öffentlicher Vernunft', in O. John and M. Striet (eds), *'. . . und nichts Menschliches ist mir fremd'. Theologische Grenzgänge. Festschrift H. Peukert* (Regensburg: Pustet, 2010), pp 59–75.

—*Religion and Public Reason* (Berlin, New York: De Gruyter, 2012).

Kant, I., *Critique of Practical Reason*, trans. L. W. Beck (Indianapolis, IN: Bobbs Merrill, 1956).

Kasper, W., *Jesus the Christ* (London: Burns & Oates, Mahwah, N. J.: Paulist Press, 1976).

Kierkegaard, S., *The Sickness unto Death*, trans. and intro. A. Hannay (Harmondsworth: Penguin, 1989).

Kuhnke, U., *Koinonia. Zur theologischen Rekonstruktion der Identität christlicher Gemeinde* (Düsseldorf: Patmos, 1992).

Lafont, C., 'Hermeneutik und *linguistic turn*', in Brunkhorst et al. (eds), *Habermas-Handbuch* (Frankfurt: Suhrkamp, 2002), pp 29–34.

Langthaler, R., and H. Nagl-Docekal (eds), 'Zur Interpretation und Kritik der Kantischen Religionsphilosophie bei Jürgen Habermas', in Langthaler and Nagl-Docekal (eds), *Glauben und Wissen* (Frankfurt: Suhrkamp, 2001), pp 32–92.

—*Glauben und Wissen. Ein Symposium mit Jürgen Habermas* (Wien: Oldenbourg, Berlin: Akademie-Verlag, 2007).

Lenhardt, C., 'Anamnestic solidarity: The proletariat and its *manes*', *Telos* 25 (1975), pp 133–155.

Bibliography

Linde, G., ' "Religiös" oder "säkular"? Zu einer problematischen Unterscheidung bei Jürgen Habermas', in Schmidt and Wenzel (eds), *Moderne Religion?* (Freiburg: Herder, 2009), pp 153–202.

Lob-Hüdepohl, A., *Kommunikative Vernunft und theologische Ethik* (Studien zur theologischen Ethik 47) (Freiburg i. Ue., Freiburg i. Br.: Universitätsverlag, 1993).

Lohmann, G., 'Moral-Diskurse', in Brunkhorst et al. (eds), *Habermas-Handbuch* (Frankfurt: Suhrkamp, 2002), pp 82–87.

—'Nachmetaphysisches Denken', in Brunkhorst et al. (eds), *Habermas-Handbuch* (Frankfurt: Suhrkamp, 2002), pp 356–358.

McCarthy, T., 'Kantian Constructivism and Reconstructivism: Rawls and Habermas in Dialogue', *Ethics* 105 (1994), pp 44–63.

Mette, N., *Theorie der Praxis. Wissenschaftsgeschichtliche und methodologische Untersuchungen zur Theorie-Praxis-Problematik innerhalb der praktischen Theologie* (Düsseldorf: Patmos, 1978).

—'Identität ohne Religion? Eine religionspädagogische Herausforderung', in Arens (ed.), *Habermas und die Theologie. Beiträge zur theologischen Rezeption, Diskussion und Kritik der Theorie kommunikativen Handelns* (Düsseldorf: Patmos, 2nd edn, 1989), pp 160–178.

—'Identität aus Gratuität. Freiheit als Prinzip von religiöser Erziehung und Bildung', in Böhnke et al. (eds), *Freiheit Gottes und der Menschen* (Regensburg: Pustet, 2006), pp 433–451.

—'Kommunikation des Evangeliums – zur handlungstheoretischen Grundlegung der Praktischen Theologie', *International Journal of Practical Theology* 13 (2009), pp 183–198.

Metz, J. B., 'Art. Erinnerung', in H. Krings, H. M. Baumgartner, and C. Wild (eds), *Handbuch philosophischer Grundbegriffe*, vol. 2 (München: Kösel, 1973), pp 386–396.

—*Faith in History and Society*, trans. David Smith (New York: Crossroad, 1980).

—'Anamnestic reason', in A. Honneth et al. (eds), *Cultural-Political Interventions in the Unfinished Project of Enlightenment* (Cambridge, MA and London: MIT Press, 1992), pp 189–194.

—'Monotheismus und Demokratie. Über Religion und Politik auf dem Boden der Moderne', in J. Manemann (ed.), *Demokratiefähigkeit* (Jahrbuch Politische Theologie I) (Münster: LIT Verlag, 1996), pp 39–52.

—'In memory of the other's suffering. Theological reflections on the future of faith and culture', in A. Pierce and G. Smyth OP (eds), *The Critical Spirit. Theology at the crossroads of faith and culture. Essays in honour of Gabriel Daly OSA* (Dublin: Columba Press, 2003), pp 179–188.

Moltmann, J., *Theology of Hope* (London: SCM Press, 1967).

—*The Crucified God. The Cross of Christ as the Foundation and Criticism of Christian Theology*, trans. R. A. Wilson and J. Bowden (London: SCM Press, 1974).

—'A living theology', in D. C. Marks (ed.), *Shaping a Theological Mind* (Aldershot: Ashgate, 2002), pp 87–96.

Bibliography

Nagl, L., 'Das verhüllte Absolute. Religionsphilosophische Motive bei Habermas und Adorno', in *Das verhüllte Absolute. Essays zur zeitgenössischen Religionsphilosophie* (Frankfurt, Berlin, Bern, Bruxelles, New York, Oxford, Wien: Peter Lang, 2010), pp 13–38.

Nagl-Docekal, H., 'Eine rettende Übersetzung? Jürgen Habermas interpretiert Kants Religionsphilosophie', in Langthaler and Nagl-Docekal (eds), *Glauben und Wissen* (Frankfurt: Suhrkamp, 2001), pp 93–119.

—'Moral und Religion aus der Optik der heutigen rechtsphilosophischen Debatte', *Deutsche Zeitschrift für Philosophie* 56 (2008), pp 843–855.

—'"Many Forms of Nonpublic Reason"? Religious Diversity in Liberal Democracies', in H. Lenk (ed.), *Comparative and Intercultural Philosophy* (Berlin, Münster: LIT, 2009), pp 79–92.

Ott, K., 'Kommunikative Ethik', in J.-P.Wils and C. Hübenthal (eds), *Lexikon der Ethik* (Paderborn: Schöningh, 2006), pp 186–194.

Outhwaite, W., *Habermas. A Critical Introduction* (Series: Key Contemporary Thinkers) (Cambridge: Polity Press, 2nd edn, 2009).

Peukert, H., 'Kontingenzerfahrung und Identitätsbildung', in J. Blank and G. Hasenhüttl (eds), *Erfahrung, Glaube und Moral* (Düsseldorf: Patmos, 1982), pp 76–102.

—*Science, Action, and Fundamental Theology: Toward a Theology of Communicative Action*, trans. J. Bohman (Cambridge, MA: MIT Press, 1984).

—'Enlightenment and theology as unfinished projects', trans. E. Crump and P. Kenny, in D. Browning and F. Schüssler Fiorenza (eds), *Habermas, Modernity, and Public Theology* (New York: Crossroad, 1992), pp 43–65.

—'Beyond the present state of affairs: Bildung and the search for orientation in rapidly transforming societies', *Journal of Philosophy of Education* 36 (2002), pp 421–435.

—'Nachwort zur 3. Auflage 2009', in *Wissenschaftstheorie – Handlungstheorie – Fundamentale Theologie. Analysen zu Ansatz und Status theologischer Theoriebildung* (Frankfurt: Suhrkamp, 3rd edn, 2009), pp 357–394.

Pröpper, T., *Der Jesus der Philosophen und der Jesus des Glaubens* (Mainz: Grünewald, 1976).

—*Erlösungsglaube und Freiheitsgeschichte. Eine Skizze zur Soteriologie* (München: Kösel, 3rd edn, 1991).

— *Evangelium und freie Vernunft* (Freiburg: Herder, 2001).

Rahner, K., 'Zur Theologie der Pfarre', in H. Rahner (ed.), *Die Pfarre.Von der Theologie zur Praxis* (Freiburg: Herder, 1956), pp 27–39.

Rasmussen, D. M., and J. Swindal (eds), *Jürgen Habermas*, vols I–IV (Sage Masters of Modern Thought) (London: Sage, 2002).

Rawls, J., *Political Liberalism* (New York: Columbia University Press, 1993).

—'The idea of public reason revisited', in *The Law of Peoples* (Cambridge, MA: Harvard University Press, 2001), pp 129–180.

Regan, E., *Theology and the Boundary Discourse of Human Rights* (Washington, DC: Georgetown University Press, 2010).

Ricken S. J., F., 'Postmetaphysical Reason and Religion', in Habermas et al. (eds), *An Awareness* (Cambridge: Polity Press, 2010), pp 51–58.

Bibliography

Ricoeur, P., *Hermeneutics and the Human Sciences. Essays on Language, Action, and Interpretation*, ed. and trans. J. B. Thompson (Cambridge, MA: MIT Press, 1981).

—*Oneself as Another*, trans. K. Blamey (Chicago, IL: University of Chicago Press, 1992).

—*The Just*, trans. D. Pellauer (Chicago, IL: University of Chicago Press, 2000).

Runggaldier, S. J., E., 'Leben wir in einem postmetaphysischen Zeitalter?', *Stimmen der Zeit* 228 (2010), pp 241–252.

Schleiermacher, F. D. E., *The Christian Faith* (ET: Edinburgh: T&T Clark, 2nd edn, 1928).

—*Hermeneutics and Criticism*, A. Bowie (ed.) (Cambridge: Cambridge University Press, 1998).

Schmidt, S. J., J., 'A dialogue in which there can only be winners', in Habermas et al. (eds), *An Awareness* (Cambridge: Polity Press, 2010), pp 59–71.

Schmidt, T., 'Religiöser Diskurs und diskursive Religion in der postsäkularen Gesellschaft', in Langthaler and Nagl-Docekal (eds), *Glauben und Wissen* (Frankfurt: Suhrkamp, 2001), pp 322–340.

—'Menschliche Natur und genetische Manipulation. *Die Zukunft der menschlichen Natur. Auf dem Weg zu einer liberalen Eugenik?*', in Brunkhorst et al. (eds), *Habermas-Handbuch* (Frankfurt: Suhrkamp, 2002), pp 282–291.

—'Nachmetaphysische Religionsphilosophie. Religion und Philosophie unter den Bedingungen diskursiver Vernunft', in T. Schmidt and K. Wenzel (eds), *Moderne Religion?* (Freiburg: Herder, 2009), pp 10–32.

Schmidt, T., and K. Wenzel (eds), *Moderne Religion? Theologische und religionsphilosophische Reaktionen auf Jürgen Habermas* (Freiburg: Herder, 2009).

Schnädelbach, H., *Zur Rehabilitierung des animal rationale. Vorträge und Abhandlungen* 2 (Frankfurt: Suhrkamp, 1992).

—'Der fromme Atheist', in M. Striet (ed.), *Wiederkehr des Atheismus. Fluch oder Segen für die Theologie?* (Freiburg: Herder, 2008), pp 11–20.

Schulz, W., *Grundprobleme der Ethik* (Pfullingen: Neske, 1989).

Schüssler Fiorenza, F., 'The church as a community of interpretation: Political theology between discourse ethics and hermeneutical reconstruction', in Browning and Schüssler Fiorenza (eds), *Habermas, Modernity, and Public Theology* (New York: Crossroad, 1992), pp 66–91.

Schweidler, W., 'Biopolitik und Bioethik. Über Menschenwürde als ethisches Prinzip des modernen Rechtsstaates', *Information Philosophie* 36 (2008), pp 18–25.

Schweitzer, F., and J. Van der Ven (eds), *Practical Theology – International Perspectives* (Frankfurt: Peter Lang, 1999) (repr. of 1993).

Siep, L., 'Moral und Gattungsethik', *Deutsche Zeitschrift für Philosophie* 50 (2002), pp 111–120.

Siller, H. P., 'Art. Autonomie III. Religionspädagogisch', in *W. Kasper (ed.), Lexikon für Theologie und Kirche,* I (Freiburg: Herder, 3rd edn, 1993), p 1297.

Sölle, D., *Die Hinreise* (Stuttgart: Kreuz Verlag, 1975). ET: *The Inward Road and the Way Back* (Eugene, OR: Wipf & Stock, 2003).

Bibliography

Sölle, D., and F. Steffensky (eds), *Politisches Nachtgebet* (Mainz: Grünewald, Stuttgart, Berlin: Kreuz, 1969).

Striet, M., 'Grenzen der Übersetzbarkeit. Theologische Annäherungen an Jürgen Habermas', in Langthaler and Nagl-Docekal (eds), *Glauben und Wissen* (Frankfurt: Suhrkamp, 2001), pp 259–282.

—'Wissenschaftstheorie – Handlungstheorie – Fundamentale Theologie. Analysen zu Ansatz und Status theologischer Theoriebildung' (Düsseldorf: Patmos, 1976), in M. Eckert, E. Herms, B. J. Hilberath, E. Jüngel (eds), *Lexikon der theologischen Werke* (Stuttgart: Kröner, 2003), pp 812–813.

Tanner, K., 'Das Ende der Enthaltsamkeit? Die Geburt einer "Gattungsethik" aus dem Geist der Diskursethik', *Zeitschrift für Evangelische Ethik* 46 (2002), pp 144–150.

Theunissen, M., 'Society and History: a Critique of Critical Theory', in Dews (ed.), trans. G. Finlayson and P. Dews, *Habermas: A Critical Reader* (Oxford: Blackwell, 1999), pp 241–271.

Thomassen, L., *Habermas. A Guide for the Perplexed* (London, New York: Continuum, 2010).

Tomberg, M., *Religionsunterricht als Praxis der Freiheit. Überlegungen zu einer religionsdidaktisch orientierten Theorie gläubigen Handelns* (Berlin, New York: De Gruyter, 2010).

Tracy, D., 'Theology, critical social theory, and the public realm', in Browning and Schüssler Fiorenza (eds), *Habermas, Modernity and Public Theology* (New York: Crossroad, 1992), pp 19–42.

Vatican Council II. The Conciliar and Post Conciliar Documents, ed. A. Flannery O. P. (Dublin: Dominican Publications, Talbot Press, 1975).

Verweyen, H., *Gottes letztes Wort. Grundriss der Fundamentaltheologie* (Düsseldorf: Patmos, 1991).

Von Soosten, J., 'Zur theologischen Rezeption von Jürgen Habermas' Theorie des kommunikativen Handelns', *Zeitschrift für Evangelische Ethik* 34 (1990), pp 129–143.

Vos, A. et al. (eds), *Duns Scotus on Divine Love* (Aldershot: Ashgate, 2003).

Wellmer, A., *Ethik und Dialog* (Frankfurt: Suhrkamp, 1986). ET *The Persistence of Modernity*, trans. D. Midgley (Cambridge: Polity Press, 1991), pp 113–231.

Wendel, S., 'Die religiöse Selbst- und Weltdeutung des bewussten Daseins und ihre Bedeutung für eine "moderne Religion". Was der "Postmetaphysiker" Habermas über Religion nicht zu denken wagt', in Schmidt and Wenzel (eds), *Moderne Religion?* (Freiburg: Herder, 2009), pp 225–265.

Wenzel, K., 'Gott in der Moderne. Grund und Ansatz einer Theologie der Säkularität', in Schmidt and Wenzel (eds), *Moderne Religion?* (Freiburg: Herder, 2009), pp 347–376.

Wiggershaus, R., *The Frankfurt School* (Cambridge: Polity Press, 1994).

Wimmer, R., *Universalisierung in der Ethik. Analyse, Kritik und Rekonstruktion ethischer Rationalitätsansprüche* (Frankfurt: Suhrkamp, 1980).

Subject Index

Subject Index

Subject Index

Subject Index

good life 32–4, 102, 131, 169n. 75,
 170n. 82, 181n. 15
gratuity 24
Grundlagen des Naturrechts 171n. 15
guilt and transcendental freedom 115

Hegel-Congress 67
Hegelianism 174n. 4
hellenisation 12
hermeneutics 7, 10–11, 17, 22, 25,
 29, 33, 40, 45, 49, 58, 63, 66, 71,
 78, 79, 80, 93, 146, 147, 159
heroic 71
Hervorgehen aus (emanating) 134
heteronomy 23, 24, 100
highest good 97, 116, 150–2, 155,
 166n. 31
historical achievements 74
historical alternatives 52
historical consciousness 77
historical justice 47
historical relativity 80
historical religion 66
Holocaust 2, 16
homoousios (of same being) 147
hope 8, 12–16, 30, 43, 55–6, 60, 62,
 103, 107, 139, 150, 152, 158,
 161, 165n. 17, 166n. 31, 167n. 39
human dignity (*Menschenwürde*) 2–3,
 20, 30, 124, 127–8, 183n. 22
hypostasis (actualization) 147

idealism 30, 33, 37, 57, 59, 63, 64, 75,
 77, 79, 85, 89, 123,
identity 8, 13–14, 21, 23–7, 30, 32–5,
 40, 49, 57–9, 63, 64, 66, 69, 81,
 97, 100, 103, 125, 130–1, 134,
 138, 142, 145–6, 162, 167n. 47,
 181n. 17, 188n. 40
ideology critique 79, 80
imago Dei 115, 133–5, 159
imitation and language theory 49–50
infallibility 143, 158, 188n. 32
innovative action and unilateral
 action risk 30–1
Institute for Social Research 2

instrumental reason 39, 137, 139
intersubjectivity 24, 36, 44, 45, 129,
 145, 172n. 15, 173n. 39, 180n. 30,
 181nn. 13, 17
 and acceptance (*Geltung*) 101
 creativity 13–14
 foundational norms and 84
 and recognition 63
 solipsism and 46–50
irrationality 106, 136, 146
Israel 9, 12, 56

justice 8, 47, 96, 113, 134, 138, 144,
 148–9, 184n. 26, 186n. 5, 187n. 23
justification 2, 25, 31, 33, 70–4, 82,
 85–93, 160, 178n. 6, 179n. 18
 modern 94
 of morality 71, 93, 100, 152
 normative 86, 90
 public basis of 187n. 23

Knowledge and Human Interests 50, 79
koinonia (living together) 21
Kultur des gemeinen Menschenverstands
 (culture of common sense) 140

language theory
 as alternative to philosophy of
 consciousness dualisms 43–6
 objections from subjectivity
 philosophers 46–56
Lebensentwürfe (life plans) 131
Lebensgewohnheiten (custom,
 habits) 73
legitimacy 66, 75, 97, 106, 123, 124,
 135, 138, 159, 161
 human dignity and 126–8
 political 187n. 23
legitimation 127–8, 135, 138, 161
Lehre (doctrine) 156
leiturgia (liturgy) 21
liberal eugenics 123, 124, 130
liberal politics 141
liberal society 118
liberation 8, 9, 145
 memory of 10–12

204

Subject Index

Subject Index

Subject Index

Subject Index

Author Index

Author Index